D1557106

METHODS-TIME MEASUREMENT

McGRAW-HILL INDUSTRIAL ORGANIZATION
AND MANAGEMENT SERIES

L. C. MORROW, *Consulting Editor*

* * *

METHODS-TIME MEASUREMENT

by

HAROLD B. MAYNARD
President, Methods Engineering Council

G. J. STEGEMERTEN
General Manager, Methods Engineering Council

JOHN L. SCHWAB
President, John L. Schwab Associates
Bridgeport, Conn.

New York : Toronto : London

McGRAW-HILL BOOK COMPANY, INC.

1948

METHODS-TIME MEASUREMENT

PREFACE

For many years management has felt the need for a procedure for establishing production standards that would eliminate the element of judgment on the part of the methods engineer. When a time study is made under the conventional time-study procedure, it is necessary for the observer to form a judgment of how the performance of the operator compares with the average or normal performance level. Regardless of the fact that such judgments can be made quite accurately by the experienced observer, because the intangible element of judgment is involved, it is difficult to prove that a correct determination has been made. There is often a tendency on the part of the worker to question the accuracy of standards determined in this manner, particularly if industrial relations are strained, and management has no way of proving the rightness of its production requirements except by studying and restudying the job until an overwhelming mass of evidence has been gathered.

This is costly and time consuming. Therefore, a procedure that eliminates the element of judgment will not only be more acceptable to labor, but it will be more economical to apply.

The methods-time measurement procedure eliminates the necessity for judging the performance level at which an operator works while being observed. The procedure is simply one of determining the motions required to perform the operation and then of assigning predetermined time standards to each limiting motion. The sum of the motion times gives the production standard for the job. True, a certain amount of judgment is required to determine what motions are necessary to perform the operation, but when the observer has an intimate knowledge of the work he is studying, this poses no particular problem. There is no judgment required insofar as the element of time is concerned, for the time standards used in the methods-time measurement have been predetermined as the result of lengthy research and investigation and are always the same for each set of motions.

The methods-time measurement procedure was originally developed as a means of methods improvement, and it is very effective when used for this purpose.   Because of the constant strain on industrial relations which is caused by the element of judgment in the work measurement process, however, management is likely to find that the improvement in industrial relations that is brought about by the use of the methods-time measurement procedure is just as valuable as the improvement in methods which inevitably follows its application.

The methods-time measurement procedure is deceptively easy to apply, and a word of warning, which is repeated frequently throughout the book, is in order.   The procedure will give accurate results only if it is properly applied.   Proper application requires not only a thorough understanding of the procedure itself, but also a thorough understanding of the motions used to perform the work under study.   When the procedure is applied away from the workplace, it is quite easy to assume that the work is performed in a certain way.   Subsequent checking by observation at the workplace will sometimes reveal that it is being done in quite a different way.   Until a job or a class of work has been closely studied motion by motion, it is dangerous for the observer to assume that he knows how it is done.

The answer to most methods improvement and work measurement problems will be found in the methods-time measurement procedure if it is properly applied.   It would be unfortunate to have a procedure as useful as this discredited, even only occasionally, by careless or inexpert attempts to apply it.   It is hoped, therefore, that methods engineers will not attempt to apply the procedure, at least for the purpose of establishing production standards, until they are certain, as the result of study, experiment, and careful checking of results, that they can apply it correctly.

THE AUTHORS

PITTSBURGH, PA.
  January, 1948

CONTENTS

PART V: APPLICATION OF METHODS-TIME MEASUREMENT

PART I

INTRODUCTION

CHAPTER 1

METHODS ENGINEERING

Since the dawn of reason, mankind has been looking for better and easier ways of performing the work that is necessary to support life and to increase material well-being. It has been recognized by the clear thinkers of all generations that in order to have, society as a group must produce. If more is to be had by the members of the group, then more must be produced. If greater leisure is desired in addition, then the goods must be turned out in less time. The capitalistic system has survived in spite of its obvious shortcomings because in the long run it has provided a higher standard of living for less work than any other system yet devised.

The capitalistic system itself does not produce. It merely provides the conditions and the incentives that cause large numbers of people to devote their time and their energies to production. Perhaps in the future some other system will be developed that will offer even stronger inducements for production. If so, mankind will be the gainer insofar as material well-being is concerned, for production is the sole basis for material prosperity. In the meantime, in the United States of America, at least, the rewards offered by the capitalistic system continue to stimulate many people to seek to produce as much as they can.

INDUSTRY'S SEARCH FOR BETTER MANUFACTURING METHODS

Since its earliest beginnings, industry has been more or less interested in better and more economical manufacturing methods. Interest is usually strongest when profits are low or nonexistent and when competition is severe. When profits are high, there is often a tendency to be satisfied with conditions as they are and a reluctance to do anything that might disturb the situation. The forces of competition, however, do not permit this to continue for long. Even the strongest and most self-satisfied company finds that it cannot neglect methods improvement indefinitely, for its competitors who do seek improvements will soon find it possible to lower prices and to take business away from it. Industries are turning more and more to methods engineering in their search for ever better manufacturing methods.

Fig. 1.— Frederick W. Taylor.

HISTORY AND DEVELOPMENT OF METHODS ENGINEERING

The foundations for modern methods engineering were laid by Dr. Frederick W. Taylor, the father of scientific management, and by Frank B. and Lillian M. Gilbreth, pioneers in the field of motion study.

In 1885, Frederick W. Taylor was made foreman of a department of the Midvale Steel Company, situated just outside of Philadelphia. As

FIG. 2.— Frank B. and Lillian M. Gilbreth (about 1912).

foreman, he was held responsible for the quantity of production turned out by his department. From the outset, he was keenly aware of the fact that his men were by no means producing as much as they easily could. This appealed to him as being an economic waste, for Taylor saw clearly that production was the foundation for material prosperity. He therefore set himself the task of doing whatever was necessary to increase the productivity of his department.

After trying various procedures and carefully noting the results, Taylor at length evolved a simple principle that forms the basis for the operation of modern industry. It was, "The greatest production results when each worker is given a definite task to be performed in a definite time and in a definite manner." The definite task was prescribed by management in the form of a job description. At first the definite time was established from records of past performance, but later, when these records proved unreliable, it was determined by the stop-watch time-study procedure that Taylor developed. The definite manner was determined by management, and was issued to the worker in the form of an instruction card.

In order to make his principle operate most effectively, Taylor found it necessary to introduce a system of paying substantial rewards for the accomplishment of the tasks that he established as the result of his studies. Thus he introduced several types of wage incentive plans into industry.

Taylor never failed to stress the importance of method in all his writings on the subject of time and motion study. The production increases that resulted from the introduction of wage incentives based on stop-watch time study were so spectacular, however, that many of those who later tried to use his procedures tended to neglect a consideration of the factor of method. It required the efforts of another pioneer to emphasize the importance of developing the best working methods before proceeding with time study and wage incentives.

A few years after Taylor began his work on the development of scientific management, a building contractor named Frank Gilbreth decided to leave the field in which he had been eminently successful and to devote his time to the study of a subject which had for a long time held his interest. The story of Gilbreth's discovery on his first day as a bricklayer's apprentice of the number of different methods used by bricklayers in the simple task of laying a brick has often been told. His interest in this discovery never lagged, and finally, with the encouragement of his wife, Lillian M. Gilbreth, he decided to give up a profitable business and devote himself to the installation of scientific management, and especially to research and application work in the field of motion study. The Gilbreths began making detailed laboratory studies of motions and methods and at length developed the micromotion study procedure that forms the basis for much of what is to follow in this book.

Both Taylor and Gilbreth won many followers in the fields in which they pioneered. Some of these followers professed to see fundamental differences in the procedures developed by these two men, and at length two groups of practitioners developed. One was the time-study group, and the other was the motion-study group. From roughly 1910 to 1930, these groups considered themselves as irrevocably opposed to each other. The time-study group could see nothing practical in the laboratory approach, and the motion-study group felt that the time-study group were unscientific and crude in their work.

At length, however, both groups began to become better acquainted with one another's work, and as is so often the case during the development stage of a new profession, began to realize that they had been calling the same things by different names. The differences were dropped, and the best features of both procedures were combined into a single, universally applicable procedure now widely known as "methods engineering."

DEFINITION OF METHODS ENGINEERING

The methods-engineering procedure integrates all of the practical devices that have been developed to bring about increased productivity into one unified procedure. Since it includes several procedures, its definition must of necessity be long.

Methods engineering is the technique that subjects each operation of a given piece of work to close analysis in order to eliminate every unnecessary operation and in order to approach the quickest and best method of performing each necessary operation; it includes the standardization of equipment, methods, and working conditions; it trains the operator to follow the standard method; when all this has been done, and not before, it determines by accurate measurement the number of standard hours in which an operator working with standard performance can do the job; finally, it usually, although not necessarily, devises a plan for compensating labor which encourages the operator to attain or to surpass standard performance.[1]

The definition definitely states that the method should be developed, standardized, and taught to the operator before the time for performing the task is measured. In theory, this is correct, and certainly the chronological order cannot be questioned. In practice, however, it has not been possible to keep methods study and time study completely separated, nor can they always be made in the theoretically correct order. Many

[1] MAYNARD, H. B., and G. J. STEGEMERTEN, "Operation Analysis," Chap. I, McGraw-Hill Book Company, Inc., 1939.

methods improvements are discovered in practice during the making of a time study. A decision as to which is the better of two or more contemplated methods cannot be made in some cases until the methods have been timed.

This difficulty, which has bothered methods engineers for years, is due to the limitations of procedures which consider methods and time separately. In reality they are inseparable. The method determines the time, and the time establishes which is the best method. It is felt that the methods-time measurement procedure which is the subject of this book and which considers method and time simultaneously solves the difficulty in cases where it is applicable.

THE GROWING EMPHASIS ON BETTER METHODS

As industry matures in any country, the opportunities for obtaining competitive advantage tend to diminish. Many factors become stabilized and uniform. Competing designs, for example, which may be radically different when a product has been newly invented, tend to become much the same as patents expire and each competitor incorporates the best design features of all the others into his product.

The possibilities for obtaining a favorable "buy" of a given material diminish as markets become developed and stable. Low wages are no longer considered as a likely source of competitive advantage. With wages tending to become more nearly the same as the result of widespread collective bargaining, this important item of cost tends to become uniform insofar as base rates are concerned.

There is one area, however, in which competitive advantage may be sought almost indefinitely, and that is in the area of better manufacturing methods. The methods engineer has demonstrated repeatedly that the method of performing a given operation can be improved again and again, if the repetitiveness justifies it, as fresh study and analysis are applied to it. Therefore, better methods are an ever-present possibility. They offer the best source of competitive advantage that exists in American industry.

PROBLEMS ARISING FROM METHODS CHANGES

It has often been said that nothing is certain but change. It has also been remarked repeatedly that it is human nature to resent change. A certain amount of change is inevitable in industry and is to be endured because its effect in the long run is beneficial. There is a large classification of change, however, which is not necessary or which, at least, can be avoided. In this classification lie the changes which must be made to correct conditions or practices which should not ever have been allowed to exist in the first place. Many of the methods changes that are made in industry belong in this category. They cause major problems in industrial relations and constitute an important obstacle in the path of effective production.

A typical example will illustrate the kinds of changes that are being made repeatedly in industry throughout the length and breadth of the country. It will be presented as a series of steps.

1. Management authorizes the design of a new product.
2. The engineer works out a design that will meet the engineering requirements of the product.
3. The tool designer develops tools that will enable the shop to produce the product.
4. The foreman receives the order, the drawing, and the tools, and assigns the job to the worker.
5. The worker, after receiving such instructions as the foreman considers necessary, begins to produce, and eventually he develops a method that results in a quality of product acceptable to the inspector. This may or may not require a considerable period of time, depending upon the product, the foreman, the worker, and the inspector.
6. On the assumption that it is a shop where time-study standards are used, the foreman requests that a standard be established on the job.
7. The time-study man analyzes the job and suggests some methods changes, which are more or less reluctantly received by the foreman and the worker who feel that their own ability to establish effective methods is being criticized.

---

8. The product is sold, and presently the sales department requests changes which will add to the salability, quality, or appearance of the product.
9. The engineer changes the design.
10. The tool designer changes the tools.
11. The foreman and the worker change the method.
12. The time-study man changes the standard.

---

13. An executive viewing the operation one day sees a different way of doing the work and orders a change.
14. The tool designer changes the tools.
15. The foreman and the worker change the method but forget to notify the time-study man.
16. Three months later, the time-study man discovers the change and restudies the job.
17. The industrial-relations department receives a grievance to the effect that a rate has been cut.

---

18. The inspection department decides that better quality is essential.
19. The tool designer alters the tools.

20. The foreman and the worker change the method.
21. The time-study man restudies the job.

---

22. Production is interrupted for several months. When it is resumed, a new operator is put on the job who develops his own method for doing it.
23. The industrial-relations department receives a grievance to the effect that the standard is too low.
24. A new time-study man restudies the job, and, finding the standard low for the method being used, revises the standard upward.
25. The operator after gaining experience improves the method and begins to make abnormally high earnings on the job.

---

26. The engineer in working on a similar product gets a new idea and revises his design for this product.
27. The tool designer changes the tools.
28. The foreman and the worker change the method.
29. The time-study man restudies the job.
30. The industrial-relations department receives a grievance because the operator can no longer make as high earnings as before.

---

31. A cost-reduction study is ordered by management to try to reduce costs in order to reduce price and, hence, increase distribution.
32. The methods man develops a new method.
33. The operator resists it, fearing a reduction of earnings and loss of job security.
34. The foreman finally convinces the operator that he should go along.
35. The time-study man restudies the job.
36. The operator soon learns to make his former earnings, but the work runs out so he is transferred to another job.

---

37. Sales increase, and soon the operator is back on the job together with three new operators, one of whom turns in a suggestion for improving the method.
38. The new method is put into effect.
39. The time-study man restudies the job.
40. The original operator receives somewhat greater earnings than before and works with less fatigue, but he turns out much more production.

This series of events could be extended indefinitely. Any one group, such as (8) to (12) or (13) to (17), may be repeated a number of times. Many variations in the sequences listed are likely to occur.

Any man with a practical shop background will recognize the type of events listed and from his own experience will be able to fill in the outline with specific products, drawing numbers, operators' names, etc. The events are typical of the kind that occur daily throughout industry. They lead to progress, to be sure, but they also lead to disturbing changes, which from the viewpoint of many of those involved are all too frequent.

METHODS CORRECTION OR METHODS ENGINEERING

An analysis of the steps given above will begin to reveal some of the reasons behind this constant change. The engineer, the tool designer, the foreman, the inspector, the time-study man, and the sales department all work relatively independently. Instead of pooling all their ideas at the start before the job is sent to the shop, they contribute their suggestions spasmodically with the result that there is constant change. The method is not carefully worked out in advance. Hence, it is corrected each time an inefficiency is discovered. Even so, it is difficult to keep the method and the standard in line, because there is no provision for teaching the method to the operator, and this in turn is due to the fact that much of the task of developing the method is left to the operator. Even when the methods man studies the job at the request of management, he is only performing a corrective function.

Certainly it would be impractical to expect that every new job could be introduced into the shop in a state of unassailable perfection. The limitations of human beings alone would prevent this happy condition, even if new materials, processes, and tools were not constantly being invented. At the same time, if the method is *engineered* by the combined efforts of all who contribute to it in advance of the beginning of production and if it is thought through in detail at the start, it is certain that better methods and fewer changes will result. In other words, subsequent methods *correction* work will be decreased in proportion to the amount of advanced methods *engineering* work that is done.

METHODS-TIME MEASUREMENT

Methods-time measurement is a useful tool for helping to engineer a method before beginning production. It has several other uses also, which will be discussed later. The procedure is a logical development that arises from the long-recognized need of being able to treat method and time simultaneously instead of separately.

The methods-time measurement procedure was developed by the authors for the reasons discussed in Chapter 3. It is a useful tool for certain kinds of methods work and meets a longfelt need. It is not intended to supplant any of the other analysis procedures used in the past—process charts, operation analysis, motion study, time study—but rather it is a supplement to them that increases their objectivity. It is an added tool in the kit of the methods engineer, which will enable him to handle certain types of methods engineering work with greater facility than was possible heretofore.

CHAPTER 2

METHODS-TIME MEASUREMENT—AN
ADVANCED STEP IN METHODS ENGINEERING

In undertaking to engineer effective methods before beginning production, one is faced with the necessity of choosing among a large number of ways of performing every operation, and even every element of every operation. For example, in performing a simple sensitive drill-press operation, the very first element will be "pick up part and move to spindle." In establishing the method for doing this, the methods engineer will have to decide such points as the following: "Where should the material be placed in relation to the spindle?" "What type of container should be used?" "How should material be placed in the container to facilitate grasping?" "Should two-handed operation be employed?" "Should more than one part be grasped at one time?" "Where should the raw material be placed in relation to the finished material?"

The decisions reached on these and similar points will determine the motions that will be required to perform the operation. In order to be in a position to decide which set of motions is the best, it is necessary to know with certainty how long it will take to make the motions. The methods-time measurement procedure, which is based upon predetermined methods-time standards, supplies the answer.

DEFINITION OF METHODS-TIME MEASUREMENT

The methods-time measurement procedure may be defined as follows:

Methods-time measurement is a procedure which analyzes any manual operation or method into the basic motions required to perform it and assigns to each motion a predetermined time standard which is determined by the nature of the motion and the conditions under which it is made.

Thus it may be seen that methods-time measurement is basically a tool of methods analysis that gives answers in terms of time without the necessity of making stop-watch time studies.

12

The procedure is called "methods-time measurement" rather than motion-time measurement because a consideration of method definitely enters into the application of the predetermined time standards that have been established. For example, it has been determined by investigation, as described in the next chapter, that the time required to make a simple Reach motion of a given length varies with the nature of the object reached for. If the object is in a fixed location, the Reach motion is made more quickly than if the object is one of several in a group in a location that may vary from time to time. The method employed in making the motion varies. In the first case, after habits of automaticity have been established by frequent repetition, the operator does not find it necessary to look at the object toward which he is reaching. He is so well oriented at his workplace that he does not need to look toward the object to locate it for his hand. In the second case, he must not only look toward the group of objects, but he must make a mental selection of the one that is to be grasped. Thus he employs a different method, and the time required is different.

PRINCIPAL USES OF METHODS-TIME MEASUREMENT

It requires a considerable period of experience with application before the full usefulness of any new procedure can be developed. At the present writing, the authors have been applying or supervising the application of the methods-time measurement procedure for about four years. This may be altogether too short a time to develop all the uses to which the procedure may profitably be put. Nevertheless, in that time the following utilizations have been made:

1. Developing effective methods in advance of beginning production.
2. Improving existing methods.
3. Establishing time standards.
4. Developing time formulas or standard data.
5. Estimating.
6. Guiding product design.
7. Developing effective tool designs.
8. Selecting effective epuipment.
9. Training supervisors to become highly methods conscious.
0. Settling grievances.
1. Research—particularly in connection with methods, learning time, and performance rating.

DEVELOPING EFFECTIVE METHODS IN ADVANCE OF BEGINNING PRODUCTION

Although the desirability of engineering effective methods before beginning production has already been stressed, the idea is sufficiently important and its application is sufficiently rare to justify further elaboration. Most methods improvement work is done on existing operations. A great deal will continue to be so done in the future, because for reasons of initial low activity, lack of available time, etc., it will not always be possible to engineer methods before work enters the factory. Nevertheless, the disturbing effects that result when an established method is changed are serious enough to make it well worth while to avoid them whenever possible.

Much methods improvement and motion-study work is done under the name of "work simplification." This is an excellent descriptive term of the philosophy underlying this approach. An existing job is studied and simplified. Unnecessary work is eliminated, and the necessary work is made less fatiguing. As a result of work simplification, production is increased, often to a remarkable extent. This is highly desirable. At the same time, change is introduced. Operators are required to produce more than they formerly were required to do. Perhaps fewer operators are required to turn out the work. It is not difficult to understand why the operators look upon this as undesirable, regardless of the economic soundness of the change.

Assume, for example, that ten operators are doing a certain task. They have been doing it together, working side by side for a number of months. The product they are working upon seems to be in good demand. The company enjoys a good position in the industry. The operators realize all this, and they have a feeling of security. Some of them are perhaps saving money with the idea of owning their own homes. All have a general feeling of satisfaction with their jobs.

Then one day the method of doing the job is changed so that five operators can produce the volume previously turned out by ten. There is no question but that the new method is better. It is in fact far less fatiguing. After a discussion with the foreman, the operators can understand that when the company reduces the price of the product by passing the saving on to the consumers, more people will buy the product, and eventually all ten operators will be needed again.

At the same time, the operators cannot help feeling disturbed. The change-over to the new method was an effort. The five operators who are left have the uneasy feeling that they may have done some of their friends out of a job, even though their friends may have been transferred to other work. The transferred operators have had to change even more, since they are on an entirely new job. They believe that the company will continue to employ them as it has promised to do, but they are also realistic enough to realize that an industrial organization is not a charitable organization and that in the long run no company can continue to make work if there is no real need for it.

Thus although everyone connected with the change is trying to face facts fairly and although all recognize the need for employing the best known methods if the organization as a whole and the individuals comprising it are to prosper, nevertheless the operators frankly would be much happier if the work-simplification man had never appeared on the scene.

This general attitude has been expressed in the past by representatives of management, labor, and government whenever the subject of methods change comes up. It is readily recognizable that when a man has worked on a given job for a period of time, he comes to look upon it as *his* job. He develops the feeling that he has a vested interest in that job, which becomes stronger the longer he holds it. As a result, his inclination is to resist change.

When the methods-engineering approach based upon the application of the methods-time measurement procedure is used, the situation is completely changed. The corrective and simplification work is done before there is any job. When at length the operation is ready for the shop, the people who are given the job welcome it as they would any new job. They undertake to learn the method just as readily as they would any new method. Because management knows what the method should be, it can see that the correct method will be taught from the start.

Because an effective method is used from the beginning, the initial price of the product will be lower. The volume may be expected to build up to the same point as in the previous example, so that the same number of operators will be employed. The process is one of steady growth, however, instead of one of growth, recession, and regrowth. The elimination of the human problems that are avoided in this manner also eliminates an important section of industrial-relations difficulties.

IMPROVING EXISTING METHODS

To be practical, it must be recognized that regardless of the amount of methods engineering work which is done in advance, there will always be a vast amount of methods improvement work which it will be profitable to do on existing jobs. Even work for which effective methods were developed before beginning production can usually be further improved as more experience is gained with it, for the familiar fundamental principle of methods engineering that any method can be improved still holds. The effect of advanced methods engineering is to reduce the number and frequency of subsequent changes and improvements, not to eliminate them altogether.

As a means of methods improvement, the methods-time measurement procedure ranks second to none in effectiveness. The authors have yet to analyze an operation by this procedure and not find practical ways of improving the method. The reason is obvious. When a method is examined motion by motion and when the exact time required to perform each motion and every other motion which might be used is known, it would be difficult indeed to find an operation on which some improvement could not be made.

ESTABLISHING TIME STANDARDS

When the times required to make every motion used to perform a given operation are totaled, the time to perform the whole operation is established. When the proper allowances for fatigue, personal and unavoidable delays, etc., are added, the result is a standard which may be used for wage-payment purposes under a wage-payment plan, or for any of the many other uses to which time standards are put. Thus the methods-time measurement procedure makes possible the establishing of accurate time standards on manual operations without the necessity of making stop-watch time studies.

Some workers prefer not to have time studies made on them. They become nervous when they feel that someone is watching and timing every move. Although operators of this type are a small minority in industry, they create a problem that is difficult to handle. The methods-time measurement procedure eliminates cases of this kind.

The methods-time measurement procedure, by its very nature, tends to foster somewhat better industrial relations than conventional time-study practices. The methods-time data consist of predetermined standards for all types and classes of motions commonly used in industry. They therefore permit the establishing of the time required to do a job as soon as the method for doing it has been determined. The time standard and the method may be brought into the shop simultaneously. The methods engineer in effect becomes the instructor and shows the operator the method that is to be used. As soon as the operator has mastered the method, he finds that he can meet the predetermined standard.

The inseparable nature of method and time are clearly demonstrated by the methods-time data. The method must be established exactly and in detail before the allowed time for using it can be determined. This forces careful analytical work with the emphasis on method as it should be. The horse is truly before the cart.

Time study all too frequently is undertaken with insufficient attention paid to methods. The time-study man may accept the method in use, which certainly is the path of least resistance. Such methods changes as he does suggest are likely to be grudgingly received or forthrightly condemned. Often not until after the standard is established does truly detailed methods improvement work begin, and then it is the operator who initiates the changes in most cases. The effect of this on the consistency of standards is self-evident. Some jobs can be improved more than others; some operators are more ingenious than others. The result is that standards, which were correctly set on existing methods, soon become out of line and inconsistent, and a series of industrial-relations problems is created.

It would be impractical to expect that no method established with the aid of the methods-time data could be subsequently improved by the operator. Human ingenuity is boundless over a period of time, and the human tendency to overlook possibilities and to make errors is always present. Nevertheless, it may be said that methods established with the aid of the methods-time data approach the ideal method much more closely than methods established in the casual hit-or-miss fashion which is prevalent throughout industry. Thus the extent of the inconsistencies that result when methods are changed by the operators is reduced.

DEVELOPING TIME FORMULAS

Time-study men have long recognized that it is uneconomical to establish large numbers of standards on a given class of work by individual time studies and that, in addition, serious inconsistencies are likely to result. They have therefore made use of time formulas,[1] or standard data, which permit the establishing of consistent time standards in a fraction of the time it would take to make a time study.

Time formulas are conventionally developed from time-study data. Standard elements are established and then the time for performing these elements is determined by studying a representative sampling of the class of work to be covered. Often several dozen time studies are required to obtain a representative set of data.

[1] LOWRY, MAYNARD, and STEGEMERTEN, "Time and Motion Study and Formulas for Wage Incentives," Chaps. XXIV–XXXV, McGraw-Hill Book Company, Inc., 1940.

On some classes of work, the methods-time measurement procedure may be substituted for time study to good advantage. When the standard elements comprising the work have been established, the method of per-- forming each element may be expressed in terms of the motions used. The time required is then determined from the methods-time data. This is considerably quicker than using the conventional time-study procedure.

An example of a formula developed from the methods-time data is given in Chapter 27. It required 2 days to develop this formula. Had it been necessary to collect time-study data, it would have taken at least 3 weeks to complete the formula.

ESTIMATING

When accurate estimates of the time required to perform a given operation are required, the methods-time measurement procedure, prop- erly applied, will give them. The method that would be used to do the job is visualized, the motions required are determined, and the methods- time standards are applied. Estimating of this type should be done only by one who has had considerable experience with the application of the methods-time measurement procedure. It is quite easy to overlook motions in the mental visualization of the method which must be made when the operation is performed, and therefore the inexperienced esti- mator is quite likely to arrive at estimates which are too low.

Estimating with the aid of methods-time data is a much more lengthy process than the over-all type of estimating, which is commonly used in industry. The conventional estimator examines a drawing or sample of the part, compares it mentally with some similar job with which he is familiar, and quickly reaches a conclusion as to the approximate time required to do the work. The whole process takes only a few minutes— seconds if the estimator is dealing repeatedly with the same class of work. Experience has shown, however, that this type of estimating leaves a great deal to be desired in the way of accuracy. It is satisfactory for small quantity or nonrepetitive work and indeed is the only practical estimating procedure to employ. When quantities are large, however, and the estimate must be exact, the methods-time measurement procedure fully justifies the additional time it consumes.

GUIDING PRODUCT DESIGN

Many products can be designed in several different ways, each of which will be equally satisfactory from a functioning standpoint. Usually one of the designs will be more economical to manufacture, however, than the others. It is therefore a growing practice in progressive organizations to permit the methods engineer to review new product designs while they are still on the drafting board, so that he can make suggestions for design changes which will reduce manufacturing costs.

Customarily the methods engineer studies the drawing of the product with an open mind and relies upon his past experience for suggestions of possible improvements. This over-all approach results in some betterment, but additional improvements are likely to be overlooked. If the quantity to be manufactured justifies it, greater results will be obtained by a more detailed study using the methods-time measurement procedure. The operations required to produce the part are first listed and studied to see if any can be eliminated by design change. Then the motions required to perform each operation are visualized and methods-time values are assigned. From this detailed analysis of motions, still further refinements in design may result. One of the most commonly encountered possibilities for improvement which this type of study uncovers is the redesign of the part to make it symmetrical so that positioning time as the part is put into work-holding devices is reduced.

DEVELOPING EFFECTIVE TOOL DESIGNS

The tool designer can obtain real assistance in doing his work effectively from the methods-time measurement procedure. A number of designs of tools are usually available to him for accomplishing a given objective. His choice will be based on such factors as accuracy obtainable, tool life, cost, etc. He will also wish to build into the tool economy of motion in its manipulation if he is as methods-minded as he should be. To accomplish this, he need only visualize the motions required to manipulate each type of tool he has under consideration. Then by assigning the methods-time standards to each motion, he can readily determine which design of tool requires the least handling time. If the design that involves the least handling time is the most costly, as is sometimes the case, then a consideration of the repetitiveness of the job will determine whether or not the tool is economically justified.

SELECTING EFFECTIVE EQUIPMENT

In cases where several different designs of machine-tool equipment can be purchased to do a given job, the methods-time data is of assistance in arriving at the proper choice. Again all that is necessary is to visualize the motions required for manipulation in each case and to apply the time standards to determine which sequence is the best.

The case frequently arises where the purchase of a machine is contemplated to eliminate a hand operation. The methods-time data make it possible to determine whether or not such a purchase is justified.

TRAINING SUPERVISORS TO BECOME METHODS-CONSCIOUS

Training in the methods-time measurement procedure is one of the best available means of developing a true appreciation of the importance of correct working methods. It is difficult for the untrained individual to place much importance on the presence or absence of a few minor motions in a given motion sequence. After he has learned to observe, record, and assign time values to motions, however, and has seen how each motion adds to the total time required to do the job, he cannot fail to realize how necessary it is to reduce motions to a minimum if the best method is to be developed.

Certain ineffective motion sequences become so familiar to the trained observer that he sees them almost automatically and begins to plan for their elimination. For example, it is quite common to see an operator pick up a small part with the left hand, transfer it to the right hand, and then move it to its destination. This involves a transfer grasp and other motions which can be eliminated if the workplace can be rearranged so that the right hand can pick up the part.

Points of this kind are seldom overlooked after training in the methods-time measurement procedure. Since correction is usually comparatively easy once the inefficiency is observed, the training is valuable not only to methods engineers but also to others who contribute to effective production methods, such as foremen, inspectors, and tool designers.

SETTLING GRIEVANCES

Methods-time measurement has proved to be extremely valuable in settling grievances in regard to the correctness of time standards. Where the procedure is used, it does not take long for all concerned to recognize the inseparable nature of method and time. A few demonstrations of the accuracy of the methods-time data are sufficient to convince workers and supervisors alike that if the proper method is followed the standard can be met without difficulty, but that if extra motions are introduced the standard will appear tight. When a grievance about a time standard is brought to a certain union steward in a department where methods-time measurement has been in use for several months, his first question to the operator is "Are you using the right method?" Practically every complaint about standards is now straightened out by the steward and the foreman without reference to the methods department, except to check occasionally on what the method was on which a questioned standard was established.

The methods-time measurement procedure is equally useful for preventing grievances from developing. For example, a certain plant had a great deal of small punch-press work. Many of the parts were quite similar, and it was the practice to establish rates on new jobs by comparison when possible in order to save time. This practice was followed in the case of the two parts shown in Fig. 3. Part A had been worked many times before. The standard established for it was considered to be

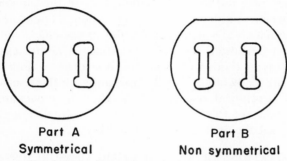

Part A
Symmetrical

Part B
Non symmetrical

FIG. 3.— Small stampings similar in general appearance.

satisfactory to everyone. When part B was issued to the shop, the rate setter, noting its similarity to part A, established the same standard. After a period of trial, the operator claimed that she could not conform to that standard.

The complaint was discussed by the foreman, the rate setter, and the union steward. All agreed that the standard for part A was satisfactory and that parts A and B were similar. No one could see why the standard for part B should not be satisfactory; yet the operator who raised the question was a skilled operator not given to complaining without justification. While the discussion was in progress, an engineer familiar with methods-time measurement came by. The problem was referred to him and his opinion was asked. He glanced at the two parts and immediately said that part B would require more time, because while Part A was symmetrical and could be positioned in any one of a number of ways, part B was nonsymmetrical and could be positioned in only one way. Thus it required more adjusting, or orienting, motions than part A.

As soon as this was pointed out, it was obvious. The complaint was immediately settled satisfactorily, and the four people involved were greatly impressed by the practical value of the methods-time measurement procedure.

RESEARCH

Methods-time measurement provides a tool of research that makes it possible to extend existing knowledge about methods and time considerably. It provides answers to such questions as "Why is one operator able to produce twice as much as another?" and "How much faster does a skilled operator working with an excellent effort perform than an operator working at the average performance level?"

Two examples of researches conducted by the authors are given in Chapters 28 and 29. One of these deals with an investigation of various assembly procedures and the other with a study of the variables existing among 21 operators all doing the same operation. These are typical of the kinds of problems in which methods-time measurement can be useful. Many other investigations remain to be made. One, for example, is a study of the way methods vary as an operator learns to do a new operation. There are many others equally fascinating for the research-minded investigator. It is hoped, now that the methods-time data are available, that many studies of this kind will be made both in universities and industry and that the findings will be published.

LIMITATIONS OF METHODS-TIME MEASUREMENT

The methods-time measurement procedure applies accurately to manual operations in which the time required to make the motion is not influenced by the process itself. For example, the time required to make a 12-inch motion when transporting a light part, as shown by Fig. 4, has been accurately established. The time assumes, however, that the part will be transported without restricting influences. If the part happens to be a shallow dish filled to the edge with a liquid, as in Fig. 5, the motion must be made slowly to avoid spilling. Again, if the operator is making the motion to apply paint to an absorbent surface, as in Fig. 6, he must slow down the motion so that the paint will flow in sufficient quantity from the brush to cover properly.

Hence, it may be seen that there are motions—usually, although not always, the Do basic element—for which it is difficult, if not impossible, to establish standards from predetermined methods-time data. In many operations, these are such a small part of the total cycle that the accuracy of the final standard will not be affected seriously if estimating is employed. Where the time is an important part of the total, however, stop-watch time study is the only accurate procedure to use. Even in such cases, the methods-time data are not without value, for if the time for all elements to which they apply is determined by their use, attention

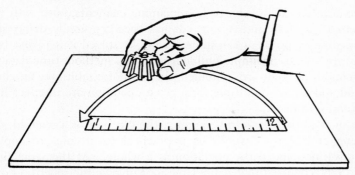

FIG. 4.— Light object moved 12 inches—no restrictions.

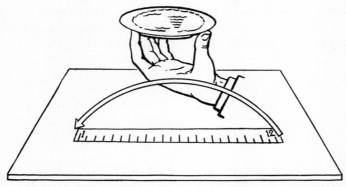

FIG. 5.— Light object moved 12 inches—motion restricted by necessity of avoiding spillage.

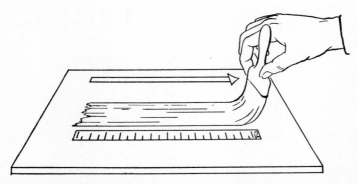

FIG. 6.— Light object moved 12 inches—motion restricted by necessity of allowing paint to flow from brush.

can be devoted exclusively to the remaining elements, both with regard
to methods analysis and timing.   It has been repeatedly demonstrated
that a complex problem can quite readily be solved if it is first broken
down into a series of simple problems.   When methods-time data application and time study are combined, the tasks of establishing an effective
method and an accurate time for a given operation are in effect broken
down and simplified.

On such work as large pit molding, the erection of a scaffold, or the
building of a ship, it would be impractical to attempt to apply the
methods-time data to the operation as a whole.   At the same time, it
should be recognized that many large jobs involve the repetition of relatively few elements only.   It is entirely practicable to establish the time
for performing individual elements by the application of the methods-
time data.   Therefore, where the activity of a class of work is sufficient
to justify the establishing of standard elemental times, the methods-time
data may be used even on long-cycle operations.

CHAPTER 3

DEVELOPMENT OF METHODS-TIME DATA

The desirability of having accurate methods-time data available has long been recognized by methods engineers. At the same time, it was felt by many that because the motions made by industrial workers in performing a variety of operations appear to be almost infinite in number, it would be a lifetime task to compile complete motion-time data. This factor tended to discourage beginning the work of collecting data.

ORIGIN OF METHODS-TIME DATA

In 1940, a methods improvement training program was conducted by the Methods Engineering Council for a large group of time-study men. The increased production reported as a result of this program was substantial. Gratifying as this was, it was recognized that the accomplishments were the result of methods correction instead of true methods engineering. It was also apparent that while inefficiencies were being corrected on one job, many other jobs were being introduced into the shop with the usual superficial consideration of methods. This resulted in the creation of new inefficiencies, which would, in turn, have to be corrected later on if true effectiveness were to be achieved.

As the result of a number of discussions of this problem, it was decided to develop a set of data, originally called a "methods formula," which would make it possible to arrive more surely at effective methods of performing operations before they were introduced into the shop. This idea eventually led to a research study that was conducted over a period of many months.

With the idea in mind of developing a methods formula for a specific line of work, the investigation was limited at first to sensitive drill-press operations. At length, however, it was found that the data which had been compiled for drill-press work applied equally well and with a very satisfactory degree of accuracy to all classes of work involving manual motions. Hence, instead of a methods formula applying merely to sensitive drill-press work, it was recognized that truly basic methods-time data had been developed.

It is, of course, clear that it is unlikely that every conceivable type of industrially useful motion will be encountered on sensitive drill-press work. Therefore the present data must be regarded as incomplete. Indeed, one who is familiar with the present data will have little difficulty in describing motions that are not yet covered. Nevertheless, the present data are found to apply just as they are to so many different industrial operations that it is felt that the major portion of the work of compiling methods-time data has been completed.

All data should, of course, be rechecked by others. Additions should be made to data as gaps in the present information are discovered. This is a task to which all who use methods-time data can and should contribute. Therefore, aside from giving a historical record, the major purpose of this chapter is to suggest, by showing what was done, how others in the future can assist in completing and perfecting the methods-time data. As a result, instead of being a lifetime task, it is believed that the work can be finished in a much more reasonable length of time.

PROCEDURE FOR COLLECTING DATA

The procedure followed in collecting data is described in the instructions that were first issued to those assisting with the work. Because the data that were collected in this manner were subsequently found to be adequate, the instructions are reproduced here.

INVESTIGATION METHODS

Methods Analysis Data Sheet. In order to assist in securing necessary data on every job investigated, a form known as the Methods Analysis Data Sheet, Fig. 7, (MEC No. 600) has been devised. This form is to be filled out for every job included in the investigation. It should be filled out as follows:

Date. Record the date the operation is observed or photographed.

Part. The name by which the part is identified on the drawing should be recorded.

Drawing and Item. To be obtained in all cases. If part number or other numbers will help to identify the part, they should be recorded directly above the drawing number.

Division and Department. This information should be sufficient to show the location in which the operation was performed.

Material. Identify by name in all cases, and give material specification number if available.

Activity. Determine from most reliable source available. Experience has shown that various individuals in an organization give widely varying estimates of activities, and where activity records are available, they should always be consulted.

Yearly Labor Cost per .0001 Hour. Yearly activity × labor rate × .0001. Direct labor rate of operator performing operation should be used rather than group rate or costing rate.

Allowed Time. Obtain setup and each-piece time from the time study department.

Operation. Describe in sufficient detail to give quick understanding of nature of operation, such as "Drill two brush-holder holes (first spindle), drill and ream two governor holes (second and third spindle), drill two stud holes (fourth spindle),

```
                        METHODS ANALYSIS DATA
  DATE OBSERVED_____ PART_____ DWG._____ ITEM_____
  DIVISION _____     DEPT. _____MATERIAL_____
  ACTIVITY _____ YEARLY LABOR COST PER .0001 HR._____ ALLOWED TIME EA. PC._____
  OPERATION_____
                                                                        B.U.

  MACHINE DESCRIPTION_____
  OPERATOR_____ SK _____ EFF_____ OBSERVER_____
```

DESCRIPTION OF METHOD	DIA.	DEPTH	SPEED	FEED	TOOL	JIG NO.	JIG COST

Methods Engineering Council
Form No. 600   Sheet No ____of____Sheets

Fig. 7.— Methods-analysis data sheet.

drill two setscrew holes (fifth spindle), and drill one mounting hole (sixth spindle)."

Machine Description. Give number of spindles and make and size of machine.

Operator. Record operator's name and initials.

Skill and Effort. Rate skill and effort shown by operator while operation is being photographed or observed, using accepted time-study rating procedure. Check rating with departmental time-study man if possible.

Observer. Record name and initials.

Description of Method. Record brief description of work done on first spindle, such as "Drill two brush-holder holes." Then follow with a detailed written description of the motions employed to do this. The description of drilling the two brush-holder holes, for example, would be as follows:

> At beginning of cycle, operator picks up a casting with left hand and blows it off with an air hose held in right hand. He also blows chips out of jig. He then places casting in a box jig and tightens one short locating screw by hand. He closes the cover of the jig and tightens it with a flat thumb nut, using an open-end wrench. He then moves three steps to first spindle and sets jig up on end. He inserts a ½-inch round bar that he himself has provided into a hole on the side of the jig and uses this during drilling to prevent the jig from turning. He drills one hole, turns the jig end for end, and drills a second hole. He then moves to next spindle.

The work performed on each spindle should be described similarly. Jig-loading time will be included in description of work done on first spindle and unloading time with work done on last spindle. Operations of applying lubricant to drills and taps, cleaning chips from the table, etc., which do not occur on each piece, may be described at end of write-up.

Diameter. Record the diameter of drill, tap, or reamer.

Depth. Record depth of holes as obtained by actual measurement.

Speed. Determine speed with rpm counter or tachometer. Experience shows that rated speed or operator's judgment of speed is not dependable.

Feed. Record "Hand" unless power feed is used, in which case, record exact feed used.

Tool. Describe tool size and material briefly. If special tool is used, sketch tool using back of data sheet if necessary.

Jig No. Record jig number as obtained from jig itself.

Jig Cost. Ascertain actual cost of jig if possible. If it is not possible, have estimate made by tool estimator.

Motion Pictures. In obtaining motion pictures for subsequent analysis, care must be taken to keep the hands of the operator in view at all times. Due to the nature of drill-press work this is not always possible, but all feasible positions from which to take the picture should be considered before the final decision is made.

The operation should be observed closely for a few minutes before the pictures are taken so that it can be determined whether or not the operator uses his standard method while being photographed. Some operators tend to improve their method while the picture is being taken in order to make a good showing, and others do just the opposite. Unless a method that is outstandingly poor is being employed, the picture can be taken, for much can be learned from it. In all probability, because of improvements that the methods investigation uncovers, few methods photographed will be the same as those finally established. Information on whether or not the operator varies his method during photographing may prove useful in other connections, however, and therefore it should be recorded.

Enough film should be exposed to get a good picture of the entire operation. On all but the very longest operations, at least two complete cycles should be observed. On short-cycle work, 10 to 15 cycles will not be too many. Certain parts of the operation, such as fixture loading, positioning of jig under spindle, etc., may justify close study. In cases of this kind, slow-motion pictures should be obtained.

Other Information. Much information about the details of the work can be obtained from the operator, and when he shows willingness to discuss the job, he should be questioned concerning it. The reasons for some of the motions he makes may be obscure until this is done, and the observer should not leave the operation until he is satisfied that he understands it thoroughly. If the operator does not appear willing to discuss the job frankly, the necessary information can usually be obtained from the foreman or group leader.

Drawings and Tool Sketches. If possible, drawings of the part and of the tools should be obtained. Many questions will arise during the course of the analysis that it will be difficult to answer without a drawing of the part or the jig. When the motion picture is taken at a sufficient distance from the operator to include his hands in it at all times, many of the details of the part and fixture are difficult to see. The drawings, however, will usually give the necessary information in cases of this kind. If drawings are not available, dimensioned sketches should be made.

When the data obtained under this procedure were subsequently analyzed, it was found that the most difficult information to determine accurately was the length of the longer motions. Hence, additional instructions were given to the investigator to make, while still at the workplace, a sketch of the machine and of the workplace layout and to place on the sketch all dimensions that it was felt would aid in determining motion lengths.

ANALYSIS PROCEDURE

All motion-picture films were subsequently analyzed, using the micromotion study film-analysis procedure described in the book, "Time and Motion Study and Formulas for Wage Incentives."[1] This gave a mass of detailed information in terms of basic divisions of accomplishment, or Gilbreth basic elements. The data were unclassified, however, and were difficult to analyze.

The next step, therefore, was to determine the standard elements which it was felt would be encountered on all drill-press work. The original list was comprised of 60 elements. Some of these were basic elements, but most of them were groups of several basic elements. All data were then posted to individual data sheets, one being used for each element. The manner in which this was done may be illustrated by the data for the element Move to Part, which in reality is the basic element Reach.

Data on the element Move to Part were collected by analyzing 1,350 feet of motion-picture film that was taken of 36 different drill-press operations; 242 values were thus obtained, some of them representing averages

---

[1] LOWRY, MAYNARD, and STEGEMERTEN, "Time and Motion Study and Formulas for Wage Incentives," Chap. XI, McGraw-Hill Book Company, Inc., 1940.

DATA FOR ELEMENT Move to Part　　　No.　D-1

Length	Motion class	Hand used	CD	PP	Elapsed frames	Skill	Effort	Allowed time	Ref.	Page	Description of motion

FIG. 8.— Form used for tabulating original methods-time data.

of a number of different observations of the same motion. In tabulating these data, a form was prepared with the following headings:

Distance moved
Motion class employed
Hand used (right, left, or both)
Change direction and/or pre-position included
Elapsed frames (at ¹⁄₁₆ second per frame)
Skill and effort rating
Reference information
Description of motion

Figure 8 shows the arrangement of this form, which also provides space for recording allowed time after leveling.

When the data were at length assembled, they were carefully analyzed on the basis of what they showed and of the information gained during the detailed film analysis. It was concluded that no single curve could be drawn for all data, but that there would be different curves, depending upon the conditions under which the motions were made.

The next step, therefore, was to classify the various conditions that were thought to exist and to plot the data in the form of tentative curves. The curves were plotted with distance moved in inches as abscissas and leveled time in sixteenth seconds as ordinates. A distinction was made in plotting points to show normal motions, motions in which Change Direction[1] occurred, and motions in which the hand was moving at the beginning or the end of the motion. Additional distinctions were subsequently made to test the effect of motion class, of hand used, of male or female operator, and of leveling factor.

Careful notes were kept of the work done and the conclusions reached. Because these notes indicate the approach used and the treatment accorded the data, the notes on the element Reach to Part will be repeated here.

ANALYSIS—REACH TO PART

After studying the available data in detail, the following classifications of the conditions under which a reach to a part might be made were established.

---

[1] Change Direction was classed as a basic division of accomplishment in "Time and Motion Study and Formulas for Wage Incentives", 3d ed., by Lowry, Maynard, and Stegemerten, and was defined as "the basic operation employed to change the line or plane along which a transport motion is made."

Class	Description	Examples
A	Reach to object in fixed location.	Control lever on machine. Object held in other hand or on which other hand rests (kinesthetic sense assists).
B	Reach to single object in location that may vary slightly from cycle to cycle.	Movable jig; small, medium, or large part; tool; bushing on machine table.
C	Reach to object in group.	Small parts jumbled together in tote pan or on table.
D	Reach to very small object or where accurate grasp is required.	Very small part either alone or in group. Small screw on jig, which can be grasped in only one way.
E	Reach to indefinite location to get hand in position for body balance, or next motion, or to get it out of way.	Drop hand from spindle lever to side; move hand out of way of hot chips during drilling.

It was further recognized that there might be two subclasses under each major classification, namely, when the object reached toward was visible and when it was not visible. No motions made to objects invisible to the operator were observed so this point could not be definitely determined.

The reasoning upon which the above classification is based is as follows. When an object is in a fixed location, the hand always moves to exactly the same point. As the motion is repeated frequently, habits of automaticity are established. Thus the hand moves with a minimum of conscious direction, or in other words the factors of plan and control practically disappear.

When the object is not fixed, its location may vary slightly from cycle to cycle. Therefore it is necessary for the operator to exert conscious physical and mental control over the motion, which will slow it up to a certain extent.

When objects are jumbled together in a group, a certain amount of Search and Select occurs. This appears to the observer as a hesitation and in this study is included in the element D-2, covering Grasp. In addition to the visible hesitation, however, it was felt that the motion to the parts might be slowed down to a certain extent because a mental Search and Select is beginning in the mind of the operator. Hence. class C was established.

When reaching for very small objects or for objects that must be grasped accurately, an unusual amount of control must be exercised over the motion. Hence, it seemed reasonable to assume that these motions would require more time than any other motions thus far considered, which led to the establishing of class D.

It was observed that occasionally an operator makes a motion off into space to secure body balance, to get his hand ready for the next motion, or to get it out of the way of some other action in the cycle. Because there is no definite destination in this case, it was felt that the motion might be made quite quickly. On the other hand, a motion of this type is seldom the one on which the operator is concentrating. Therefore it might be slowed up for this reason. In any event, it was decided to establish a class E tentatively and to confirm or disprove its existence by quantitative analysis of the data.

In addition to the five classifications, it was recognized that there might be other variables which would affect the time required to make a motion within each classification. These were listed tentatively as motion class, length, hand used, change direction, pre-position, and whether or not the hand was in motion at the beginning or end of the movement.

The analysis up to this point laid out the general course to follow in analyzing the data further. First each observed motion was classified as A, B, C, D, or E, in accordance with the classifications listed above. The data for class A were then tabulated for convenience on a separate data summary sheet, with information being recorded under columns headed: Hand, Class, Distance, Time, CD, PP, Ref, Hand in Motion, and Notes. In the column headed Time, the number of elapsed frames leveled by applying the standard leveling factors used in time-study work was recorded.

The data were next plotted on a curve sheet identified as Tentative Curve D-1, case A. A distinction was made in plotting points to show plain motions, motions in which CD appeared, and motions in which the hand was already moving at the start. The points indicated three separate curves, and lined up exceptionally well. A distinction was also made between third-, fourth-, and fifth-class motions, but the data did not show that motion class measurably influenced motion time.

The data for case B were next plotted on Tentative Curve D-1, case B. A distinction was made in plotting the points among motions including CD, plain motions, motions where the hand is in motion at the start, and motions including PP. Inspection of the points showed that the points where the hand was in motion lined up markedly lower than the rest. The rest, however, all apparently lined up together so an average curve was drawn. There were several points that did not line up well with the curve. The original films for these points were then reanalyzed, and in every case but one, it was found that either number of frames or distance had been recorded incorrectly. When revisions were made, the points fell on the curve. In the one case where the data appeared to be correct, the actual setup was observed again in the shop. It was then found that the camera angle of the original picture was such that it was almost impossible to determine from the picture the correct distance of

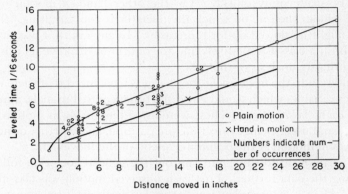

Fig. 9.— Original data—case *B* Reach.

the motion. When the distance as determined by actual measurement was used, the point lined up on the curve. The curves for case *B*, together with the original points from which they were determined, are shown by Fig. 9.

It was not expected to find the motions with change direction requiring the same time as those without. Therefore, the data were studied further in this connection. It was found that of the points where the motion included CD, 10 were above the tentative curve, 6 on the curve, and 7 under. Of the points with no CD, 6 were over the curve, 27 on, and 25 under. The fact that more points with CD were above the curve than under, coupled with the fact that more points of plain motions were under the curve than above, does give a slight indication that CD may have some influence on time. If two curves are plotted, however, the curve with CD would have 10 points on the curve and 13 under, while the curve of plain motions would have 25 points on and 33 over. Neither of these curves would therefore be as satisfactory as the average curve. When it is further recognized that some of the off points can be due to the inaccuracy of the measuring process, as will be explained presently, it is felt that the average curve best fits the points.

It is not difficult to see why change direction may have little effect on this type of motion. When a motion is being made rapidly as in the case of class A motions, a change direction will slow it down measurably. When a class B motion is made, however, it is already slowed down due to the amount of control which is necessary. Because the motion is already slowed down and controlled, a change direction can be made without slowing it further. The data bear out this reasoning.

Points were next plotted for class C motions. They lined up just as for class B. It was impossible to distinguish between motions with CD and plain motions, so an average curve was drawn. Three motions had both CD and PP. Two points were on the curve; one was below. The curve drawn passed through the majority of all points. It was slightly higher than the curve for class B as was expected.

The majority of the points for Tentative Curve D-1, case D, came from one study. Eight additional points obtained from five other studies lined up quite well. Therefore, although more studies would be desirable, it is felt that the curve is fairly well determined.

Only six points were available for plotting Tentative Curve D-1, case E. These points, however, determine a curve that analysis shows might be expected. It has the same slope as all other curves. When compared with the class A curves, it is higher than the curve for the plain class A motion but lower than the class A motion that includes CD. This bears out the initial analysis, which felt that a class E motion would be made quite quickly but might be slowed up due to the fact that the operator was not primarily concentrating on the motion.

The curves plotted as described line up so well that it appears that the initial analysis was sound. All the points, of course, do not fall exactly on the curves. The very nature of the measurement process will make this inevitable. In the first place, the time factor is measured only to the nearest $\frac{1}{16}$ second. Although this appears to be a very small increment of time, the majority of elapsed times are in the range of 4, 5, and 6 sixteenths of a second. Five-sixteenths is 25 per cent more than four-sixteenths. If the true time for a motion were halfway between, it would have to be measured either as $\frac{5}{16}$ or $\frac{4}{16}$ second. In either case, a point would be obtained that is appreciably off from the true value.

The distance factor also introduces an element of inaccuracy. Distances were judged from the film to the nearest inch with the majority of distances being judged as 4 inches, 6 inches, 8 inches, 12 inches, 24 inches, 30 inches, and 36 inches. An error of judgment of an inch or more is quite probable in many instances, and therefore this may also be expected to affect the data.

The plotting of curves that average the points therefore seems to be the logical course to pursue until more accurate measuring means are possible. Consequently this was done. Two pictures taken in slow motion were available for study. In these, the error in the time factor was considerably reduced. It is, therefore, significant to note that the data from these pictures fall on the curves.

It was assumed from inspection of the data that there would be no measurable difference in the time for motions performed with the left and the right hands. To check this further, separate curves were plotted for right- and left-hand data for case B. They showed no measurable difference.

It was also assumed that all elapsed times should be leveled. Although the curves of leveled points were most satisfactory, it was felt desirable to plot curves of unleveled points to see how they would appear. This was therefore done. The leveling factors used were as follows:

Number of Occurrences	Leveling Factor
5	1.00
3	1.02
1	1.03
1	1.035
1	1.05
1	1.065
6	1.08
4	1.095
4	1.11
1	1.115
2	1.13
1	1.175

Because all of the operators who were studied ranged from average to excellent in performance, the range of performance studied was quite limited. If studies of performances ranging from poor to super were available, it would be much easier to show conclusively the effect of leveling on the raw data. As it is, the only conclusion which can be drawn at this time is that leveling improved the data somewhat.

In view of these check tests and the way in which the data bear out the analysis, it was decided to accept the curves as plotted for use in determining values of Reach to Part. The curves were therefore plotted on one curve sheet in order to put them into a form convenient for use. When this was done, several very interesting and significant facts developed. It was found that the curve of case A with change direction coincided very closely with the curve of case B (hand not in motion). Indeed the curves are so nearly the same that any difference may be attributed to a variation in judgment in drawing the curves through the points rather than to any actual difference in the time required to perform these motions. These two curves may therefore be combined into one single curve.

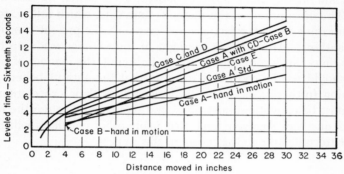

FIG. 10.— Final curves for Reach.

The curve for case C coincided exactly with the curve for case D. In other words, the time required to move to an object in a group is the same as the time for moving to a very small object or where accurate grasp is required. Perhaps the mental reaction necessary to select a part from several jumbled-together parts is the same as that involved in deciding how the very small object or the part which requires an accurate grasp must be handled. Perhaps instead, the mental reaction in the first case requires the same time as the physical control in the second case. There is no way of determining this under the procedure employed. It is clearly determined, however, that the time for the two cases is the same; therefore the two curves may be combined.

Chart D-1 (Fig. 10) shows the final curves, as determined by this analysis, for element D-1.

CONCLUSION

The foregoing paragraphs were taken from notes covering the analysis of the first set of data studied. The findings reported were subsequently checked and verified by additional studies.

All other data were developed and analyzed in a similar manner. When the elements that were composed of a group of basic elements were analyzed, it was found preferable to break them down into basic elements. When this was done, it was found that all elements except those involving the basic elements Do and Examine could be handled with the seven tables for methods-time data which were eventually developed.

This chapter is designed to aid those who wish to contribute to the development of methods-time data. It includes reference to the uncertainties and doubts which must accompany every search for new knowledge. The descriptions of the methods-time data, which follow, for the most part omit all such references and give only the present conclusions of the authors. Although, in the light of the findings made up to the present time, this information is felt to be sound, the manner of presentation should not be construed to mean that the authors believe there is nothing further to be learned. Indeed it is their expectation that there must be corrections, additions, and refinements before the task is finished, and they sincerely hope that many other engineers will find it possible to contribute in the future in this respect.

PART II

BASIC INFORMATION

CHAPTER 4

METHODS-TIME DATA

Before going on to a detailed discussion of what has been learned in regard to the characteristics of each type of motion studied, it seems advisable to present in summarized form the methods-time data that have thus far been checked and accepted as being satisfactory for application and use. By viewing the data in the few condensed tables that it has been possible to construct, an idea can be gained of the comparative simplicity of the methods-time measurement procedure.

METHODS-TIME DATA TABLES

Tables of time data have been compiled for the following motions:
1. Reach
2. Move
3. Turn (including Apply Pressure)
4. Grasp
5. Position
6. Disengage
7. Release

These tables are shown on pages 42 and 43. For convenient use in application, it has been found practical to place them on two pages, 8½ x 11 inches in size, as shown to a reduced scale by Figs. 11 and 12.

These tables have several blank spaces in which no time standards are shown. These represent motion lengths or cases of positioning that have not yet been observed and analyzed in detail by the authors. Although in practical application no serious error will probably be caused by extending the curves or interpolating in the positioning table, it does not seem wise to publish standards obtained in this manner as being acceptable and accepted.

The seven tables cover all types of manual motions that have thus far been observed by the authors in their studies of a wide variety of industrial operations. They do not cover body and leg motions or eye time which occurs as a separate element in certain types of inspection work. Walking time is discussed separately in Chapter 12 because it appears to be sufficiently different in nature from hand and arm motions to justify individual treatment. Some body and leg motions are described in Chapter 13.

When the tables are applied with an understanding of the character-

METHODS—TIME DATA

TABLE I – REACH

Case	Description	DISTANCE MOVED INCHES	LEVELED TIME TMU'S					
			A STD.	A HAND IN MOT	WITH AC D or B	B HAND IN MOT	C OR D	E
A	Reach to object in fixed location or to object in other hand or on which other hand rests	1			2.1		3.6	
		2			4.3		5.9	
		3			5.9		7.3	
B	Reach to single object in location which may vary slightly from cycle to cycle	4	6.1	4.9	7.1	4.3	8.4	6.8
		5	6.5	5.3	7.8	5.0	9.4	7.4
		6	7.0	5.7	8.6	5.7	10.1	8.0
		7	7.4	6.1	9.3	6.5	10.8	8.7
C	Reach to object in group	8	7.9	6.5	10.1	7.2	11.5	9.3
		9	8.3	6.9	10.8	7.9	12.2	9.9
		10	8.7	7.3	11.5	8.6	12.9	10.5
		12	9.6	8.1	12.9	10.1	14.2	11.8
D	Reach to very small object or where accurate grasp is required	14	10.5	8.9	14.4	11.5	15.6	13.0
		16	11.4	9.7	15.8	12.9	17.0	14.2
		18	12.3	10.5	17.2	14.4	18.4	15.5
		20	13.1	11.3	18.6		19.8	16.7
E	Reach to indefinite location to get hand in position for body balance or next motion or out of way	22	14.0	12.1	20.1		21.2	18.0
		24	14.9	12.9	21.5		22.5	19.2
		26	15.8	13.7	22.9		23.9	20.4
		28	16.7	14.5	24.4		26.3	21.7
		30	17.5	15.3	25.8		26.7	22.9

TABLE II – MOVE

Case	Description	DISTANCE MOVED INCHES	LEVELED TIME TMU'S				MULTIPLYING FACTOR	
			A	B or E	C	D-B HAND IN MOT	WEIGHT	FACTOR
A	Move object against stop	1	1.7	1.7	1.7		Up to 5	1.00
		2	3.6	4.2	4.2		10	1.03
		3	4.9	5.7	5.7		15	1.05
B	Move object to approximate location	4	6.1	6.9	7.3	4.3	20	1.08
		5	7.3	8.0	8.7	5.0	25	1.11
		6	8.1	8.9	9.7	5.7	30	1.14
		7						
C	Move object to exact location	8	9.7	10.6	11.8	7.2	35	1.16
		9	10.5	11.5	12.7	7.9	40	1.19
		10	11.3	12.2	13.5	8.6	45	1.22
		12	12.9	13.4	15.2	10.0	50	1.25
D	Toss object aside	14	14.4	14.6	16.9	11.4		
		16	16.0	15.8	18.7	12.8		
		18	17.6	17.0	20.4	14.2		
E	Move object to indefinite location	20	19.2	18.2	22.1	15.6		
		22	20.8	19.4	23.8	17.0		
		24	22.4	20.6	25.5	18.4		
		26	24.0	21.8				
		28	25.5	23.1				
		30	27.1	24.3				

TABLE III – TURN

DEG. TURNED	LEVELED TMU'S	DEG. TURNED	LEVELED TMU'S
30°	2.8	120°	6.8
45°	3.5	135°	7.4
60°	4.1	150°	8.1
75°	4.8	165°	8.7
90°	5.4	180°	9.4
105°	6.1		

Small — No load or parts up to 2 lbs. Use table value

Med-ium — Loads from 2.1 to 10 lb. 1.57 x table value

Large — Loads from 10.1 to 35 lbs. 3 x table value

Apply pressure 16.2 TMU'S

Turn is a special case of Reach or Move. It is accomplished by a turning or torsional motion during which the hand and wrist turn. When turn is combined with a normal Reach or Move, determine time for Turn and Reach or Move from the tables and use larger value.

FIG. 11.— Methods-time data.

istics of the motions covered, as discussed in the next several chapters, it will be found that they make it possible to establish with remarkable accuracy the time required to perform the vast majority of industrial manual operations.

UNIT OF TIME

The unit of time used in deriving the original data was $\frac{1}{16}$ second, the time that elapses between successive exposures when a motion picture

METHODS- TIME DATA

TABLE IV—GRASP

Case	Description	LEVELED TIME T.M.U's
la	Pick up Grasp-Small, medium, or large object by itself-easily grasped	1.7
1b	Very small object or tool handle lying close against flat surface	3.5
1c	Interference with Grasp on bottom and one side of object	8.7
2	Regrasp	5.6
3	Transfer Grasp	5.6
4	Object jumbled with other objects so that Search and Select occur	8.7
5	Contact, Sliding or Hook Grasp	0

TABLE V — POSITION

CLASS OF FIT	EASY TO HANDLE			DIFFICULT TO HANDLE		
	SYMM.	SEMI-SYMM	NON SYMM	SYMM.	SEMI SYMM.	NON SYMM.
1 Loose-No pressure required	5.6	6.6		9.0	13.7	16.3
2 Close-Light pressure required		14.1	21.9	19.6	25.5	27.2
3 Exact-Heavy pressure required	39.4	43.9	53.1			

SYMMETRICAL	SEMI-SYMMETRICAL	NON-SYMMETRICAL
Object can be positioned in an infinite number of ways about the axis which coincides with the direction of travel	Object can be positioned in several ways about the axis which coincides with the direction of travel	Object can be positioned in only one way about the axis which coincides with the direction of travel

*Distance moved to engage-1"or less

TABLE VI—DISENGAGE

Class of Fit	EASY TO HANDLE	DIFFICULT TO HANDLE
1 Loose-very slight effort-Blends with subsequent move	4.0	5.7
2 Close-Normal effort-Slight recoil	7.5	11.8
3 Tight-Considerable effort-Hand recoils markedly	22.9	34.7

TABLE VII— RELEASE

Case	Description	
1	Normal Release performed by opening fingers as independent motion	1.7
2	Contact Release	0

FIG. 12.—Methods-time data (continued).

is taken at a camera speed of 16 frames per second. In preparing the final tables, the desirability of using as the unit of time seconds, decimal minutes, or decimal hours was considered. It was decided that decimal hours would be a desirable unit to use because of the widespread prac-

tice of establishing production standards in terms of decimal hours. A
major disadvantage was apparent, however, in that when the very small
time intervals used in the methods-time measurement procedure are
expressed in decimal hours it becomes necessary to resort to a large number of decimal places. The normal time for a simple grasp, for example,
is $\frac{1}{16}$ second. This is the equivalent of .00001735 decimal hour, which is
an awkward figure to use.

Table	Example	Significance
I	R8C	Reach, 8 inches, case C
	R12Am	Reach, 12 inches, case A, hand in motion
	R14ACD	Reach, 14 inches, case A with Change Direction
II	M6A	Move, 6 inches, case A, object weighs less than 5 pounds
	M16B15#	Move, 16 inches, case B, object weighs 15 pounds
III	T30°S	Turn 30°, small part
	T90°L	Turn 90°, large part
	AP	Apply Pressure
IV	G1a	Grasp, case 1a
V	P1NSD	Position class 1 fit, nonsymmetrical part, difficult to handle
VI	D2E	Disengage, class 2 fit, easy to handle
VII	RL1	Release, case 1

Fig. 13.— Conventions for recording motion classifications.

The difficulty was eventually overcome by arbitrarily choosing as the
unit of measurement .00001 hour, which was given the name Time Measurement Unit. This is readily abbreviated to TMU. When the time for
a simple grasp is expressed in these units and the time is carried out to
only one decimal place, the time becomes 1.7 TMU. This system gives
simple, easily remembered numbers with which to work. They may
readily be converted to decimal hours by multiplying by .00001. Thus if
the time required to perform a given series of motions is found to be 325
TMU, the time in decimal hours is 325 × .00001, or .00325 hour.

Some engineers prefer to express their standards in terms of decimal
minutes, while a fewer number prefer to use seconds. The conversion
factors in these cases are .0006 minute and .036 second, respectively.

The tables are set up, therefore, in terms of leveled TMU. They show
the number of .00001 hours required by the operator of average skill
working with average effort to make the motion under average conditions. When the total number of TMU required to perform any cycle

has been determined, conversion to other units may be made with the following factors:

$$1 \text{ TMU} = .00001 \text{ hour}$$
$$1 \text{ TMU} = .0006 \text{ minute}$$
$$1 \text{ TMU} = .036 \text{ second}$$

The tables do not include any allowances for fatigue, personal necessities, or unavoidable delays.

CONVENTIONS FOR RECORDING METHODS-TIME DATA

It has been found convenient to develop a code for referring to the various classes of motions. It would be awkward, for example, to have to refer to a "case B Reach, 10 inches long, with hand in motion" in so many words every time a motion of that sort was encountered. Therefore, for convenience, this is coded as R10Bm. The above table (Fig. 13), which gives the coding for all types of motions, is self-explanatory.

CHAPTER 5

REACH

In order to apply the methods-time measurement procedure accurately, a thorough understanding of the nature of each type of motion must be obtained. Although a misinterpretation of one type of motion may have an insignificant effect on the allowed time for an element or operation in which the motion occurs only once or twice, the same error occurring in an operation in which the motion is performed several times during the operation cycle can result in a serious discrepancy in the final time value.

In the following nine chapters, explanations of the method used for measuring each type of motion, their characteristics, and the manner in which they may best be recognized will be given in detail.

DEFINITION OF REACH

The definition[1] for the Gilbreth Basic Element of Reach is as follows:

Reach is the basic element employed when the predominant purpose is to move the hand to a destination or general location.

This basic element was originally called "transport empty." This name always caused confusion, however, when the hand contained an object. For example, a sewing-machine operator often keeps a pair of scissors in her hand during the entire cycle. Most of the time the scissors are palmed. They do not interfere with the action of the fingers, and therefore the operator retains them in the hand at all times because it is more convenient to keep the scissors in the hand than it is to set them down and pick them up again repeatedly. When a Reach was performed with the scissors in the hand, it was always a question as to whether the basic

[1] The definitions of all Gilbreth basic elements which follow are those which at the present writing have been tentatively adopted by a subcommittee of the Committee for the Standardization of Therbligs, Process Charts, and Their Symbols, working under the sponsorship of the American Society of Mechanical Engineers. Members of this committee are: Prof. David B. Porter, chairman, Ralph M. Barnes, Clifton H. Cox, Dr. Lillian M. Gilbreth, Joseph O. P. Hummel, Harold B. Maynard, Joseph A. Piacitelli, and Gideon M. Varga.

element should be classified as a transport empty or as a transport loaded. Some contended that because the scissors were "only going along for the ride," so to speak, the classification should be transport empty. Others insisted that because the hand carried an object, the classification must be transport loaded, reasoning that the weight of the object transported would have an important effect on the time required to make the motion. Analysis and investigation conducted to develop the methods-time measurement procedure definitely showed, however, that the major influencing factor was the predominant purpose of making the motion, not

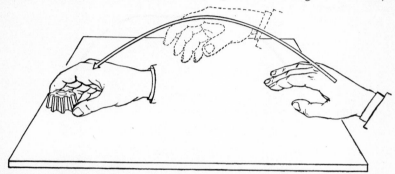

Fig. 14.— Standard Reach—hand not moving at beginning or end of Reach.

the weight of the object carried, at least in the case of light objects. For example, the movement of a pair of tweezers to a tray of parts where the tines must first be carefully positioned before the part can be grasped was found to require a greater amount of time than a motion of the same length in which the hand carries the tweezers without any intent of using them after arriving at the destination. In the light of these findings, the basic element Transport Empty was redefined, and the more descriptive name Reach was selected.

STARTING AND STOPPING POINTS

There are three different general types of Reach, which may be described as follows:

1. Hand is not moving at beginning and at end of Reach.
2. Hand is in motion at either beginning or end of Reach.
3. Hand is in motion at both beginning and end of Reach.

The first type, illustrated by Fig. 14, is known as the "standard motion" because it occurs most frequently. The hand starts, accelerates, moves for a while at its maximum rate of travel, decelerates, and stops. A curve of rate of travel vs. distance moved would appear as in

Fig. 15. The curve from A to B represents the period of start and acceleration. The curve from B to C represents the period of movement at constant rate of travel. The curve from C to D shows the period of deceleration and stop.

To measure the time consumed by a standard Reach motion when motion pictures were being analyzed, the motion was considered to begin at the frame before the frame in which the first noticeable motion

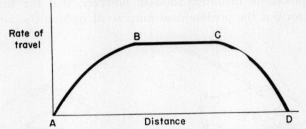

FIG. 15.— Rate of travel vs. distance moved—standard Reach.

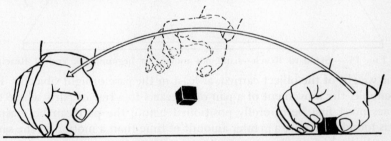

FIG. 16.— Type 2 Reach—hand in motion at beginning of Reach.

takes place. It was considered to end at the frame where noticeable motion has ceased. In most cases observed, the starting and stopping points were not at all difficult to determine.

In the second type of motion, the hand is in motion either at the beginning or the end of the Reach. Thus the period either of start and acceleration (AB, Fig. 15) or of deceleration and stop (CD, Fig. 15) is eliminated. It is obvious, therefore, that a motion of this type consumes less time than the standard motion where both acceleration and deceleration are present. Figure 16 illustrates a type 2 Reach. Here a part has been disposed of by drop delivery as the hand travels to the next part to be grasped. As soon as the part is released, Reach begins. Because it is unnecessary to slow down at the point of release, the hand is in motion at the beginning of Reach.

The amount of the difference in time between type 1 and type 2 Reaches varies with the case of motion and also slightly with the length of motion. The difference in TMU for cases *A* and *B* is shown by the table, Fig. 17.

Distance moved, inches	Difference between type 1 and type 2 Reach, TMU	
	Case *A*	Case *B*
4	1.2	2.8
5	1.2	2.8
6	1.3	2.9
7	1.3	2.8
8	1.4	2.9
9	1.4	2.9
10	1.4	2.9
12	1.5	2.8
14	1.6	2.9
16	1.7	2.9
18	1.8	2.8
20	1.8	
22	1.9	
24	2.0	
26	2.1	
28	2.2	
30	2.2	

Fɪɢ. 17.— Difference in TMU between type 1 and type 2 Reaches, cases *A* and *B*.

In the third type of motion, the hand is in motion at both the beginning and the end of the Reach. This is illustrated by Fig. 18. This type of motion is made the most quickly of all, because both "start and accelerate" and "decelerate and stop" are eliminated. No formal research has yet been undertaken to determine the time for this motion, because no motions of this type were encountered in the original study. A number of type 3 motions were encountered in a subsequent application study, however. In assigning a time to them, the time was computed by subtracting from the time for the standard motion, twice the difference between the type 1 and the type 2 Reach, as shown in Fig. 17. Thus the time for a type 3 case *B* Reach, 10 inches long, R10B2m, was computed as $11.5 - 2 \times 2.9 = 5.7$ TMU. The total cycle time determined when treating the type 3 Reaches in this manner checked closely with the total actual cycle time; therefore it may be concluded tentatively that this is a satisfactory method of determining the time for type 3 Reaches until more data are available.

When the hand is in motion at the beginning of a Reach, the starting point is taken to be the frame that marks the termination of the preceding basic element. In the instance illustrated by Fig. 16 where the part is disposed of by dropping it on the way to get the next part, the Reach is considered to begin as soon as the Release of the part has been completed.

When the hand is in motion at the end of a Reach, the stopping point is taken to be the frame that marks the beginning of the next basic element. For example, assume that the hand moves to a small flat part

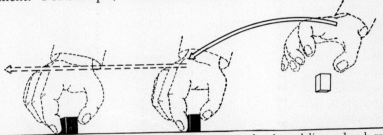

FIG. 18.— Type 3 Reach—after disposing of a part by drop delivery, hand grasps next part on the fly.

lying on a smooth surface and without hesitation makes a Contact Grasp and slides the part along in the same direction the hand was moving at the instant of contact. The stopping point of the Reach would be the frame in which contact with the part is made.

On light, repetitive work, it has been found that operators, after a period of practice, tend to replace type 1 motions with type 2 and type 3 motions. This constitutes a change in method, which will be discussed at greater length in another chapter.

DETERMINING LENGTH OF MOTION

The greatest chance for error in applying the methods-time data to the motion of Reach lies in the determination of the length of the motion. The most accurate method of determination is, of course, by actual measurement. In measuring, the only precautions to observe are that the true path of the motion is measured—not just the straight-line distance between the two terminal points—and that the measurement is made at the same part of the hand at the beginning and the end of the motion. The knuckle at the base of the index finger is a convenient point to use in many cases.

Frequently it is not practical to measure motion lengths, in which case they must be estimated. Great care should be exercised in estimating distances. Experience has shown that most people are poor estimators of distance. They improve with practice and eventually achieve reasonable accuracy, but at first their estimates are usually far from correct. Accuracy of estimating will be increased if the analyst will make the motion himself, duplicating as nearly as possible the motion made by the operator, and then measure the distance his own hand moves, using a 12-inch flexible rule. This does not have to be done at the work station, as long as the analyst has a good mental picture of the location of the object to which the Reach is made.

The motions from which the data were derived were all normal Reach motions made over straight or normally curved paths. Motions where the hand travels a circular path have not at the present writing been subjected to detailed study. In application, however, it has been found that if the distance the hand travels, namely, the circumference of the circle described by the hand, is used as the length of the motion, the results appear quite satisfactory. This practice may therefore be followed until more data are available.

REACH MOTIONS INVOLVING BODY MOVEMENTS

Many Reach motions involve a certain amount of body movement. The most common occurrence is when the body or shoulders move in the same direction as the direction of the Reach. In this case, the body assists the Reach. It speeds up the Reach motion relative to the object, for the movement of the hand imparted by the body is added or over-lapped with the movement of the hand imparted by the arm.

To determine the time for a Reach where a minor body movement occurs in the same direction as the Reach, the table of Reach times is used. For example, in Fig. 19, the operator's hand begins the Reach at A with B as its final destination. To perform the Reach with the shoulder and body held in a fixed position would be unnatural, fatiguing, and time consuming. Therefore the body and shoulder move toward B at the same time that the hand moves from A to B. Since these motions are combined, the distance which determines the time for the Reach is actually the distance which must be moved by the hand minus the distance moved by the shoulder. If the distance moved by the shoulder were 4 inches, and the total distance moved by the hand were 16 inches, the time allowed for the Reach motion would be that of a $(16-4)$ or a 12-inch Reach.

Thus, when the body assists the arm and hand in a Reach to a destination by simultaneously moving in the same direction as the hand, the length of the Reach is considered to be the distance traversed by the hand minus the distance moved by the shoulder or body.

In a study of a foundry operation, a case was found where the body moved in the opposite direction from the hand. In this case, the length of the Reach was considered to be the distance moved by the hand plus the distance moved by the body. A check of the actual time consumed

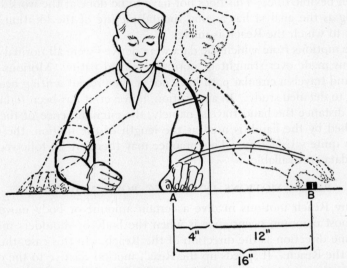

Fig. 19.— Reach accompanied by a body motion made in the same direction as that traveled by the hand.

against the computed time showed close agreement and indicated that this was the proper way to handle this type of motion.

When a Reach is accompanied by a turning or pivotal movement of the body, as when an operator turns to reach for something in back of him, the assistance given to the movement of the hand by the body is greatly increased. This may be readily seen by considering what happens when a yardstick is swung with one end acting as a pivot, as shown by Fig. 20. When the yardstick is swung through 90°, the 12-inch mark travels 18.82 inches, the 24-inch mark travels 37.64 inches, and the 36-inch mark travels 56.46 inches.

The same thing happens in the case of Reaches accompanied by a pivoting of the body. The distance from the vertical axis of the body to the shoulder is approximately 6 inches. When the arm is partly extended to a normal working position, the distance from the shoulder to the hand is approximately 24 inches. Therefore, when the shoulder moves 1 inch as the body pivots, the hand moves 4 inches. Thus to determine the time for a Reach accompanied by a body pivot, the length of the Reach motion is considered to be the distance moved by the hand minus four times the distance moved by the shoulder when the arm is partly extended to the normal working position. If the arm is fully extended, the distance from the shoulder to the hand is approximately 30 inches, and the multiplier thus becomes 30 ÷ 6, or 5. In all the cases of com-

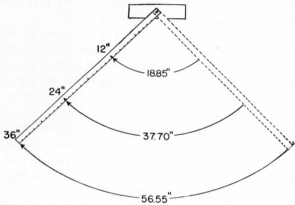

Fig. 20.— Distance moved by the 12-, 24-, and 36-inch marks on a yardstick when it is pivoted 90° about one end.

bined body and hand movement described above, it is assumed that the movement of the hand attributable to arm motion requires more time than the movement of the hand attributable to body motion, or in other words, that the arm movement is limiting. In all cases studied thus far, this condition exists; therefore it is assumed that when body movement and arm movement are combined, the operator will instinctively accomplish the major part of the movement with the faster moving member, or the arm, and will use the body motion only as a means of assisting the arm motion.

CLASSIFICATIONS OF REACH

In addition to the length and the type of Reach, the time required to perform the Reach is influenced by the nature of the object toward which the Reach is made. Analysis of available data has led to the establishing of five classifications of destinations. These classifications, or cases, may be explained as follows:

Case A. Reach For Object in Fixed Location or For Object in Other Hand or on Which Other Hand Rests. This is the fastest case of Reach, for the amount of conscious direction required to make the motion successfully is reduced to a minimum. A common example of an object in a fixed location is a control lever on a machine. Because the operator must reach constantly toward that control lever, after a number of repetitions, he learns exactly where that lever is in relation to the rest of the workplace. He becomes so oriented that he can move to the lever from other parts of the workplace without having to look for the lever with his eyes. He develops a set of habits of automaticity that enable him to perform the Reach in a minimum amount of time.

Most operators who qualify for factory work learn to make case A motions to objects in a fixed location by the time they have practiced the job sufficiently to develop average skill. With further practice and the development of greater skill, the better operators tend to use case A motions for Reaches which are to objects which are not truly in fixed positions. A machine molder in an iron foundry, for example, worked at the same type of machine for many years. He habitually kept his bag of parting sand on the head of the machine in the same location. An analysis of a motion picture of this molder performing his molding operation showed that he reached for the parting sand in the time ordinarily attained only in reaching to an object in a fixed location. Other molders less experienced than the first were found to require the time for a case B motion, or the time for a "reach for a single object in a location that may vary slightly from cycle to cycle." The indication is, therefore, that with constant repetition a case B motion can be changed to a case A motion. This is interesting, for it indicates one way in which a highly skilled operator can outperform an operator of average skill.

When the Reach is toward an object held in the other hand, the same sense of orientation exists as when the Reach is toward an object in a fixed location. One hand is able to find the other with a minimum of conscious direction and without the aid of sight. The situation is similar if one hand rests on an object close to the point to be grasped by the other hand. Three examples of the case A Reach are illustrated by Fig. 21.

Case A Reaches may be type 1, type 2, or type 3 motions, as indeed is true for any other case of Reach. Case A Reaches are quite commonly encountered, although they are not as common as case B Reaches on most jobs.

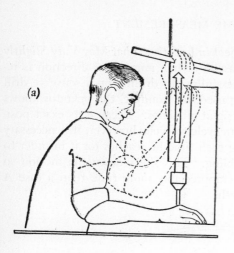

(a)

(b)

FIG. 21.— Examples of case A Reach.
(a) Reach to a machine lever; (b)
Reach to a part in other hand; (c)
Reach to a part on which other hand
rests.

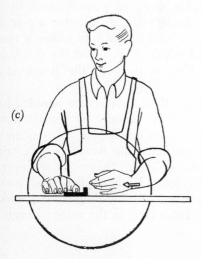

(c)

Case B. Reach For Single Object in Location That May Vary Slightly from Cycle to Cycle. In this case, a certain amount of direction is required to make the motion successfully. In drilling on a sensitive drill press on which a box jig is being used, for example, the operator knows the approximate location of the jig at all times. Because its exact position may vary an inch or two from cycle to cycle, however, it is necessary for the operator to look at the jig each time he reaches for it in order to be able to grasp it without fumbling. This slows down the motion so that the case *B* Reach consumes appreciably more time than a case *A* Reach of the same type and length.

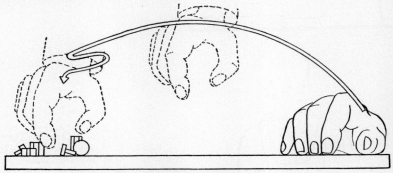

Fig. 22.— Reach to an object in a group.

Examples of the case *B* Reach are numerous. Reaching for a setscrew on a jig, reaching for a pencil in one's pocket, reaching for a single part in a jig, and reaching for a part by itself on a workbench, as shown by Fig. 14, are all examples. Case *B* Reaches are usually easy to identify, although when the other hand is resting on a part some distance from the point of grasp, it is sometimes difficult to decide whether a case *A* or a case *B* Reach is employed. A good rule of thumb to follow is that the other hand must rest on the part within 3 inches of the point of grasp to justify the case *A* classification. Otherwise, the Reach is a case *B*.

Case C. Reach for Object in Group. When objects are jumbled together in a group, as shown in Fig 22, it is necessary for the mind to make a selection before one of the objects can be grasped. This extends the time for grasping, and it also slows down the Reach to a certain extent. Case *C* Reaches are easy to recognize, for they occur whenever material or other objects are jumbled together haphazardly. Small parts jumbled together in a tote pan or parts in an unstacked pile on a workbench cause case *C* Reaches. In the latter case, as the material begins

to be used up, occasionally a part will become separated from the pile
and will lie by itself on the bench near the pile. In this case, the Reach
to this part may be only a case *B* Reach. The last part or two from the
pile will also be reached with a case *B* Reach. In establishing the time
for a cycle of this kind, however, it is satisfactory to assume a case *C*
Reach in all cases, for the slight reduction in time attained through the
employment of a case *B* Reach will be offset in all probability by occasional fumbles.

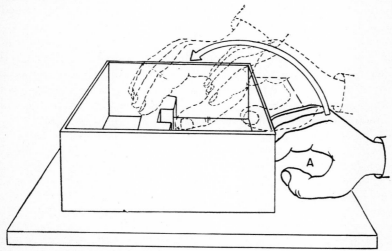

Fig. 23.— Reach to an object where a sharp reversal of direction occurs.

*Case D. Reach For Very Small Object or Where Accurate Grasp Is
Required.* When a very small hard-to-grasp object is reached for, the
time for Reach is extended by the necessity for controlling the motion
accurately. It is not clear at present whether the slowness of the motion
is caused by the necessity for focusing the eye on the very small object or
by the need for additional muscular control. In any event, the time for
the case *D* Reach is the same as the time for the case *C* Reach. In the
few cases observed where the Reach was for a very small object which
was also in a group, the same time applied, indicating that there is no
pyramiding effect when the conditions of case *C* and case *D* coincide.

*Case E. Reach to Indefinite Location to Get Hand in Position For
Body Balance or Next Motion or Out of Way.* This case of Reach
occurs quite frequently and may cause the inexperienced analyst some
difficulty. Often when a case *E* Reach is made, the other hand is
performing the limiting operation, and therefore the case *E* motion

need not be considered. When the Reach is made for the purpose of getting the hand in position for the next motion, a limiting case E motion frequently occurs. For example, assume a box with sides 12 inches high, Fig. 23. The hand starts at point A outside the box close to the side of the box and close to the table on which the box is resting. It moves to an object inside the box along the path shown by the arrow. This motion, if the bend is very sharp at the top of the motion, would be classed as a case E Reach on the way up and a class B or C Reach on the way down, depending upon the situation of the object to be grasped— that is if it is by itself or is jumbled in a group. The chief perplexity in this case would be to decide whether to class the upward motion as a type 1 or a type 2 class E motion. If the motion can be observed, the choice is easy to make. If the motion is continuous with no noticeable pause at the top, it is type 2. If, however, there is a noticeable slowing down or hesitation, it is type 1. The latter appears to be the more common and should be used in estimating.

CHAPTER 6

MOVE

The basic element Move has many of the same characteristics as the basic element Reach. The same three types have been identified. The starting and stopping points of the motion are determined in much the same way. The procedure for determining motion length when body movement is involved is exactly the same. In the discussion that follows, therefore, a detailed description of these factors will be omitted. The points of difference, however, will be emphasized.

DEFINITION OF MOVE

Move is the basic element employed when the predominant purpose is to transport an object to a destination.

Move was originally called "transport loaded." Because of the confusion caused, however, when an object is carried in the hand but not used, it was felt that the revised name and the revised definition are better. Thus in the case previously cited, if a pair of scissors is carried against the palm of the hand as when a sewing-machine operator reaches for a piece of material, the basic element would be classified as Reach. If, on the other hand, the operator moves the scissors to a thread for the purpose of cutting it, the basic element would be classified as Move. Thus by considering the predominant purpose of the basic element, the correct classification is readily determined.

STARTING AND STOPPING POINTS

In collecting the methods-time data, the standard, or type 1, Move was considered to begin at the frame before the frame in which the first noticeable motion takes place. This same point, in most cases where the Move follows a Grasp, marks the termination of the Grasp. Move is considered to end at the frame where noticeable motion ceases.

The hand is sometimes in motion at the beginning of a Move. A common example is when a light part has been secured with a Contact

Grasp and the Move is made in the same direction as the preceding Reach. The Move is considered to begin as soon as the Contact Grasp has been made. This same frame, of course, also marks the termination of the Reach.

The hand may also be in motion at the end of a Move. This occurs when a part is moved aside and released, employing drop delivery. If the hand continues on in the same direction, there is no noticeable slowing down. Thus the Move and the following Reach are type 2 motions. The Move in this case would be considered to end on the frame where the part is released.

As in the case of Reach, practiced operators on light manual operations tend to replace type 1 Moves with type 2 or type 3 Moves. The amount of time which this saves is shown by the table, Fig. 24, for a

Distance Moved, Inches	Difference in TMU between Type 1 and Type 2 Moves Case B
4	2.6
5	3.0
6	3.2
7	3.2
8	3.4
9	3.6
10	3.6
12	3.4
14	3.2
16	3.0
18	2.8
20	2.6
22	2.4
24	2.2

FIG. 24.— Difference in TMU between type 1 and type 2 Moves, case B.

case B Move, the only case on which data are at present available. The time for a type 3 case B Move may be determined, until further data have been compiled, by subtracting from the time for the type 1 case B motion twice the difference between a type 1 and type 2 motion of the same length, as shown by the table.

Although type 2 motions for cases A, C, and E have not yet been studied in detail, a few observations have indicated that they may be handled satisfactorily for the time being by using the time for the type 1 motion minus the difference between type 1 and type 2, shown in Fig. 24.

CLASSIFICATIONS OF MOVE

Moves have been classified into five different cases as was done for Reach. The cases, however, are quite different from the Reach cases. The existence of additional cases is considered probable, but they have not yet been isolated.

Case A. Move Object against Stop. When an object is moved against a stop, as illustrated by Fig. 25, the necessity for subsequent

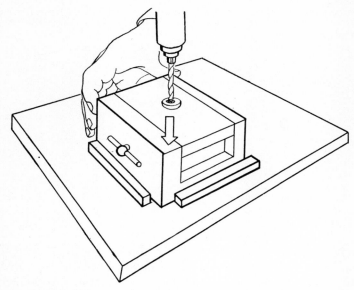

FIG. 25.—Case A Move—object moved against a stop.

positioning is reduced or eliminated. Thus the provision of stops and guides materially reduces the time required to perform many operations. This is because positioning is eliminated rather than because the Move is speeded up to any appreciable extent. Present data indicate that the case A move is slightly faster than a case B Move up to 14 inches, but that for the longer motions, it requires more time. The case A Move is faster than the case C Move throughout, but the difference is not so great as might at first be expected.

The reason appears to be that it is not practical to bang an object up against a stop at a high rate of speed. The object might be damaged, or it might bounce back from the stop. The stop might be knocked out of position, or the hand might lose its grasp on the object. Any or all of these possibilities make it necessary to perform the Move fairly carefully with a controlled motion, so that when the object reaches the stop, it is not traveling too rapidly.

The available data for this case indicate that there are at least two kinds of Moves against a stop. These have tentatively been identified as

1. Moves where the object is primarily controlled by the operator.
2. Moves where the object is partly controlled by mechanical means.

If the object is not attached to any other object, all control must be exerted by the operator. In the case of a lever attached to a machine, however, one end of the lever is controlled mechanically. In many cases,

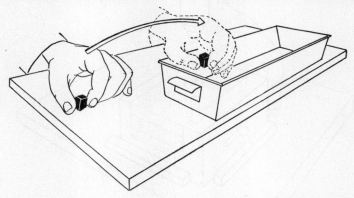

Fig. 26.— Case *B* Move—object moved to an approximate location.

the direction in which it may be moved is also controlled. Under these conditions, it would seem reasonable to suppose that the case A Move would be made more quickly than when the operator was required to exercise complete control. The data show some confirmation of this although not enough to justify setting up two subdivisions.

Case B. Move Object to Approximate Location. A case B Move occurs when an object is moved to a general location but where no special care has to be taken to line up the object exactly. The most common occurrence is when a part is laid aside in a container, as illustrated by Fig. 26. The part must be placed in the container, but if it is not to be stacked in an orderly manner, it makes no particular difference in which part of the container it is placed. The location of the part is only approximate, and therefore a case B Move may be employed.

Case C. Move Object to Exact Location. When an object is moved to a location where it must be brought into exact relationship with another object, a case C Move occurs. A case C Move is nearly always followed by Position, although a very practiced operator may be able to control the Move so exactly that no positioning is required. Common examples of the case C Move are "move part to jig," illustrated by Fig. 27, "move thread to eye of needle," and "move tool to tool holder." Case C Moves are quite common on assembly operations.

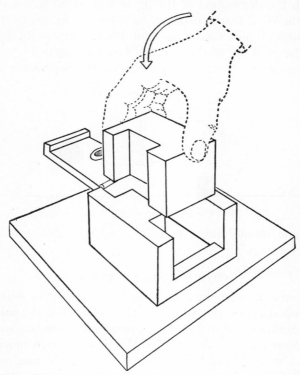

Fig. 27.— Case C Move—object moved to an exact location.

Case D. Toss Object Aside. Frequently objects are disposed of by tossing them aside, as shown by Fig. 28. If the hand continues in the same general direction after the object has been released, without noticeable hesitation, a case D Move occurs. This is a type 2 sort of motion, so that it is not surprising to find the time for a case D and a type 2 case B Move coinciding. Indeed case D might well be considered to be merely a special case of the type 2 case B Move, but it occurs so frequently that for the time being at least, it was thought advisable to establish a separate classification.

When a part is tossed aside and the hand stops and then starts off in another direction, the Move should be classed as a case E Move.

Case E. Move Object to an Indefinite Location. One example of a case E Move has just been given. Another instance occurs when an operator picks up a drill jig to brush chips off the drill-press table where the jig had been resting, as shown by Fig. 29. The operator is not concerned with the destination of the jig as long as he gets it out of the way. He therefore moves it off to an indefinite location. The Move may be limiting from a time standpoint, because he cannot do anything else until the jig is out of the way, but his chief interest is centered on what he is going to do next, rather than on the destination of the jig.

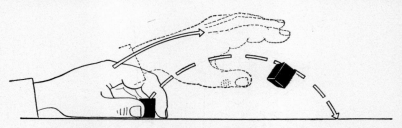

FIG. 28.— Case *D* Move—object tossed aside.

This example should suffice to explain what is meant by the term "indefinite location."

OTHER CASES OF MOVE

In the course of collecting data, three cases were encountered where a jig was bumped against the drill-press table to jar loose the part that was in it. It was thought that this might prove to be a special case of Move. Notes made at the time showed that the time per inch moved up and down was 1.88, 1.81, and 1.72 TMU. If this were classed as a case *E* Move on the way up and a case *A* Move on the way down, the time per inch for Moves up to 4 inches would be as follows:

Length of Bumping Motion, Up or Down	Average Time per Inch, TMU
1	1.70
2	1.95
3	1.77
4	1.63

In view of the closeness with which this checks with the observed data, this would appear to be a satisfactory way of handling bumping Moves.

One case of hammering was observed. The motion made by the hand was about 6 inches in length although the mallet head traveled further.

The average leveled time per inch of hand travel was 1.13 TMU. If the downward motion were considered as an *M6A* and the upward motion were considered as an *M6Em* (type 2 because of the rebound of the hammer), the average time per inch of a 6-inch hammering motion would be computed as $[8.1 + (8.9 - 3.2)] \div 12 = 1.15$ TMU. Although there seems to be some basis for this reasoning, the treatment is

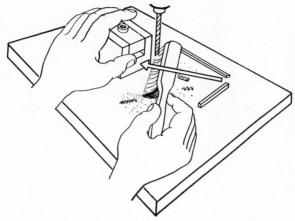

Fig. 29.— Case E Move—object moved to an indefinite location.

admittedly empirical. It is described here, however, to give other investigators an opportunity to prove or disprove its correctness and to offer a means of computing hammering time for estimating purposes until further data are available.

Only a few observations were available where the object was slid along a surface instead of being picked up and carried. Further investigation is necessary, but for the time being, the regular Move time for the proper classification may be used for cases of this type.

WEIGHT FACTORS

It is recognized that the weight of the object moved will have an effect on the time required to make the Move. Experiments with minimum motion times have shown that every ounce of weight increases the time for a Move when it is performed at maximum speed. Industrial motions are not ordinarily made at maximum effort. Therefore, when a light object is moved at a normal effort, it appears that the control of the motion is the limiting factor rather than the weight of the object so that small differences in weight do not affect time.

A study was made of the effect of weight on Move time, using all available data. Only 18 observations were available on the moving of objects weighing more than 3 pounds. The results of the study were somewhat disappointing due to their lack of consistency. Of the 18 points, 9 fell on the curve already determined for small objects. Nine were above the curve. On the basis of these findings, it may be assumed that weight does have some influence on time but that all the variable factors have not yet been identified and measured.

In the meantime, in order to have some means of handling the weight factor, a curve of weight vs. the per cent that time of Move is greater than base curve has been developed. Although the points were undesirably scattered, there appeared to be enough of a trend to justify drawing a curve using a liberal amount of judgment. This curve in tabular form is included in Table II of the methods-time data. It should be used with a full understanding of its limitations.

CHAPTER 7

TURN

The Reach and Move elements, as described thus far, are accomplished by moving the hand in a straight line or along a normally curved path. The same basic elements are also sometimes accomplished by a turning or torsional motion. For purposes of the methods-time data, all such motions are classed as Turns.

DEFINITION OF TURN

Turn is not a Gilbreth basic element, but is merely a special way of performing a Reach or a Move. In these cases, it may be called a Reach-turn or a Move-turn. It will be pointed out presently that the omnibus basic elements Use and Assemble often may be broken down into a number of Reaches, Grasps, Moves, and Releases for the purpose of time determination. The Reaches and Moves may be of the type covered by Tables I and II or they may be Reach-turns and Move-turns.

A Turn is also used occasionally to perform the basic element Preposition. Turn may be defined as follows:

Turn is the motion employed to turn the hand either empty or loaded by a movement that rotates the hand, wrist, and forearm about the long axis of the forearm.

A separate table of time values has been set up for Turn because the motion is distinctive and requires a different time to perform than the normal Reach or Move. The procedure for measuring the length of the motion is also different.

STARTING AND STOPPING POINTS

Analysis would indicate that there are three different types of Turn just as there are three different types of Reach and Move. At the present time, however, only the type 1 Turn where the hand is not moving at the beginning and at the end of Turn has been encountered. In estimating, if it is necessary to determine the time for a type 2 Turn, the value from Table III less 1.4 TMU may be used until further data are

67

available. The fact that no type 2 Turns have been encountered in all the studies which have been made would indicate that they are not common.

A type 1 Turn is considered to begin on the frame preceding the frame in which the first noticeable movement of the hand occurs. It is considered to end at the frame where noticeable motion ceases.

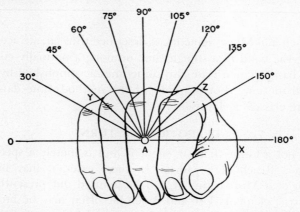

Fig. 30.— Concept employed in determining length of Turn motion.

LENGTH OF TURN MOTION

The length of Turn is measured in terms of degrees turned. Figure 30 represents a closed hand. As the hand is rotated in a clockwise direction about point A, which represents the end of the long axis of the forearm, the number of degrees turned is shown by the lines radiating from point A. In determining the number of degrees the hand turns, the points x, y, and z, or the thumb knuckle, the little finger knuckle, and the index finger knuckle, in descending order of desirability are the best parts of the hand to observe. If an object is held so that it protrudes from the hand, the displacement of the object may be observed.

Table III of the methods-time data contains the time values in TMU for Turns ranging from 30 to 180° in increments of 15°. These data were established after a very careful film analysis of many types of operations, and hence are considered quite accurate. It is realized, however, that in the application of the data, cases will arise in which it is extremely difficult if not impossible to determine with exactness the number of degrees turned in making the motion. When this situation arises, it is sound practice to consider the Turns occurring in 45° steps, rather than to attempt to break them down into steps of 15°.

COMBINATION MOTIONS

Turn is frequently combined with Reach or Move. For example, a part held in the hand may be turned 180° while the object is moved several inches along the path of a normal Move, as illustrated by Fig. 31. In such cases, the motion is considered to be first a Turn and then a Move. The values are determined from Tables II and III, and the larger of the two is used. For example, assume that a part is turned 90° during the course of an *M5B* Move. The time for a 90° Turn is 5.4 TMU.

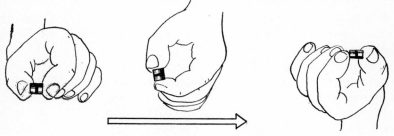

Fig. 31.— Combination Move and Turn.

The time for an *M5B* Move is 8.0 TMU. The Move is limiting; therefore the time of 8.0 TMU would be used.

Again, assume that a *T180S* occurs in combination with an *M3C*. The times are 9.4 TMU and 5.7 TMU respectively. Here the Turn is limiting; therefore the time of 9.4 TMU is used.

CLASSIFICATIONS OF TURN

It seems reasonable to suppose that the time for Turn will be affected by the predominant purpose of the motion. Therefore there would be one set of time values when the Turn is made for the purpose of reaching and another set when the Turn is made for the purpose of moving. Furthermore the Reach-turn could be subdivided into the same five cases as the normal Reach and the Move-turn into the same five cases as the normal Move.

This is an assumption which should be checked in detail before being either accepted or rejected, even though data available at present indicate that only one class exists. The motion is difficult to measure accurately, both with respect to degrees turned and elapsed TMU. The total length of time consumed by Turn is so small that the fact that the measuring process employed measures only to the nearest $\frac{1}{16}$ second makes it impossible to measure accurately the minor variations which may be present. The available data all plot up quite smoothly into a single curve. Hence, for the time being, no classifications of Turn have been established. Although this point should be investigated further so that greater knowledge of motion times and characteristics may be had, from a practical standpoint, the accuracy of the results obtained from the application of the methods-time data will not be materially affected by neglecting to establish the various cases of Reach-turns and Move-turns if they do exist.

INFLUENCE OF WEIGHT OF OBJECT ON TURN

It is apparent that more time will be required to turn heavy parts than to turn light parts. In all probability, time varies with weight along a smooth curve. As a matter of fact, this assumption was tested by plotting a curve of weight vs. the time for 90° Turns during the course of the original investigation of Turn. Sufficient data were available to yield a fairly good curve, thus bearing out the above analysis.

Because of the limited amount of data available, however, it was decided to handle the weight factor in the case of Turn by establishing three classifications as follows:

Small—No load to parts up to 2 pounds in weight.
Medium—Loads from 2.1 to 10 pounds.
Large—Loads from 10.1 to 35 pounds.

The time for turning small parts, for which there were considerable data, was next determined. Then the additional time in per cent required to turn the very few medium and large parts studied was determined. The percentages were averaged, and finally factors of 1.57 for medium objects and 3.0 for large objects were established. These factors multiplied by the time for turning a small object give the time for turning medium and large parts.

SPECIAL CASES OF TURN

The turning of screws with a screw driver presents some interesting problems. Assume that the screw driver is supported by one hand and turned with the other, as shown by Fig. 32. If the resistance offered to turning is small, the screw driver will be turned by a series of Reaches and Moves performed by the fingers rather than by the Turn motion. They may be classed as R2E and M2B and values of 4.3 and 4.2 TMU, respectively, may be used. The Grasp will be a Simple Grasp, G1a, and the Release will be a Simple Release, RL1, so that the total time is 11.9 TMU's per turn.

If the resistance to turning is moderate, a true Turn motion will be employed. The Grasp will still be a G1a and the Release will be an RL1. Even if resistance increases considerably, this same combination of Turn, Release, and Grasp motions is used.

The same situation applies in the turning of small circular handles, such as the handle on a radiator valve.

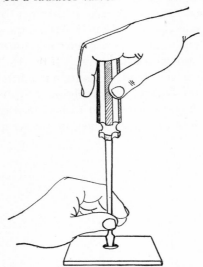

Fig. 32.— Screwdriver in position for use.

APPLY PRESSURE

In studying the tightening of screws, it was noted that when the screw was turned down as far as it would go, the operator would give it a final tightening, during which considerable pressure was applied without causing any appreciable movement of the screw. This was called "Final Tighten," and a value of 16.2 TMU was assigned. Later it was found that whenever pressure was applied to a part, whether with a turning motion or with some other type of motion, such as a pull or a push, the time consumed came out at 16.2 TMU quite consistently. The operation was, therefore, renamed Apply Pressure, and a value of 16.2 TMU was established for all cases. The value appears in the table for Turn, largely because it was in connection with the study of Turns that this element was first identified.

Apply Pressure is not a recognized basic element at the present time. It occurs on a surprisingly large number of operations but is likely to be overlooked by the inexperienced observer. It is easy to recognize by observation, however, for it appears as a slight pause or hesitation followed by a noticeable application of force.

A great many cases have occurred which indicate that Apply Pressure, as it has been set up, includes a G2 Grasp, or Regrasp, or its equivalent, and that the true application of pressure consumes $16.2 - 5.6$, or 10.6 TMU. A value of approximately 10 TMU for Apply Pressure has been encountered sufficiently often to make it worthy of mention. The fact that values of approximately 16 and 10 TMU are the only values thus far measured for Apply Pressure is also interesting, for it indicates that the act of applying pressure is basic in nature. If the 16.2 value does include a Regrasp, it may be stated that the Regrasp is not recognizable as a visible adjustment of the fingers. It does, however, consist of a very minor adjustment of the fingers, perhaps to make sure that there will be no pinching of the flesh of the fingers when pressure is applied.

CHAPTER 8

GRASP

Grasp may be performed under so many different conditions that it is quite apparent that all possible cases of Grasp have not yet been identified, described, and measured. The cases which are listed below, however, are the ones which occur most commonly. It is probably safe to say that they cover well over 98 per cent of all Grasps which are likely to be encountered in industrial operations.

DEFINITION OF GRASP

Grasp is the basic element employed when the predominant purpose is to secure sufficient control of one or more objects with the fingers or the hand to permit the performance of the next required basic element.

Grasp can be performed by no other body member than the fingers or hand. It does not occur, therefore, when control of a part is secured by a mechanical agent actuated by the hands. For example, when an object is secured by a pair of tongs, the motion is not a Grasp basic element. Instead it would be classed as a Move. This conforms to the methods-time data, which would determine the time for closing the tongs around the object by considering the motion made by the hand as a case A Move.

STARTING AND STOPPING POINTS

In determining the time for Grasp, the basic element was considered to begin when the preceding basic element ended. This was usually a Reach. Grasp was considered to end when the next basic element began. By treating Grasp in this manner instead of trying to judge it by the movements of the fingers, not only was it measured more accurately but the influence of other factors such as Search and Select was determined. It was found that these latter factors were more easily measured through their effect on other basic elements than by direct measurement.

CLASSIFICATIONS OF GRASP

There are two fundamentally different kinds of Grasp, the Pickup Grasp and the Contact Grasp. In the Pickup Grasp, the object is actually picked up. Sufficient control is obtained so that the object may be carried from one point to another. In the case of the Contact Grasp, the object is constrained in some other way than by the fingers. Because of this the fingers need only touch it to enable the hand to move it from one point to another.

Either of these types of Grasp may be performed under a wide variety of conditions. In general, the Contact Grasp is quicker than the Pickup Grasp, and it should be employed wherever practical. The following cases of Grasp have been established thus far.

Case G1a. Pickup Grasp—Small, Medium, or Large Object by Itself, Easily Grasped. This is by far the most commonly encountered type of

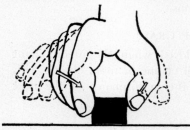

Grasp. Any object in a position that permits easy grasping by a simple closure of the fingers is grasped with a G1a Grasp when it is picked up. Examples are a small part on a table by itself, as in Fig. 33, a box jig on a drill-press table, a pencil lying on a desk, or a pen in a desk penholder. This type of Grasp is also employed in grasping the spindle

Fig. 33.— Pick-up Grasp.

lever of a drill press, a thumbscrew on a jig, or the handle of a handwheel on an engine lathe. In the latter cases, the object is not actually picked up, to be sure, but the fingers are closed around it in a manner equivalent to a Pickup Grasp.

The time for a G1a Grasp has been established as 1.7 TMU. This was the value obtained in all occurrences that were measured. Actually the time may be somewhat less than this, but because the films studied in collecting data were for the most part exposed at the normal speed of 16 frames per second, the smallest unit measured was 1 frame, or $\frac{1}{16}$ second, or 1.7 TMU. Many of the operators filmed gave performances above average, but in recognition of the fact that the G1a Grasp might actually take less than 1 frame, the 1.7 TMU values obtained by film analysis were not leveled. In view of the accuracy of the results obtained when applying the methods-time data, it is not felt that this manner of treating the data introduced any appreciable error.

Case G1b. Pickup Grasp—Very Small Object or Tool Handle Lying Close against a Flat Surface. When it is necessary to grasp a tool handle lying close against a flat surface, as shown by Fig. 34, by wrapping the fingers securely around it so that the tool can be used with the applica-

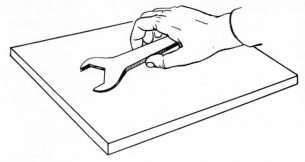

Fig. 34.— Case G1b Grasp of tool handle lying close to a flat surface.

tion of considerable force, a G1b Grasp occurs. This consumes 3.5 TMU. It should be recognized that it occurs only under the conditions specified, namely, a handle or similar object lying close to a flat surface. In grasping the spindle lever of a drill press, although the fingers must

Fig. 35.— Pick-up Grasp—cloth or paper stacked in layers

be wrapped securely around it so that force can be applied, the handle is easy of access so that a 1.7 TMU Grasp is always possible.

In grasping a very small part, ⅛ × ⅛ inch or less in cross section, more control is necessary than if the part were larger. Hence, it is logical that a greater amount of time should be consumed by Grasp. Analysis of available data showed that the leveled average of 16 cases was 3.5 TMU. Therefore, very small parts are included in the G1b classification.

Another instance of a 3.5 TMU Grasp is found where thin, flexible material is stacked in layers, such as paper in a pad or cloth in a pile, as illustrated by Fig. 35. In grasping the top piece, the operator will place his hand on the stack near one corner with the thumb and fingers separated. Then applying light pressure, he will separate the top sheet from the pile by moving the fingers toward the thumb (assuming that the fingers are nearer the edge of the stack). This forces the section of the top piece of material between the thumb and fingers away from the stack and raises it upward between the thumb and fingers, thus providing a condition suitable for maintaining control of the part with a light grasp. A study of this type of Graps shows that it requires 3.5 TMU to perform; therefore it too has been included in case G1b.

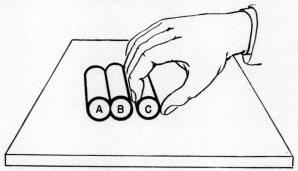

FIG. 36.— Cylindrical parts in contact with one another.

Case G1c. Pickup Grasp—Interference with Grasp on Bottom and One Side of Object. Case G1c was established to cover the situation that exists when cylindrical parts are placed in a box or on a table touching one another, as shown by Fig. 36. If an attempt is made to pick up part C, it will be found that securing control of the part is interfered with on the bottom by the surface on which the part is resting and on the side by the adjacent piece. To grasp the part, it will be necessary to work the fingers in between parts B and C and the thumb under part C. In the occurrences of this type of Grasp that have been analyzed, the time for the Grasp was found to run 8.7 TMU consistently. A value of 8.7 TMU has therefore been established for case G1c.

Case G2. Regrasp. Perhaps one of the most important accomplishments in the compilation of the methods-time data has been the identification and measurement of Regrasp. It occurs on a large number of operations, often more than once. Until it was identified, it caused endless perplexities and inconsistencies, which have since vanished.

When an object is held by the fingers, Regrasp is accomplished by opening the fingers, and moving quickly so as not to lose control of the object, closing them again at or near the point of the original Grasp.

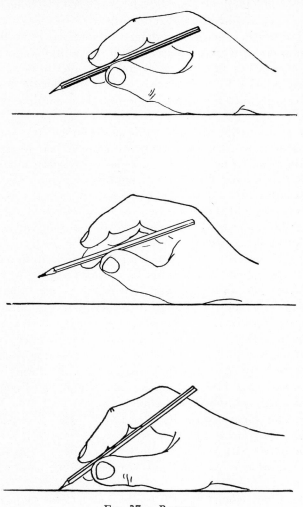

Fig. 37.— Regrasp.

Figure 37 illustrates a typical Regrasp. The purpose of Regrasp is usually either to secure a better control of the object or to shift the object about in the hand. In the latter case, the Regrasp or a series of Regrasps may accomplish the element of Pre-position.

A common occurrence of Regrasp to secure better control occurs in writing. When a pencil is moved to a piece of paper for the purpose of writing, a Regrasp is almost always performed either en route or just before the pencil is used. If considerable writing is to be done, the pencil will be regrasped frequently, either to turn it to secure a sharper edge of the lead or to relieve muscular fatigue in the fingers or both.

A common use of Regrasp to accomplish pre-positioning occurs when the pencil is picked up near the eraser end. In order to bring the pencil into a better position for writing, it is worked through the hand with a series of Regrasps until the fingers come to a good grasping position for writing.

Regrasp occurs frequently just before positioning. If a small part is to be placed in a jig, a common sequence is move part to jig, Regrasp, and position in jig. The suspected presence of Regrasp in conjunction with Apply Pressure has already been commented upon.

Regrasp consistently requires 5.6 TMU to perform. It is recognizable as a quick opening and closing of the fingers and can be readily observed by anyone who understands the nature of the motion and who knows where to expect its occurrence.

Case G3. Transfer Grasp. When a part is passed from one hand to the other at normal effort, a Transfer Grasp takes place. At high effort levels, the part may be tossed from one hand to the other with the release of one hand and the grasp of the other occurring simultaneously. At the normal performance level, when the transfer begins, the empty hand grasps the object. There then appears to be a brief delay before the other hand releases, probably while the mind is assuring itself that the part is securely grasped. Finally the Release occurs, during which the hand which has grasped the part remains idle holding it. Figure 38 illustrates the normal Transfer Grasp sequence.

The Transfer Grasp consumes 5.6 TMU. Its occurrence should always raise a question as to why it is necessary. Often it is quicker to pick up the object with the hand which is to carry it to its destination than to pick it up with one hand and transfer it to the hand which completes the move.

Case G4. Grasp when Object Is Jumbled with Other Objects So That Search and Select Occur. When objects are jumbled together in a group, the time for Grasp is prolonged. This is probably partly due to the presence of the basic elements Search and Select and partly due to interferences with Grasp of the kind described under case G1c.

The time for a G4 Grasp checks quite consistently at 8.7 TMU. A certain amount of variation may naturally be expected, however, due to the fact that when parts are jumbled together haphazardly, it will sometimes be easy to single out a part for grasping and sometimes difficult.

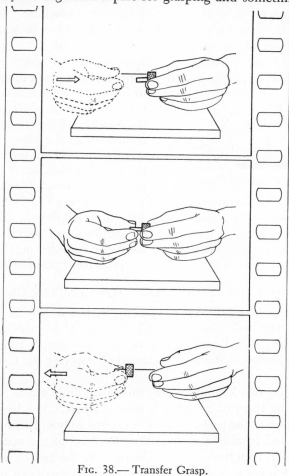

FIG. 38.— Transfer Grasp.

When parts are so jumbled together that they are interlocked and must be separated, the G4 Grasp time does not apply, for several other motions must be made to accomplish the separation.

Case G5. Contact, Sliding, or Hook Grasp. Various names have been given by various writers to the grasp that is primarily a Contact

Grasp, so that several names are here included until standardization can be achieved. The principal characteristic of this type of Grasp is that partial control is obtained by making contact with the object. The rest of the control is provided by the surface on which the object rests or by mechanical means, as in the case of a lever on a machine. The control obtained by the fingers is partial, but it is nevertheless sufficient to permit the performance of the next required basic element.

A Contact Grasp is customarily employed when an object is to be slid along a surface, as in Fig. 39. It would be used when a hinged cover is to be swung shut on a box drill jig under certain conditions. Because the motion of the cover is largely controlled by the hinge, it is necessary for the operator only to push on the cover to close it. A pushing action requires only a Contact Grasp.

FIG. 39.— Contact Grasp.

No measurable amount of time for performing a Contact Grasp was observable under the measurement procedure employed. Therefore, a value of zero TMU has been assigned. Although no time is allowed for Contact Grasp, its presence should always be recorded on the Methods Analysis Chart in order to provide a complete description of the method.

SYNTHESIZING TIME VALUES FOR COMPLEX GRASPS

Special cases of Grasp occur occasionally, but usually they are combinations of the basic Grasp element with one or more other motions. Cases of this type can readily be recognized and proper time standards applied by identifying the motions and then applying the time standard for each.

The grasping of a handful of very small parts from a tote pan preparatory to placing them on a table is a good example. The hand is closed around a group of the parts, pressure is exerted to hold them together en route, the hand is raised 6 inches above the level of the material in the tote pan, and is then turned before the move to the table is begun. The Turn is performed to avoid dropping loose or free parts en route to the destination. The motions employed in this operation are

Motion	TMU
$G4$	8.7
AP	16.2
$M6E$	8.9
$T180S$	9.4
Total	43.2

Other cases can be calculated similarly and just as easily once the motions employed are identified.

GRASP AT HIGH PERFORMANCE LEVELS

Operators working in the excellent and excessive performance ranges tend to eliminate Grasp as a separate element by blending it in with Reach and Move. A motion sequence at the average performance level might consist of

$$R6B$$
$$G1a$$
$$M10B$$

At a higher performance level the operator might change this to

$$R6Bm$$
$$M10Bm$$

The object would be scooped up on the fly, as it were, and the Grasp would be blended into the Move. This constitutes a change in method and shows another way in which highly practiced operators working with high effort will out perform operators working at the average performance level.

Fig. 40.— Work station arranged to permit simultaneous motions with both hands.

TWO-HANDED OPERATIONS

In two-handed setups, as in Fig. 40, if the parts to be grasped are within the normal working area, and if they can be secured with a simple

Pickup Grasp, the Grasp will be performed simultaneously by the right hand and the left hand.   If the parts are more widely separated, first one hand and then the other will perform the Grasp.   Under this condition, twice the Grasp time must be allowed.   Where the Grasp is a G4 Grasp, twice the time for a single Grasp must always be allowed for two-handed operation, regardless of proximity of the parts.

CHAPTER 9

POSITION

Perhaps the most difficult motions to understand and apply are those required to join or position one part to another. At the same time, these motions are most important from the standpoint of methods improvement, as well as that of accurate determination of time. Because this group of motions occurs frequently in every type of industrial work, and because the time required to perform them often represents a large percentage of the handling time for the entire operation, it is evident that misinterpretation of the positioning motions by the analyst can result in a serious error in the time value which he establishes.

THE IMPORTANCE OF POSITION

Until the analyst applies the methods-time measurement procedure, he scarcely realizes how often the motions making up Position are used. In a sensitive drill-press operation involving the use of a simple jig for the drilling of one hole, these motions occur at least three times and may represent as much as 20 per cent of the total handling time. In an operation, such as the placing of two parts together and then making a permanent joining with a screw, lockwasher, and nut assembly, tightened by an electric screw driver, the act of Position occurs five times and represents over 90 per cent of the total operation time.

Position is the basic element employed to align, orient, and engage one object with another object where the motions used are so minor that they do not justify classification as other basic elements.

Those who are familiar with the older micromotion-study procedure will recognize the reasoning underlying this definition. When two objects are brought together, directly after the Move there is a period of hesitation and adjustment until the objects are finally fitted together successfully. It was the practice to classify the aligning and orienting as Position and the engaging as Assemble. When the depth of engagement was not great, however, the motion by which the engagement was accomplished was so minor that it was difficult to distinguish it, even on a motion-picture film.

In compiling the methods-time data, an attempt was made at first to separate Position and Assemble. It was soon found impossible to make the separation accurately and consistently, so the two were then measured together. This gave much better results. This experience, which has been confirmed by others, led the authors to decide that if Position and Assemble as covered by the older definitions could not be accurately identified and measured, it would be better to redefine them into basic elements which were more readily measurable. Hence, it was decided that the term "Position" should cover not only aligning and orienting but should also include minor motions of assembly. In methods-time data application practice, a minor motion of assembly is one which follows immediately after or is combined with alignment and orientation and is not greater than 1 inch in length. Any assembly that requires a motion greater than 1 inch to complete is handled by treating all motion in excess of 1 inch as a Move or a Move-turn. If another motion such as Regrasp intervenes between alignment and orientation and the motion of engagement, then the motion of engagement is considered to be a Move or Move-turn regardless of its length, and additional time is allowed for it.

STARTING AND STOPPING POINTS

Position begins at the frame which marks the termination of the preceding basic element, which is usually Move. In order to avoid measurement difficulties, Position, Assemble used in the sense explained above, and Release were measured as a group. This made it possible to obtain consistent data, for the termination of Release could be definitely determined by considering that it ended at the frame which marked the beginning of the next basic element, which is usually Reach.

In some operations, there is no Release following Position. Two parts may be positioned together, for example, and then moved directly into a kick press for staking. In setting up Table V in its final form, it was decided that it should cover Position only. Therefore the time for Release, which has been established at 1.7 TMU, was subtracted from the data as originally compiled to yield Table V, shown in Chapter 4.

Because of the advantage in the form of increased accuracy resulting from the procedure of measuring Position and Release together and then subtracting 1.7 TMU, it would seem advisable to continue this practice on any new studies that are made.

VARIABLES AFFECTING POSITION

There are three major variables that affect positioning time. They are

Class of fit
Symmetry
Ease of handling

It is thought probable that size or weight may also affect positioning time. The heaviest work analyzed up to the present time was foundry work where weights up to approximately 35 pounds were involved. The data in Table V seemed to cover all positioning done on this work quite satisfactorily, which would seem to indicate that weight is not a variable. It would be unwise, however, to consider this a final conclusion until additional analyses have been made.

CLASS OF FIT

Three classes of fit have been established as follows:

Class 1—Loose. No pressure required.
Class 2—Close. Light pressure required.
Class 3—Exact. Heavy pressure required.

When two objects can be put together easily without exerting any pressure, the fit is considered to be loose. There will be appreciable clearance between the two parts, even after the engagement has been completed. The parts go together so easily that the observer is often inclined to feel that no positioning was required, since he could observe no appreciable hesitation. Nevertheless as long as the objects must be brought together into a predetermined relationship, analysis and meas-urement show that position does occur and must be allowed for.

When it is necessary to exert heavy pressure to put two objects together because they are so very nearly the same size, the fit is considered to be exact, or class 3. An observer watching this class fit will receive the impression that the operator is having real difficulty in getting the objects together. From 1.5 to 3 seconds are required, which is a readily notice-able amount of time.

The class 1 and the class 3 fits represent the extreme conditions. All other situations are identified as class 2. If the fit is close enough to require careful aligning and orienting, a class 2 fit exists whether or not any noticeable pressure is required to bring the parts together. In any case of doubt as to the class of fit, class 2 should be selected. It is by far the most commonly encountered.

Studies of positioning to a line have shown that the equivalent of a class 2 fit exists. A study was made of the dipping of a small cylindrical object into a liquid, as shown in Fig. 41. The part had to be immersed exactly to the line marked A. Measurement showed that the time required to do this corresponded to the time of a class 2 fit. This was subsequently checked on other studies of positioning objects to lines.

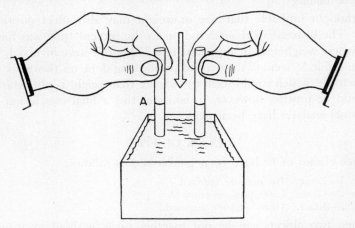

FIG. 41.— Cylindrical parts to be dipped in liquid by immersing to line A.

SYMMETRY

Class of fit affects the time required for aligning and engaging one object with another. Condition of symmetry affects the time for orientation. The three classes of symmetry are defined as follows:

Symmetrical. Object can be positioned in an indefinite number of ways about the axis that coincides with the direction of travel.
Semisymmetrical. Object can be positioned in several ways about the axis that coincides with the direction of travel.
Nonsymmetrical. Object can be positioned in only one way about the axis that coincides with the direction of travel.

The three classifications of symmetry are quite easy to recognize. Symmetry is judged by the condition of symmetry at the point of initial engagement. For example, a certain electrode holder was cylindrical in shape except for a single projection located as shown by Fig. 45. This projection fitted in a slot in a drill jig. In classifying the Position which occurred as the part was placed in the jig which was itself cylindrical in shape except for the slot, the part was classed as nonsymmetrical because it could go in the jig in one way only. Analysis of the data, however, showed that the time for Position was lower than it should be for a nonsymmetrical part. A further study of the method was then made, which showed that the part was oriented either by pre-positioning it while transporting it to the jig or by turning it so that the projection lined up with the slot after the piece was part way in the jig. The part

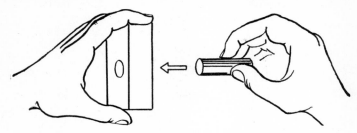

Fig. 42.— Cylindrical object to be placed in a circular hole.

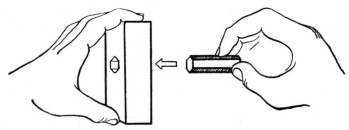

Fig. 43.— Hexagonal object to be placed in a hexagonal hole.

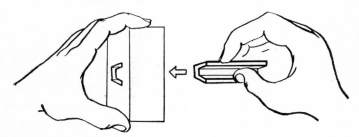

Fig. 44.— Irregularly shaped object to be placed in hole of same shape.

was therefore seen to be symmetrical insofar as the performance of the Position basic element was concerned.

In another instance, an operator was placing irregularly shaped parts into the cavities of a dial on a dial-feed machine. There was a considerable interval between each indexing of the machine. The operator therefore had plenty of time to orient the part in her fingers while waiting for the machine to index. Thus when she placed the part in the dial cavity it was already oriented and could be positioned in the same time as a symmetrical part.

These two examples show two rather unusual conditions which changed the classifications of symmetry from those which would ordinarily have been chosen based upon the shape of the parts.

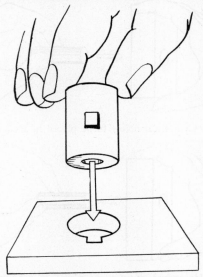

FIG. 45.— Cylindrical electrode holder
with boss.

EASE OF HANDLING

Parts are classed as either easy to handle or difficult to handle when considering positioning. When a stiff object, small or medium in size, can be grasped close to the point of initial engagement, the part is considered as easy to handle. If the part must be grasped some distance from the point of initial engagement, the part becomes difficult to handle. The distance from the point of initial engagement which differentiates easy to handle from difficult to handle varies with several conditions, chief of which are size of part and closeness of fit. A $\frac{1}{16}$-inch diameter rod inserted in a closely fitting hole would have to be grasped within about $\frac{1}{2}$ inch of the point of initial engagement, i.e., the end of the rod which goes in the hole first, to justify the easy-to-handle classification. A 3-inch diameter rod of light plastic inserted in a large hole with clearance all around would be easy to handle if it were held 4 or 5 inches from the point of initial engagement.

All flexible parts, such as thread, flexible wire, and string, are classed as difficult to handle under all conditions except when there is a very loose fit with the Grasp very close to the point of initial engagement.

Among very small parts, flat, thin pieces are difficult to handle, while irregular parts with projections which offer grasping advantages are classed as easy to handle. These examples will indicate the distinction between the two classifications.

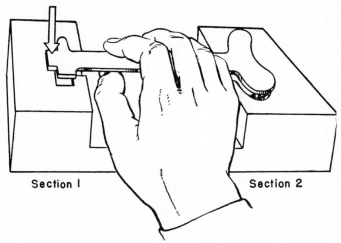

Section 1   Section 2

Fig. 46.—Multiple Positioning.

SPECIAL CASES OF POSITION

Cases are occasionally found in industry where the fitting of one part to another involves a multiple positioning motion. In cases of this type, close analysis of each situation must be made, and the types and number of basic Positions that are required must be determined. However, once a thorough understanding of the basic element Position is gained, little difficulty is encountered in applying the methods-time measurement procedure to these cases.

An example of a multiple positioning is shown in Fig. 46. A punch-press die is constructed with the contour of each end of the part built into sections 1 and 2 with a 4-inch space between these sections. Each end of the part is placed into its contour as it is held by the hand in the center.

Since the part is long and narrow, and the ends are irregular and nonsymmetrical, the part cannot be controlled accurately enough by an operator giving a normal performance to assemble both ends simultaneously. Therefore the operator positions one side in Section 1 and then the other in Section 2, the two Position elements occurring in succession. The Position element for the first end is *P1NSE*; but the position element for the second end is *P1SE* because it is mechanically controlled.

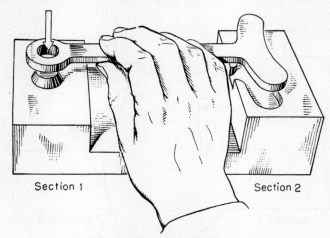

Section 1   Section 2

FIG. 47.—Multiple Positioning.

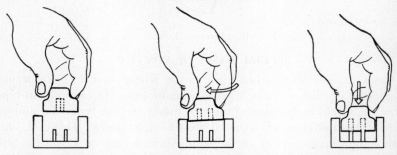

FIG. 48.— Multiple positioning—part positioned in jig and then to locating pins.

If one end of this part were located by a tapered pin instead of an irregular recess with the other end held as shown before, as illustrated by Fig. 47, a *P1SE* would be required to Position one end to the pin. The positioning of the other end to its contour in the die would be a *P1SE*, as before. The time standard for this condition should, therefore, be the sum of the two *P1SE* motions.

Cases of this type are especially prevalent where flexible materials or parts are handled. Here movement of one end or side of the part does not necessarily result in the other side moving simultaneously. In folding a wide piece of cloth where each end is held by the fingers of each hand, the positioning of the corners occurs successively rather than simultaneously.

Figure 48 illustrates another example of this condition. The drill jig is so constructed that very little clearance exists between the walls. To assemble the part to the drill jig, it must first be positioned into the body of the fixture and then to the locating pins. Thus a *P1SE* is followed by a *P2SSE*.

THEORY OF POSITIONING MOTIONS

During the investigation conducted to develop the methods-time data and the subsequent compilation of the data tables, a theory of the nature of the minor movements that occur when one part is joined to another was developed. A description of this theory is included so that a better understanding of Position and its application may be gained. It is felt that it may serve as a guide in the further study of Position. In the meantime, it provides a logical basis for developing time standards for those classifications in the Position table for which standards based upon actual measurement do not exist.

The theory presupposes that any Position can be accomplished by the use of four movements occurring in varying sequences and combinations according to the conditions under which Position is performed. With the exception of Align, these motions occur in operations other than positioning and have been carefully studied, as was discussed in previous chapters. As a result, they have been assigned accurate time standards. The four motions are

1. Align
2. Turn
3. Regrasp
4. Apply Pressure

These motions, individually or in various combinations, cover every variable encountered in the basic element of Position. The motion Align brings one part into approximate relationship with the other. The motion Turn brings it into final orientation. Combinations of Align and Turn, therefore, cover such variables as symmetry of the part, number of locating points, etc. The variable of tightness of fit is covered by Apply Pressure. Regrasp is employed when difficulties are encountered in placing the part due to its size, shape, or restrictions in movement caused by the working location or tools.

The theory of positioning motions is based upon the following assumptions:

1. That the orientation of one part to another involves the use of the basic element Turn, in a constant number of degrees when an average performance is given.

2. That the necessity for a Regrasp, or G2, in an assembly operation is responsible for the Difficult to Handle classification.

3. That the amount of pressure required to push a part to its final position is constant regardless of the symmetry and difficulty of handling of the part when average effort is exerted.

Description		Values derived by synthesis, TMU	Values derived by motion-picture analysis, TMU
Easy to Handle			
Fit	Part		
Loose	Symmetrical	5.6	5.6
Close	Symmetrical	16.2	
Exact	Symmetrical	43.0	39.4
Loose	Semisymmetrical	9.1	6.6
Close	Semisymmetrical	19.7	14.1
Exact	Semisymmetrical	46.5	43.9
Loose	Nonsymmetrical	10.4	
Close	Nonsymmetrical	21.0	21.9
Exact	Nonsymmetrical	47.8	53.1
Difficult to Handle			
Loose	Symmetrical	11.2	9.0
Close	Symmetrical	21.8	19.6
Exact	Symmetrical	48.6	
Loose	Semisymmetrical	14.7	13.7
Close	Semisymmetrical	25.3	25.5
Exact	Semisymmetrical	52.1	
Loose	Nonsymmetrical	16.0	16.3
Close	Nonsymmetrical	26.6	27.2
Exact	Nonsymmetrical	53.4	

FIG. 49.—Comparison of Position values developed by synthesis with those established by motion-picture analysis.

By following this line of reasoning, a table of Position values has been developed which, for the most part, agrees closely with the values established through motion-picture analysis. Both tables are shown in Fig. 49 so that a comparison can be made.

Align. Every assembly operation requires the basic element Align, but the motion occurs alone only on rare occasions. For example, it occurs alone when a tapered cylindrical pin is placed loosely into a hole or, conversely, when a part with a round hole is placed over a rounded pin. Other examples of Align occurring alone would be the placing of a part roughly to a line, placing a round dowel rod loosely into a square hole, or inserting a ball into a box.

Align, either alone or in combination with other assembly motions, can be readily recognized by the eye. It usually occurs at the end of a Move, and appears as a definite though slight hesitation. This motion requires close muscular and visual coordination and probably is affected by the indefinite elements of eye-focus time, Search, and Select.

The methods-time value for the basic element is 5.6 TMU. Thus the minimum normal time allowance for a Position operation would be the time for performing the Align, the simplest type of assembly.

The act of placing one part into another need not always mean that a Position occurs. Tossing a part into a large container or dropping a cone into a hole point downward, as shown in Fig. 50, would merely be a releasing of the part. A good rule to follow is to consider that a Position occurs when the difference in size between the mating parts at the point of initial engagement is one-half inch or less.

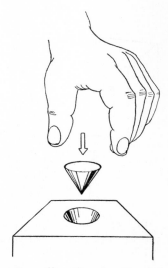

FIG. 50.—Conical part dropped into a hole point downward—no positioning occurs.

In the methods-time data tables, the time value for Align is the value for *P1SE.*

Turn. Once a loose-fitting symmetrical part has been aligned, the Position operation can be considered complete. However, if the mating parts are semisymmetrical or nonsymmetrical, an orienting, or turning, of the part must be made before the proper joining of the two parts can occur.

Basically, this orienting motion is a Turn motion, made with the fingers, and is almost imperceptible. In the basic element of Position, it is never found alone, but always occurs with and is preceded by the Align motion.

In the assembly of a semisymmetrical object, such as a square rod to a square cavity, it is impossible consistently to place the rod into the cavity with a direct aligning motion without an orienting or turning motion to bring the mating faces of the rod and cavity into proper relationship. A turn of approximately 45°, as illustrated by Fig. 51, would be the maximum required to orient one part to the other once the parts had been aligned. Thus if the rod were loose fitting, the time for the assembly would be the sum of the Align time (5.6 TMU) plus the 45° Turn time (3.5 TMU), or 9.1 TMU.

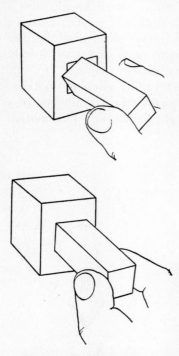

The number of degrees turned in orienting the part will of course vary with the shape of the object to be assembled. Obviously an octagonally shaped object would never require more than a 22½° Turn, while an object that could be positioned in only one of two ways could conceivably require a Turn of 90°. A careful analysis of semisymmetrical assembly operations disclosed that in 84 cases studied, 66 required an average Turn of 45°, 7 cases required an average Turn of 30°, and 11 cases required an average Turn of 90°. In the last instance,

FIG. 51.—Semisymmetrical part requiring aligning and orienting in order to position.

all observed cases were those in which the part could be assembled in only two ways. In observing the operations as performed by qualified operators, it was noted that the parts were roughly prepositioned during the Move, thus reducing the number of degrees turned in the orienting motion to approximately 45°. In accordance with these findings, the orienting of a semisymmetrical part during the Position may be considered as a 45° Turn and the time value of 3.5 TMU applied.

Nonsymmetrical objects, or those which can be positioned in only one way about the axis which coincides with the direction of travel, are oriented by turning in exactly the same manner as semisymmetrical objects, with the exception that the number of degrees turned is greater.

From data accumulated as the result of extensive observations, variation was found to exist ranging from 120 to 20° or less. In analyzing the data, however, it was found that the most highly skilled operators turned the parts the least number of degrees, while the new and unskilled operators were the ones who turned the parts the greatest number of degrees.

Therefore a new study was made. While observations were made to determine the number of degrees the part was turned in the orienting motion, the operators who were observed were also rated for skill and effort. A summary of the data thus obtained is as follows:

> 16 cases DD^* to $C1C1$...60° to 90°
> 21 cases $B2B2$ to $A1A2$..30° to 60°

Thus it was found that the more highly skilled and energetic operators were able to pre-position the part more effectively during the Move of the part to the die, thus improving their performance.

Because the methods-time data express the time required for an operator giving an average performance to perform a given motion, the number of degrees the part is turned by the operator of average skill and effort is the one on which the time value should be based. Therefore, the Turn value for 75° of 4.8 TMU has been established for nonsymmetrical parts. Thus the time for positioning a loose-fitting nonsymmetrical part would be the Align value of 5.6 TMU plus the Turn value of 4.8 TMU, or 10.4 TMU.

Ease of Handling. All the cases of Position previously described are for parts that can be easily handled without moving the fingers or relocating the hand before the Position is completed. This, of course, cannot always be done. A number of cases are found wherein the fingers must move to a new location once the part has been aligned and oriented. In Fig. 52, a small flat part is being assembled to a die. The part is held between the thumb and forefinger, and it is apparent from the illustration that the finger must be removed and the thumb must push the part to its final position before the assembly is completed. This constitutes the equivalent of a Regrasp of the part.

As previously pointed out, the difference between the easy-to-handle classification and the difficult-to-handle classification is that the latter

---

* See Performance Rating Table, "Time and Motion Study and Formulas for Wage Incentives" by Lowry, Maynard, and Stegemerten, McGraw-Hill Book Company, Inc., 1940, p. 233.

classification requires a Regrasp. Thus the time standard for any classification of fit and symmetry will be 5.6 TMU greater for a difficult-to-
handle part than for an easy-to-handle part.

FIG. 52.— Positioning of
difficult-to-handle part that
requires Regrasp.

Apply Pressure. When joining two parts
that fit closely, an additional force is necessary to push the parts to the final location
once the alignment and orientation of the
parts to one another has been completed.
This force is known as "Apply Pressure." It
occurs in every assembly operation where the
force of gravity is not sufficient to bring the
part being assembled to its final location.

In Chapter 7, in which Apply Pressure was
discussed at length, it was stated that this
element, for which a time standard of 16.2
TMU was determined, probably contains a
Regrasp and that a number of occurrences of
Apply Pressure without the Regrasp had
been observed. The standard for this type of
pressure was found to be 10.6 TMU. The
majority of these occurrences were found in
positioning operations requiring light pressure, and accordingly a value of 10.6 TMU
has been established as the time standard for
an Apply Pressure occurring in a positioning operation where only light pressure is
required.

The reasoning behind this is clear. When
a close-fitting part is being aligned and
oriented, the hand maintains more than
normal control of the part; hence, when
the pressure is applied, no additional grasp-
ing force need be applied during the Pressure motion, if only light
pressure is applied. Therefore the time value for the positioning of a
close-fitting part would be the value for the loose classification plus
10.6 TMU.

When the fit is exact and a heavy pressure is required to push the
part in place, the grasping force is not sufficient to maintain control of
the part while the heavy force is exerted by the arm, and the part must
therefore be regrasped. In addition, it is evident that parts of an exact
fit will assemble more slowly, because friction, air pressure, and the like

must be overcome. Hence, for an exact fit, it has been reasoned that following the alignment and orientation of the part, and the first Apply Pressure, the part must be regrasped to permit firmer control, and pressure must be exerted twice more before the assembly can be completed. No additional Regrasp is included for the third pressure, for the grasping force has been applied and would not need to be reapplied. The time value for the positioning of a part where the fit is exact would therefore be the time for aligning and orienting plus the time for the Regrasp and three 10.6 TMU Apply Pressures.

In positioning to a line where close control must be maintained, as in the example given where parts were carefully immersed into a liquid to a given mark, no pressure is exerted to force one part into another, but a retarding force is applied that prevents the hand from immersing the part beyond the allowable limits. Several studies of similar operations where this retarding force was used have indicated that the time to apply this force coincides very closely with the 10.6 TMU allowed for the positive pressure. Operations, such as carefully placing a part within $\frac{1}{16}$ inch of a line or object, moving a center-punched part under a drill for drilling, and the like are typical examples of cases in which this retarding force is present.

CHAPTER 10

RELEASE LOAD

The basic element that requires the shortest time of any to perform is Release Load. Values of 1.7 TMU and 0 TMU have been assigned to the two cases thus far established. Undoubtedly the value of 1.7 TMU is high. It was obtained as the result of the measuring procedure employed when collecting data. Even in slow-motion pictures, Release Load is often found to consume only one or two sixty-fourths of a second, which would give values of approximately .4 or .8 TMU.

Release Load is so quick that its presence must usually be determined by analysis rather than by observation. In compiling the methods-time data, it was thought possible that Release Load might be ignored altogether in application. It was found after numerous checks with and without recognizing Release Load that the accuracy of the results was somewhat increased by including time for releasing. This may be attributable to the manner in which the data were compiled, i.e., time may have been assigned to Release Load which actually belongs to Move and Reach. Regardless of this, however, since the recognition of Release Load increases the accuracy of the methods-time data in application in their present form, it should be included in the manner outlined below.

DEFINITION OF RELEASE LOAD

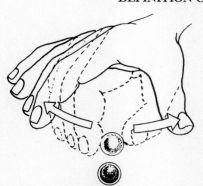

FIG. 53.—Normal Release Load.

Release Load is the basic element employed to relinquish control of an object by the fingers or hand.

The opening of the fingers, or hand, permitting the part to be free, as shown by Fig. 53, is the motion employed. It should be noted that, like Grasp, the definition limits the basic element of Release Load to releases which are performed with the hand only. If a part is released by opening a pair of tongs, it is accompanied by performing the basic element Move.

STARTING AND STOPPING POINTS

In compiling the methods-time data, Release Load was considered to begin at the frame which marked the termination of the preceding basic element, which was usually Move or Position. It was considered to end at the frame which marked the beginning of the next basic element, which was usually Reach. This was also checked by considering that Release Load begins at the last frame in which the fingers are closed on the object and ends when the fingers have moved from the object. The latter method will always give a one-frame, or a 1.7 TMU, Release. By the first method, however, a value of 1.7 TMU was also obtained in practically every case, so that the results obtained were the same.

CLASSIFICATIONS OF RELEASE LOAD

Only two classifications of Release Load have been identified. They may be described as follows:

RL1. Normal Release Performed by Opening Fingers as Independent Motion. When an object has been secured by a Pickup Grasp of any type, a normal Release, characterized by opening the fingers, is employed to let go of it. If the object is sticky so that it adheres to the fingers and must be shaken off, the relinquishing of all control will, of course, require more than 1.7 TMU. In terms of the methods-time data, however, other motions in addition to the motion of opening the fingers would be employed for which additional time would have to be allowed. Such cases have not yet been fully analyzed.

RL2. Contact Release. When control has been secured of an object with a G5, or Contact Grasp, control is usually relinquished by employing a Contact Release. The Release begins and is completed at the instant the following Reach begins. A Contact Release, therefore, consumes no measurable amount of time. It is always shown on the Motion Analysis Chart, however, to provide a complete record of the method employed.

Occasionally, following a Pickup Grasp, the fingers are loosened about the object during a succeeding motion. When at length the Release Load occurs, it is a Contact Release. This occurs at times in the manipulation of levers or handles. The lever is grasped with a G1a Grasp. As it is moved, the hand is opened so that contact with the lever is maintained only by the palm of the hand. Thus when it is time to relinquish complete control, the operator has only to take his hand from the lever by performing the Reach basic element.

CHAPTER 11
DISENGAGE

. The time for taking apart two pieces which have been assembled together can be established correctly only if the manner in which this is accomplished is properly analyzed. If the entire act of unscrewing one part from another is called "Disassemble," it may be seen that the term becomes an omnibus term which includes a number of basic elements. For purposes of methods-time data application, therefore, it has been decided to cover only the act of final taking apart by the basic element Disengage, and to handle all motions preliminary to this as Moves, Releases, Reaches, Grasps, Turns, and the like.

DEFINITION OF DISENGAGE

Disengage is the basic element employed to break the contact between one object and another, and it is characterized by an involuntary movement occasioned by the sudden ending of resistance.

In effect, it consists of the application of a certain amount of pressure in the form of a tug or a pull. If the fit is tight, the pull must be harder than if the fit is loose. As the objects are pulled apart, the resistance to pulling that they offer suddenly ends. The hand and one part move quickly away with a motion that may be described as a recoil. The operator must bring this motion under control before he can perform the next basic element, which usually is Move. He therefore checks the movement of recoil, and in so doing, usually causes a perceptible break in the motion. The length of the motion of recoil varies with the amount of resistance to disengagement offered by the objects, or in other words, with the closeness of the fit. When a part is disengaged carefully to eliminate injury to the hand or parts, even though the separation can be accomplished without overcoming resistance, a Disengage is considered to occur.

STARTING AND STOPPING POINTS

Disengage was considered to begin, when gathering data, when the Reach to the object to be disengaged ended. Disengage was considered to terminate when the motion of recoil had been checked. This was the frame that marked the beginning of the next Move. By collecting data in this manner, the time for Grasp was included. Further experience in application showed that Grasp did not always precede Disengage, for the hand might have been holding the part prior to disengaging. A check of the disengaging data previously collected showed that the type of Grasp which was employed was a G1a. Therefore, to eliminate the time for Grasp from the table for Disengage, 1.7 TMU were subtracted. The resulting data were then tabulated in Table VI, shown in Fig. 12.

VARIABLES AFFECTING DISENGAGE

Only three variables have been found to affect the time for Disengage. These are

Class of fit
Ease of handling
Care of handling

Weight would also seem to be a logical variable, but, within the range studied, its influence could not be measured.

The classifications of class of fit and ease of handling are not necessarily the same for Disengage as those assigned when considering the basic element Position. When an object is positioned to a line, for example, it would be considered as a class 2 fit, as has already been pointed out. When the object is removed from the line, no disengagement would take place. When a needle is threaded with a light thread, the thread would be considered to be difficult to handle. In unthreading the needle, however, the thread would present no especial handling difficulties, and therefore would be considered as easy to handle.

CLASS OF FIT

Three classes of fit have been established for Disengage, as follows:

Class 1—Loose. Very slight effort—Disengage blends with subsequent Move.
Class 2—Close. Normal effort—slight recoil.
Class 3—Tight. Considerable effort—hand recoils markedly.

These are illustrated by Fig. 54.

If two objects are put together in an unrestricted location so loosely that there is complete clearance between them, the objects are disengaged merely by lifting one from the other. In this case, the motion is the

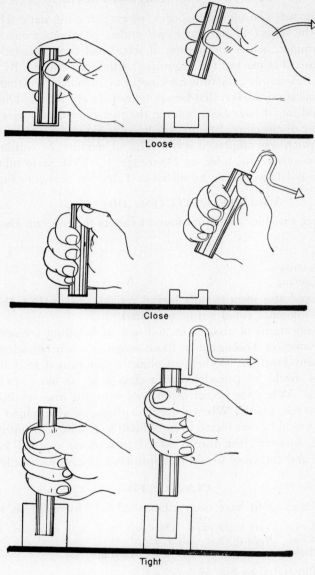

Fig. 54.— Classes of Disengage.

equivalent of a Move, and no Disengage within the meaning of the basic element takes place.

A class 1, or loose, fit offers a slight resistance to disengaging. The resistance is so slight that the motion of recoil which takes place as the two objects come apart blends with the subsequent move so closely that it is often difficult to determine by observation whether or not a Disengage occurs. If the observer will perform the operation himself, however, he will have no difficulty in telling whether there is a recoil and then a Move or merely a pure Move.

The class 2, or close, fit is the one which has been encountered most commonly in the studies made thus far. The Disengage is identifiable by a motion of recoil not more than 4 or 5 inches in length. At the end of this motion, the hand comes to a complete stop and may even return slightly in the direction opposite to the motion of recoil as the muscles of the arm check the motion of the hand. During the motion of recoil, the hand is under slight control if any.

A class 3, or tight, fit requires an easily observable tug or pull to accomplish the disengaging. The hand recoils somewhat violently as the separation takes place and moves a distance of from 5 to 10 or 12 inches. Because of the muscular effort required, this is a fatiguing basic element to perform.

When a fit is so tight that two objects cannot be disengaged with a single pull, other basic elements are considered to take place. Only the final separation involves the Disengage basic element.

EASE OF HANDLING

As in the case of Position, parts are considered as easy to handle or as difficult to handle. Parts which can be grasped securely and which can be disengaged without the possibility of binding, if the pull is not straight, are considered as easy to handle.

Three examples of the difficult-to-handle classification are (1) where the object cannot readily be grasped; (2) where there are obstructions which must be considered in separating the objects (for example, part in drilling fixture with cover raised and lowered by cam action, where the cover in the open position is only a short distance from the back of the hand as the part is grasped prior to disengaging); (3) where objects are flexible, and hence may bind during disassembly.

The distinction between the easy-to-handle and the difficult-to-handle classifications is often hard to make. In such cases, the difficult-to-handle classification should be used, as this appears to occur most frequently.

CAREFUL HANDLING

If a part is removed, or disengaged, from a restricted location where damage to the part or injury to the fingers of the person removing the part could occur unless great care is exercised, the motion is greatly slowed down. Removing a part by hand from between a punch and die, where a clearance of 2 inches or less exists, or removing an internal lap from a small finished bushing are good cases of a Disengage that requires careful handling. Even though the Disengage occurs without resistance, the extra care required greatly slows down the motion. It has been found satisfactory to allow the time for a class 2 Disengage in such cases.

CHAPTER 12

WALKING

Operations that involve walking occur frequently in industry. There-fore a detailed study of walking time and methods is necessary if the methods-time data are to be applied to this class of work. Such a study has been begun, and although it is far from complete, has yielded enough information to justify including a discussion here.

STUDY PROCEDURE

An oval course was laid out on a gymnasium floor. This gave an unobstructed course about 275 feet long, for the most part straight but with four rounded corners that could be negotiated without apparent slowing down.

Observations were made on approximately 125 people. The group was comprised of both office and shop workers. Ages ranged from 17 to 65 years. Heights ranged from 5 feet to 6 feet 4 inches.

Each person participating in the study was required to walk around the course from three to five times on each trial. Before beginning, it was explained that there were 6 degrees of effort at present recognized: poor, fair, average, good, excellent, and excessive. Each degree was described briefly. The operator was then requested to walk around the course maintaining as nearly as possible constant speed, giving what-ever degree of effort he wished. After a rest, he was required to go around the course again three to five times at a different effort level and so on until observations had been made at all effort levels.

The data obtained did not include starting and stopping time. The operator began each trial about 10 feet in back of the starting line and thus was walking at full speed as timing began. He continued at full speed past the finishing point so that there was no slowing down at the end of the trial.

Each trial was observed by three to five experienced time-study men. The operator did not announce the effort level he was trying to main-tain, so that the judgment of the observers was not influenced by the operator. Each observer was required to record his rating of effort in writing before the ratings were announced for recording. Thus one observer did not influence the others. The consensus of the raters was chosen as the correct rating for the trial. No attempt was made to rate skill as it was felt that this factor, which is defined as "proficiency at following a given method," did not enter into straight-away walking.

As the operator crossed the starting point, timing was begun. One observer counted the number of steps taken by the operator per lap. On a prepared data sheet, the following information was recorded: name, age, height, weight, hip to floor measurement, time per lap, steps per lap, and the effort rating. In the case of women, the height of the heels on their shoes was also noted.

CHARACTERISTICS OF WALKING

The test data obtained on male operators were analyzed in detail. The following conclusions were thus obtained and apply to male operators only.

The factors that influence walking time at the average performance level are age and weight. Although the length of step taken by the operator increases as the height of the operator increases, the data show definitely that when the effect of age and weight are eliminated, walking time per foot at the average performance level is a constant.

The data showed that there is a "best weight" as far as walking is concerned. In all age groups, the indications were that walking time was a minimum at 170 pounds. As weight decreases below this point, walking time per foot increases. As weight increases above 170 pounds, walking time also increases. This relationship is shown by the curve illustrated in Fig. 55.

As effort increases above average for any age and weight, walking time per foot decreases. As effort decreases below average, walking time per foot increases. The percentage of increase or decrease in walking time per foot is shown in the second column of Fig. 56.

As effort increases, the length of step increases. As effort decreases, the reverse is true. A typical curve showing how length of step and time per step vary with effort is shown by Fig. 57. This change in length of step is a change in method from the viewpoint of the methods-time data. The effect that this has on walking time per foot is shown in the third column of Fig. 56. The combined effect of effort and methods change is found by multiplying the two factors together, and this gives the combined factors shown in the fourth column.

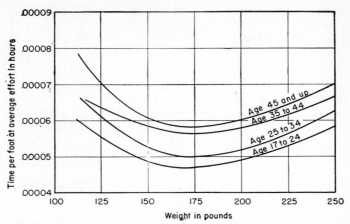

FIG. 55.— Effect of age and weight upon walking time per foot at average effort level.

Effort level	Effort	Methods change	Combined
A1	1.39	1.25	1.71
A	1.30	1.20	1.56
A2	1.2	1.175	1.41
B1	1.18	1.15	1.36
B	1.15	1.125	1.29
B2	1.12	1.10	1.25
C1	1.09	1.07	1.17
C	1.06	1.045	1.11
C2	1.03	1.02	1.05
D	0	0	0
E1	.97	.965	.93
E	.93	.94	.87
E2	.91	.915	.83
F1	.88	.885	.78
F	.85	.86	.73
F2	.83	.83	.69

FIG. 56.— Percentage of increase or decrease in walking time per foot at various performance levels attributable to effort and methods change.

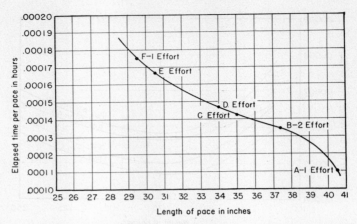

Fig. 57.— Typical walking-time curve—length of pace against time per pace at different performance levels.

Effort level	Combined factor from Fig. 56	Skill and effort leveling factor for corresponding performance level	Difference
A1	1.71	1.28	.43
A	1.56	1.265	.295
A2	1.41	1.25	.16
B1	1.36	1.21	.15
B	1.29	1.185	.105
B2	1.25	1.16	.07
C1	1.17	1.11	.06
C	1.11	1.08	.03
C2	1.05	1.05	0
D	0	0	0
E1	.93	.91	.02
E	.87	.865	.005
E2	.83	.82	.01
F1	.78	.72	.06
F	.73	.665	.065
F2	.69	.61	.08

Fig. 58.— Comparison of walking-time effort factors with manual leveling factors.

Although it was never the intention that the original leveling factors should be applied without checking to any but manual operations, nevertheless, many times engineers have used them to level walking time because no other factors had been made available. The extent of the error which this would introduce into time standards on elements which consist of walking is shown by Fig. 58, which compares the combined rating factors shown in Fig. 56 with the skill and effort factors of conventional leveling for the same effort level. The error over the entire range from F-2 to B does not exceed 10.5 per cent and ranges down to 0. Because this would affect the elements involving walking only and because the majority of time-study ratings lie between E-2 and C-1, where the errors are small, it may be seen that the use of the manual leveling factors would not cause any appreciable difficulty.

DETERMINATION OF WALKING TIME

In order to know how long it will take any male operator to cover a given distance by walking with average effort with no load, the time per foot determined by his age and weight must be multiplied by the distance walked. To determine how long it will take at any other performance level, this figure must be multiplied by the combined rating factor for walking shown by Fig. 56.

If a time study is made of walking, it should be leveled by using the combined rating factor in Fig. 56 rather than by using the manual-performance rating factors. This will give walking time at average performance for an operator of the same age and weight as the one studied. If it is desired to establish a standard on some other basis of age and weight, then the curves shown by Fig. 55 should be used.

Because age and weight definitely affect walking time, they must be taken into account if it is desired to determine how long it will take a particular operator to walk a given distance at a given effort level. It is not the usual practice to establish standards for each operator, however, so that it will be more practical to select an average age level for a particular plant and base all standards accordingly. The standard for walking in a plant employing elderly precision workers would thus be higher than the standard in a plant largely employing boys under 21.

Many plants have operators of all ages. In this case, a reasonable standard appears to be .000053 hour, or 5.3 TMU per foot. This is 3.57 miles per hour, which checks closely with the standard used or advocated by several other companies and engineers. When the usual 15 per cent

is included for fatigue and personal and unavoidable delays, this is
reduced to 3.1 miles per hour.

If this figure is accepted as a reasonable standard, then walking time,
not including starting and stopping, may be obtained from Fig. 59.

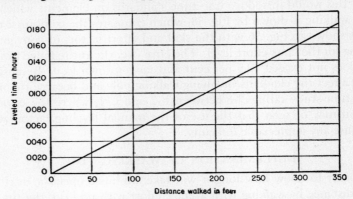

FIG. 59.— Walking time—no load, level surface, average effort—
no allowances included.

ACCURACY OF WALKING-TIME DATA

There are undoubtedly other minor variables which affect walking time
which have not been isolated and measured.   There are physiological,
psychological, and physical differences among individuals, which the data
do not attempt to cover separately.   These and other minor factors
undoubtedly account for some of the scattering of the data when attempts
are made to plot them.   Nevertheless, the trends seem to be clearly
discernable, and because the group studied seemed to be a normal industrial group, it is felt that the curves presented are quite representative.

CHAPTER 13

OTHER MOTIONS

Although motions of the fingers, hands, and arms are those most used in performing productive operations, other body members and the body itself are frequently used either to accomplish a definite result in the operation cycle or to assist another body member in the performance of a motion. In operating a small, bench foot press, for example, the leg delivers a kick to actuate the ram of the press. When an operator seated at a bench requires an additional supply of materials, he may arise from his chair, walk to the supply, stoop to collect a quantity, arise, straighten up, and return to his chair where he seats himself before resuming the performance of the operation. In a bench operation involving large bulky parts that cannot be located within the maximum working area, a step, side step, or turn of the body is frequently necessary to bring the hands within reach of the parts. In this instance, the body motion is usually the limiting motion, and time must be allowed for its performance.

Foot, leg, and body motions differ from arm and hand motions in that they are usually not used to perform motions which are accurate, probably because they are incapable of being as closely controlled. Thus they are not subject to as many variables affecting the time for their performance. Movements of the body are made primarily to bring the body into an approximate location from which the hands and arms can work to accomplish a task, while foot and leg movements are usually either mechanically guided, as by a foot treadle or kick-press ram, or are used to actuate levers and treadles, which are fixed in definite locations and require little control to locate and operate.

MEASUREMENT PROCEDURE

The time standards for body, foot, arm, and leg motions that are shown in Fig. 60 were determined by a combination of the methods-time measurement procedure and time study.

111

A number of shop operations were first selected, which included a motion for which a time standard was to be established. The motions for which methods-time data were available were then analyzed and the operation time value was established from the data. A time study was next taken of the operation, and the performance was rated for skill and effort by three experienced observers.

Motion description	Symbol	Distance moved, inches	Time, TMU
Foot motion—hinged at ankle	FM	Up to 4	8.5
Foot motion with heavy pressure	FMP		19.1
Leg or foreleg motion	LM	Up to 6	7.1
		Each add. inch	1.2
Side Step, Case 1	SSI	Less than 12	Use Reach or Move time
		12	17.0
		Each add. inch	.6
Side Step, Case 2	SSII	12	34.1
		Each add. inch	1.1
Bend, Stoop, or Kneel on one knee	B,S,KOK		29.0
Arise from B, S, or KOK	AB,AS,AKOK		31.9
Kneel to floor on both knees	KOBK		69.4
Arise from KOBK	AKOBK		76.7
Sit	Sit		34.7
Stand from sitting position	Std		43.4
Turn Body, Case 1	TBI		18.6
Turn Body, Case 2	TBII		37.2
Walk, per foot	W1'		5.3
Walk, per pace	W		15.0

Fig. 60.— Methods-time data for body, leg, and foot motions.

In working up the study, all cycles that were not performed in accordance with the predetermined method were excluded. The pure average time value was then established and adjusted by leveling to the time required when a normal performance is given.

To determine the time for the motion being studied, the methods-time value for the operation (which did not include this time) was subtracted from the leveled time value for the complete operation. The result was accepted as the standard time for that particular motion. Twenty to thirty time studies of this type were taken on operations involving each of the body, leg, and foot motions, and these results were averaged to establish the standard motion time.

FOOT MOTIONS

Foot motions are those where the foot is moved with the ankle serving as a hinge. It is usually made in a vertical direction, the heel of the foot serving as a fulcrum. Figure 61 is an illustration of a setup involving the use of a typical foot movement required in industrial work. When the analysis of foot movement times was begun, it was felt that the time would vary in accordance with the distance moved by the toe. Investigation showed, however, that few foot motions require a movement of

Fig. 61.— Typical foot motion.

greater than 3 inches (when measured at the toe) with the greatest distance found in the study being 4 inches. Because of the fatigue involved in moving the foot alone for a greater distance and/or in holding it in the unnatural position that would be required if the movement were of greater length, it has been found impractical to set up methods where a foot motion of more than 4 inches is required.

Under the procedure used to determine this motion time, it was impossible to determine any variation in the time value in relation to the distance moved by the toe. It was further found that few cases existed where the toe moved less than 2 inches. Accordingly, a constant time value of 8.5 TMU was established as the average time for this motion.

Several cases in the study involved foot motions where the instep served as the fulcrum of the motion. This created little variation in the time values.

When heavy pressure is required, a noticeable increase in the time required for the motion was noted. Many studies of this type of foot motion were made, and the normal time was developed in the manner previously described. The difference in time between the foot motion where normal pressure was required and that where pressure was exerted at the completion of the free movement of the foot was found to be 10.6 TMU, a value identical with that required for the hand motion of Apply Pressure where no Regrasp is involved.

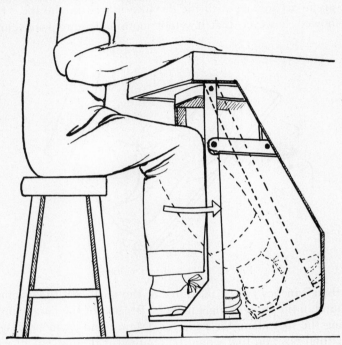

FIG. 62.— Leg motion pivoted about the knee.

LEG MOTIONS

Leg motions are movements of the foreleg or the entire leg where either the knee, as in Fig. 62, or the hip, as in Fig. 63, serves as a pivot. It was originally assumed that there would be a difference in time between a foreleg motion and one requiring a full leg movement. The studies made of these motions indicated, however, that the leg motions are similar to the motions of the arm, where it was found that no measurable difference in time was evident because of the point at which the body member was hinged.

In the studies made of these motions, no cases were found where leg motions of less than 6 inches were employed. Accordingly, the minimum time for a leg motion is the time required for the minimum distance analyzed or 6 inches. It has further been found that because of the nature of the leg motion, it would be impractical in many cases to shorten the motion to a distance of less than 6 inches. For example, when a leg motion is used to exert force normally, as in the operation of a small foot-operated punch press, momentum must be gathered before the blow is made if the desired results are to be accomplished with a minimum of fatigue. If the foot traveled less than 6 inches, sufficient momentum could not be gained to accomplish the desired result.

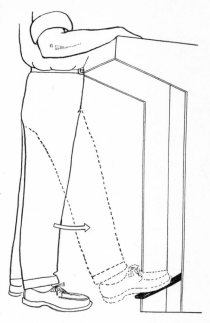

FIG. 63.—Leg motion pivoted about the hip.

SIDE STEP

A Side Step occurs where the body must be displaced sideways from one location to another in the immediate area without turning or taking more than one step. Examples of this would be the movement of the body from the first to the second spindle of a two-spindle sensitive drill press or in stepping from between a chair and a desk after arising.

Two cases of Side Step were found to occur. Case 1, illustrated by Fig. 64, occurs where the Side Step is completed when the leading leg makes contact with the floor. When contact is made, the hands can immediately begin their work and the lagging leg is brought up to its normal position as a balancing motion that is not limiting. In the case of the drill press previously mentioned, the right hand could begin its Reach toward the drill-press lever as soon as the leading leg touched the floor with the lagging leg being brought to position as the spindle was being lowered.

Case 2, illustrated by Fig. 65, occurs where the lagging leg must be brought into position beside the leading leg before the next motion can be made. For example, after arising from a chair at a bench or desk, the body is restricted from free movement. To get clear of the restricted

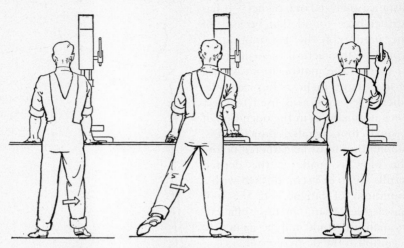

FIG. 64.— Case 1 Side Step—hand begins Reach motion as soon as leading leg touches the floor.

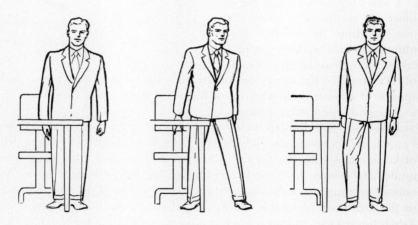

FIG. 65.— Case 2 Side Step—lagging leg must be brought into position before the next motion can be made.

area so that one can begin walking, the body must be moved away from the area by a side step. When the leading leg makes contact with the floor, the body still is not free; the lagging leg must be brought to position alongside the leading leg and body balance regained before the body can be turned and walking begun.

Case 2 is always encountered where body balance must be regained before work can be begun. Further examples of case 2 would be moving the body to a new location where an excessively long Reach or Move is the first succeeding motion after arrival, carrying or sliding a heavy object during the move of the body, or moving sideways in a very narrow and restricted space.

The length of the Side Step motion is determined by the distance the body is moved, which is not necessarily the same as distance moved by the feet. When the distance moved is less than 12 inches, the hands are seldom, if ever, prevented from performing the limiting motions of the operation. Hence, the Side Step is overlapped with the limiting motions and does not affect the time. When the body is moved a distance of 12 inches or more, the time value should be determined from the table shown by Fig. 60.

TURN BODY

The motion Turn Body is in reality a variation of the Side Step. It occurs in cases such as the turning of the body to a new location while stepping away from a bench. Two cases of Turn Body exist. Case 1 occurs when the hands take over as the leading leg makes contact with the floor. Case 2 occurs when the lagging leg must be brought alongside the leading leg before work can begin. The cases are identical to those encountered in the Side-step motions.

The time values shown in Fig. 60 are for body turns of 90° or less. When the body must be turned a full 180°, the body performs first a case 2 followed by either a case 1 or another case 2 Turn Body. On the assumption that the movement is to the right and that the body must turn a full 180°, the right leg moves out as the body turns, the right foot touches the floor, the left or lagging leg is brought alongside, and body balance is regained. The right leg can then once again move out as the body turns to the final destination.

BEND, STOOP, AND KNEEL ON ONE KNEE

Bend is said to occur when the body is bowed at the waist with the upper portion of the torso being lowered to bring the hands within reach

of an object that cannot be obtained when the body is held erect. When
the body is lowered by bending the knees, a Stoop occurs. If the Stoop
is accompanied by a lowering of one knee until the knee touches the
floor so that the body gains additional support, a Kneel on One Knee is
performed.

A Bend begins with the downward motion of the shoulders and ends
when the hands are at the level of the knee or slightly below, with the
arms fully extended. It is made as a separate and distinct motion and
is readily recognized for it never blends smoothly with the preceding

FIG. 66.— Bend.   FIG. 67.— Stoop.

motion. It frequently occurs with or follows a Side Step. Figure 66
shows a typical Bend.

Care must be used so that Bend is not confused with a Reach or Move
by the analyst. When the body is only slightly bent during a Reach or
Move, the body movement is overlapped with the limiting motion of
the arm. Bend occurs only when it is made as a separate and distinct
motion with the destination of the hand at or below the level of the
kneecap.

A Stoop begins with the downward movement of the body and ends
when the hands touch the floor or object close to the floor. Like Bend,
it is a separate and distinct motion easily recognized by the analyst as
may be seen by comparing Fig. 67 with Fig. 66. With this motion, too,
care should be exerted so that a normal Reach or Move with its accom-
panying slight body movements is not considered as a Stoop.

A Kneel on One Knee begins with the downward movement of the
body and ends as the knee touches the floor. Like the others, it is an
easily recognized and distinctive body movement (see Fig. 68).

Because motions such as these are fatiguing and time consuming, they should be eliminated if possible. It is not always possible to do this, however, because of machine construction, limitations in the working area, and the like.

In collecting the data, these three motion types were analyzed individually, and the time values for each type were determined separately. The time values, however, were found to be practically identical, and therefore one value was chosen to represent the time required for performing Bend, Stoop, or Kneel on One Knee.

The motions of arising from the positions assumed in performing Bend, Stoop, or Kneel on One Knee are readily recognizable. As in the case of the other body movements just described, no appreciable varia-

Fig. 68.— Kneel on One Knee.

tion in time for the Arise motions was found. Hence, the time for them has been included in Fig. 60 as a constant value.

KNEEL ON BOTH KNEES

When the body is lowered to kneel on both knees, a Kneel on One Knee is first performed, after which the remaining leg is lowered to its proper position. In arising from this position, one foot is first placed on the floor, following which, the body is raised to an erect position. Time values for both the lowering and arising motions are included in Fig. 60.

SIT AND STAND FROM A SITTING POSITION

Sit, or the seating of oneself, begins when the body is positioned at the location from which the body can be lowered to a chair, or bench, without further movement of the body or feet, and ends when the body is seated. It frequently follows a case 2 Side Step. It does not include any other motions that may occur after the body reaches its destination, as, for example, the grasping of the chair and moving it closer to the workbench, or desk.

Stand begins when the feet are in position on the floor and ends when the body has assumed an erect stance. Like Sit, it includes time for none of the preceding motions necessary to prepare the body for the motion. The times for these preparatory motions are selected from the methods-time data in Fig. 12 or from the leg-motion times in Fig. 60.

ACCURACY OF BODY, FOOT, AND LEG METHODS-TIME STANDARDS

Although the measurement procedure used to establish these standards was not as refined and accurate as that used in the development of the hand and arm data, the standards shown in Fig. 60 will serve satisfactorily until more accurate studies have been made to prove or modify them. They have been used many times and have proved satisfactory in practical application. Because these motion times usually represent only a slight proportion of the total operation-cycle time, any inaccuracies that may exist will have only a minor effect on the total time allowed for the operation.

CHAPTER 14

PRINCIPLE OF THE LIMITING MOTION

In performing industrial operations, it is usually undesirable to have only one body member in motion at a time. Two or more body members should usually be in motion simultaneously if the most effective method for doing the job is to be used. The reason for this becomes evident when a simple example, such as the reading of a letter while riding to work, is considered. While being transported to a destination, the reading of the letter is accomplished. On the assumption that the time required for traveling is 15 minutes and the reading time is 5 minutes, both tasks are accomplished within the 15 minutes of traveling time. In this instance, the traveling time would be the limiting factor. If the letter were read after arriving at the destination, the time required for the two operations would be 15 minutes of traveling time plus 5 minutes of reading time, or 20 minutes in all. By combining the reading of the letter with the traveling, the time for performing the two operations is reduced by 25 per cent. The same reasoning applies to motions. If two or more motions are combined or overlapped, all can be performed in the time required to perform the one demanding the greatest amount of time, or the limiting motion.

COMBINED MOTIONS

Combination motions are those which occur when two or more motions are performed by the same body member at the same time. For example, in turning a part in the hand while moving it to a destination, the Turn is performed in combination with the Move. Similarly, the hand may shift to a new grasp on the part while moving to a destination or two parts may be positioned and assembled during a Move. Combination motions in almost every instance have a Move as one of the motions.

Combination motions are relatively easy to evaluate. To do so, the analyst must first recognize all the motions performed. The motion requiring the greatest amount of time is considered the limiting motion,

121

and the standard value for the limiting motion is the value for the combination motion.

When an irregularly shaped part is grasped and moved 12 inches to a fixture, the hand must pre-position the part by turning it approximately 180° during the 12-inch Move. Since the Move value is 15.2 TMU, and the Turn value is 9.4 TMU, it can be seen that the Turn can be accomplished during the Move time. Therefore, the Move is the limiting motion, and the time allowed for the combination motion is 15.2 TMU. If, in the above case, the part were moved only 4 inches, the Move time would be 7.3 TMU. Because the Turn value is 9.4 TMU, the Turn would be limiting, and the 9.4 TMU value would be applied.

In methods-improvement work, the attempt is often made to bring parts and tools as close to the point of use as possible. It may be seen, however, that it is useless to bring irregularly shaped or jumbled parts to within two or three inches of the point of use. No saving would be made because the time for Turn would be limiting. A less congested workplace layout and one which would be just as efficient will result if the parts are located so that the Move time and the Turn time are equal.

Care must be exercised by the analyst in evaluating combination motions, for the tendency is, in most cases, to be too conservative in rating these motions. If there is doubt as to whether or not a Turn must be made while moving a part 4 inches, the Turn should be recognized as being present and allowed for in the evaluation. Although some parts will be in position, thus eliminating the necessity for a Turn, the majority will undoubtedly require the Turn.

SIMULTANEOUS MOTIONS

Perhaps the most difficult part of the methods-time measurement procedure is the recognition of and the application of time standards to motions performed simultaneously by two or more body members. With a proper understanding of the findings of the methods-time measurement studies, however, and with experience in application, these motions can be handled just as accurately as individual motions.

Simultaneous Reaches and Moves are the easiest simultaneous motions to recognize. When both hands travel the same distance, the motion time allowed for both Reaches would be the value allowed for one Reach of that distance. When the distances moved simultaneously are unequal, the natural rhythm of the body tends to make the arms begin and end their motions at the same time. In this case, the longer of the two motions is the limiting motion.

Simultaneous motions can occur when the hands perform identical, similar, or dissimilar motions. For example, both hands may be called upon to perform R10C motions simultaneously; again, the right hand may perform an R10C as the left hand performs an M12A; finally, the right hand may be required to perform a Disengage as the left hand turns a locator screw.

Figure 69, below, shows a chart which indicates the basic elements which can easily be performed simultaneously, those which can be performed simultaneously within certain limitations, and those which cannot be performed together except under special conditions.

Motion	Reach	Move	Turn	Grasp	Position	Dis-engage	Release	Apply Pressure
Reach	A	A	A	B	B	B	A	B
Move	A	A	A	B	B	B	A	B
Turn	A	A	A	B	B	B	A	B
Grasp	B	B	A	B	C	C	A	C
Position	B	B	B	C	B	C	A	C
Disengage	B	B	B	C	C	A	A	A
Release	A	A	A	A	A	A	A	A
Apply Pressure	B	B	B	C	C	A	A	A

A. Occur frequently in combination—readily performed simultaneously.
B. Occur occasionally in combination—can be performed simultaneously by highly skilled operators. Performance of accurate motions with both hands very difficult unless performed within the area of normal vision.
C. Rarely in combination. Performance of accurate motions with both hands impossible unless performed within the area of normal vision.

Fig. 69.— The basic elements frequently, occasionally, and rarely performed simultaneously.

SIMULTANEOUS GRASPS

All G1 and G2 Grasps can be made simultaneously regardless of their location, provided that they are made within the normal working area. Even though one of the Grasps must be performed outside the area of normal vision, an operator qualified to perform the operation will be able to accomplish these motions simultaneously with ease after he has familiarized himself with the workplace layout. The time value for these Grasps performed simultaneously is the time value for performing one Grasp.

Simultaneous Grasps involving two different types of Grasp are accomplished in the time required to perform the limiting, or slowest,

Grasp. If the objects to be Grasped fall outside the area of normal vision, a glance toward the object requiring the simpler Grasp to locate and direct the hand to the object is made during the Reaches of the hands, after which the eyes shift to the object requiring the more difficult Grasp. The mind and eyes are concentrated on the latter until the object is secured. The easier Grasp is accompanied by balancing delay, with control of the object delayed until the instant the more difficult Grasp is completed. For simultaneous Grasps of this type, the slower Grasp is limiting, and its time standard must be allowed.

G4 Grasps cannot be performed simultaneously. The eyes keep one part constantly in focus during the Reach to the part and the selection of the part. While the first part is being secured, the eyes shift to the second part before the other Grasp can be accomplished. The time required to perform this type of motion, therefore, is the time to perform two distinct G4 Grasps.

SIMULTANEOUS POSITIONS

Because of the complexity of the motions involved, the basic element Position can be performed simultaneously only when both parts are positioned within a distance of no more than 4 inches of one another. The time standard for the simultaneous Position is the time value for the limiting Position. When the distance between the locations in which the Positions occur is greater than 4 inches, the time value for each Position must be allowed.

When Position is performed by one hand, only relatively uncontrolled motions can be performed by the other hand. Grasps, Turns, Moves, and Reaches to precise locations cannot be performed simultaneously with Position. Reaches or Moves to indefinite locations can be performed, however. In a situation where the right hand positions a part following which the left hand must obtain another part from a group jumbled together at the operator's side, the left hand will move to the approximate location of the parts while the Position is occurring. Until the Position is completed, however, the left hand will be unable to select and grasp the part.

SIMULTANEOUS ARM AND STEPPING MOTIONS

Simultaneous motions of the arms and legs occur most often when a step is combined with a transportation, as, for example, in moving the body from one spindle of a drill press to another while the hand reaches for the drill-press spindle. In such cases, the same reasoning applies as in handling simultaneous arm motions—the motion requiring the greater amount of time is the limiting motion.

The purpose of moving the body from one location to another is primarily to bring the arms and hands into a new working area. The body, therefore, is moved directly to the front of the area in which the work can most effectively be performed. Since the final destination of the hands may be at a location other than the effective work area, an additional motion or two of the hands must be accounted for in measuring movements such as these.

When the body is moved by a step, or side step, it will assume a balanced and comfortable position. Even though the operation preceding and succeeding the move requires the body to be bent or stooped or the arms to be extended, the body straightens to an erect position and the hands move toward the body so that the body is balanced during the stepping motions. Thus, a type 2 Reach or Move precedes the step, and at the completion of the step, another type 2 Reach or Move occurs to bring the hand to its final destination.

Observations of a wide variety of operators have indicated that the hands are carried most comfortably at a distance of approximately 6 inches from the body at any level of the torso. Thus the weight of the hands, arms, and any object being moved is close to the center of gravity of the body with all weight and strains distributed throughout the body. It is also apparent that the elevation of hand during the body movement is unimportant physically if the upper arm is held close enough to the body to distribute strain and fatigue to the back muscles.

Therefore, in applying motion-time standards to combination arm and stepping movements, the motion preceding the combination movement will bring the hand to within 6 inches of the body along the vertical plane in which the motions directly preceding this motion were performed. During the step, the hand will move in a vertical direction as close to the plane of the final destination as possible while remaining within a distance of 6 inches from the body. At the completion of the step, the hand will then travel to its final destination from this point with a type 2 Move or Reach.

In Fig. 70, the operator is at location A. The right hand has just released a lever at B, a distance of 14 inches from the operator's body. The operator must now side-step 30 inches to location C to perform work in the area indicated by D. Before any work can be accomplished, a part located at E, 20 inches from the operator's side when at position C, must be grasped by the right hand.

The motions occurring between the release of the lever and the grasp of the part at the new location would be

Reach (14 — 6) or 8-inch type 2
Side Step 30 inches as the hand drops to the approximate level of the next Reach
Reach (20 — 6) or 14-inch type 2

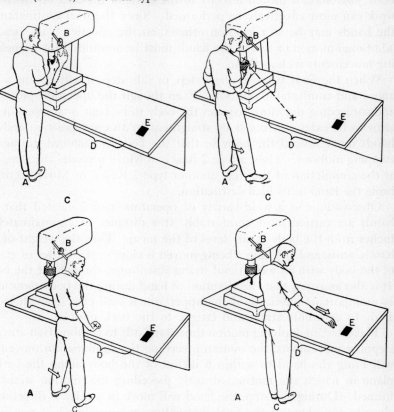

FIG. 70.— Combination arm and stepping movements.

The movement of the hand from X to X would be performed as a combination motion in which the 30-inch Side Step is limiting; hence, no time is allowed for it in the evaluation.

SIMULTANEOUS FOOT OR LEG AND ARM MOTIONS

Simultaneous motions of the arms and foot or of the arms and leg are common in industry in such occupation as punch-press work, resistance-welding operations, sewing-machine work, and the like. With a few exceptions, they are performed simultaneously in the same manner as simultaneous arm motions and are evaluated in the same manner; the motion group is analyzed, the motions occurring are identified, and the time value for the limiting motion is considered to be the time value for the group.

Two frequently occurring exceptions are (1) where a considerable pressure or force must be applied by the foot or leg, and (2) where the hand or arm must be removed from an area to avoid injury before the foot or leg can begin its motion.

In the former case, such as operating a resistance-welding machine requiring heavy foot pressure, attention is concentrated on performing the foot motion. As a result, the hands can perform only relatively uncontrolled motions. In this instance, the motions of the foot or leg and arms occur in succession rather than simultaneously, and their individual time values should be allowed.

In a punch-press operation where the foot or leg motion lowers a punch that would injure the hand if it were not moved out of the way, the time for the removal of the hand must be allowed. The return motion of the foot or leg which raises the punch can be combined or performed simultaneously with other motions, including the return of the hand to the danger area. The rule governing the application of time to simultaneous motions applies here also—the limiting motion is the one requiring the greatest amount of time.

COMPLEX SIMULTANEOUS MOTIONS OF THE BODY

The cases of complex simultaneous motions which occur in industry are too numerous and too varied to discuss in complete detail. They are, however, handled in the same manner as explained in the preceding paragraphs. The motions must be identified, the limiting motion determined, and the time value for the limiting motion applied.

An example of one of the many complex simultaneous motions occurring in industry is encountered in foundry work. An operator performing a machine-molding operation dusts the pattern with parting sand shaken from a bag held in his right hand and then lays aside the bag with the right hand on the top of the machine. He then reaches to the floor to grasp a riddle, preparatory to filling it with sand.

During the operation of reaching for the riddle, the operator performs the following three motions simultaneously:

Motion	Distance, inches	Time value, TMU
Move Hand to Riddle, case *B*	30	25.8
Stoop		29.0
Turn Body, case 2		37.15

In the case shown above, the turn body, case 2, requires the greatest amount of time, and hence it is the limiting motion. The time required to reach for the riddle by this method would therefore be 37.15 TMU.

If, in performing this operation, the bag had been laid aside by the left hand, the body could have been brought into a position more favorable for the reach to the riddle. During the laying aside of the bag, the right hand would have moved downward to the hips and the body would have turned to bring the right arm in line with its desired destination. Thus, these movements would be overlapped with the laying aside of the bag and the body would be pre-positioned for the Get Riddle element without additional chargeable time. With the body turned, the case 2 Turn Body movement would not be required. A case 1 Side Step in combination with the Reach of the hand and the Stoop of the body would be sufficient to bring the hand to the riddle. With this method, the following motions would be performed simultaneously:

Motion	Distance, inches	Time value, TMU
Move Hand to Riddle, case *B*	20	18.6
Side Step, case 1	18	20.6
Stoop		29.0

In this case, the Stoop of the body is the limiting motion, and the time value of 29.0 TMU must be allowed.

Great care must be taken in evaluating complex motions similar to the one just illustrated. Actually in the first example, the hand traveled a distance of 80 inches. Were the analyst to consider this purely as a Reach instead of a simultaneous motion, a time value of 61.7 TMU would be allowed instead of the proper value of 37.15 TMU. Since this and similar motions occur frequently in work such as molding, errors serious enough to make the study worthless from either a methods comparison or rate-setting standpoint would result from such a misinterpretation.

CHAPTER 15

ACCURACY OF METHODS-TIME STANDARDS

One of the most important questions that can be raised in connection with any newly developed measurement procedure is "How accurate is it?" This was, of course, a question which was uppermost all during the period when the methods-time standards were being developed. As soon as the standards were ready for application, therefore, a number of tests for accuracy were made. The tests of necessity had to start with the assumption that the leveling procedure itself was accurate, for unless an average performance was observed, the familiar problem of performance rating and the adjusting of data to the average performance level had to be faced. Thus in effect two variables were being checked simultaneously, the methods-time data and the leveling procedure. The fact that unexpectedly good results were obtained tends to lend weight to the conclusion that both the methods-time measurement procedure and the leveling procedure, when properly applied, will yield time standards of highly acceptable accuracy. It is the purpose of this chapter to report briefly on some of the tests that have been made.

PRELIMINARY TESTS OF ACCURACY WITH MOTION-PICTURE FILMS

The first tests for accuracy were made with the aid of motion-picture films. Nine rather simple operations, which had not previously been analyzed, were selected for the purpose. The procedure employed in each case was as follows: The motion picture was first projected at normal speed, and the performance of the operator was rated by three observers experienced in performance rating. The consensus of the three was accepted as the standard rating, and was not changed thereafter. Then one cycle of the operation was selected for study. The film was run through the projector shown in Fig. 71, which is a Keystone projector, especially equipped with a frame counter and speed-control device for motion-study work. The limiting motions were observed and recorded, and the actual elapsed time consumed by the cycle was determined.

FIG. 71.— Keystone projector especially equipped for motion-study work. (*Courtesy of Prof. David B. Porter and Dr. Louis P. Granath.*)

Next the actual time was multiplied by the leveling factor determined from the previous performance rating to give actual leveled time. Then the methods-time standards were assigned to the limiting motions previously recorded and totaled to give allowed TMU. The results were tabulated as follows:

Film No.	Operation	Actual leveled time, TMU	Allowed time, TMU
61	Crimp leads (old method)	199.5	200.5
61	Crimp leads (new method)	169.0	171.0
61	Dip swab (old method)	135.8	132.5
82	Cut web belting to length	42.4	43.8
82	Best method of wrapping 2-inch compresses	256.2	259.0
82	Same (wrapping only)	131.9	132.8
82	Label tube (new method)	173.0	175.0
82	Pack creosote solution (new method)	436.0	440.0
82	Place ampoule in envelope (normal speed)	180.2	178.8
Total		1,724.0	1,733.4

This appears to be a highly satisfactory check. It was recognized, however, that the procedure probably helped to arrive at some of the answers. For example, the fact that a given positioning consumed a certain number of frames could not help but be noted. This would create a tendency to classify it as more difficult than one that took only a few frames. Therefore, a different procedure was established for the next check.

TESTS OF ACCURACY AGAINST TIME-STUDY DATA

During a second investigation, a methods engineer checked in 27 cases the results of applying the methods-time measurement procedure by observation with the results of time studies made by a time-study man. Both men studied each job at the same time, so the factor of method was held constant. The time-study man made a stop-watch time study. The methods engineer observed the operation and applied the methods-time data. He also rated the performance of the operator for skill and effort, since he was more skilled at this than the time-study man who was a comparatively new man. Both men worked up their studies independently. The leveled time obtained from the time study was then checked with the time obtained from the methods-time measurement procedure.

The results obtained are shown by the following tabulation:

| Part No. | Department | Leveled time, dec. min. | |
		Time study	Methods-time data
E 21879	Forming	.0810	.0828
E 9113	Forming	.0950	.0887
E 26312	Forming	.0461	.0422
E 17780	Forming	.0428	.0400
E 2518	Forming	.3474	.3504
E 24060	Forming	.0330	.0336
E 25837	Switch	.0954	.0942
E 2486	Sundries	.1800	.1788
6174	42	.1452	.1452
6197	42	.1260	.1320
5612	Switch	.1210	.1220
6208	43	.6798	.6780
E 24769	Forming	.0640	.0640
E 4646	Forming	.0570	.0570
E 25921	Receptacle	.1080	.1086
C 2040	Switch	.1680	.1740
C 10	Switch	.0588	.0594
87145	43	.1260	.1200
73752	Sundries	.1247	.1135
Cat. F56	Switch	.1420	.1432
F 6233	Switch	.1060	.1056
E 25993	Switch	.1260	.1218
FS 5	Switch	.0730	.0733
E 3854	Forming	.0680	.0620
E 24060	Forming	.0330	.0330
E 23975	Forming	.0343	.0381
E 20486	Forming	.1800	.1800

The total time allowed by time study for the 27 jobs was 3.4615 minutes. The total time allowed by the methods-time measurement procedure was 3.4414 minutes. This is a difference of less than six-tenths of 1 per cent.

STUDY OF GAUZE-FOLDING FILM

A number of similar tests in other plants were subsequently made, which need not be discussed here, since they only served to confirm the findings reported above. As a result of these checks, the investigators began to accept the fact that the methods-time standards, properly applied, were highly accurate. On the basis of this assumption, they were used as a means of checking the accuracy of performance ratings in a study made to check the application of the leveling procedure.

A motion-picture film was prepared, which consisted of pictures of 21 different operators performing a simple gauze-folding operation. One operator was photographed working at two different performance levels, so that the film contained 22 different scenes or observations. At the time that the motion pictures were made, the performance of each operator was rated by three observers in terms of skill and effort as defined in the leveling procedure for evaluating performance. The consensus of the three observers was established as the temporary standard rating.

The film was then turned over to a methods analyst who was trained in the application of the methods-time data. The analyst proceeded to make a thorough analysis of the gauze-folding film. In all, 105 cycles were analyzed into terms of the methods-time data. At the outset, the actual time taken by the operator to perform each motion was leveled, using the temporary standard rating, and compared with the equivalent value from the methods-time data. It was felt, however, that this detailed comparison might cause the analyst to vary his estimate of the length of motions to cause close agreement, so presently this procedure was abandoned.

It was decided instead to analyze each complete cycle without observing the number of frames taken for each basic element, so that no comparison could be made until the end of the cycle. The over-all actual time for the cycle was then leveled and compared with the standard predicted by the methods-time data.

In this way, the analyst was sure that he was not being influenced by the methods-time data in his analysis of each basic element and that he was not consciously or unconsciously making the leveled time agree with the standard determined from the methods-time data. After each cycle had been analyzed, it was accepted as final without reanalysis, regardless of how well the leveled actual time for the cycle agreed with the time predicted by the methods-time data.

It was found, when the results were eventually compared, that the standards arrived at from the leveled actual time and from the methods-time data checked quite closely. In 74 of the 105 cycles analyzed, the difference between the two standards was 3 per cent or less. In only seven cycles was there a difference of 6 per cent or more, and in only one case was the difference as great as 9 per cent. Thus, in every case the difference was less than the plus or minus 5 per cent accuracy that has been established as the reasonable limit of accuracy of the leveling procedure.

Operator, clock number	Observer	Average elapsed time	Leveled time from formula	Difference, per cent	Leveling factor, per cent	Rating	
						Skill	Effort
45	JTO	.000525	.00068	129	125	A2	A2
60	JTO	.000685	.000635	93	100	D	D
20	WD	.000551	.000635	115	111	C1	C1
38	JTO	.000657	.000635	97	100	D	D
33	JTO	.00175	.00205	117	119	B1	B2
38	JTO	.000567	.000635	112	116	B2	B2
25	JTO	.000825	.00090	109	111	C1	C1
29	E	.000564	.000635	112	116	B2	B2
51	JTO	.000784	.000895	114	111	C1	C1
20	SJ	.000567	.000635	112	108	C2	C1
5	WD	.000450	.000590	131	127	A1	A2
40	JTO	.000570	.000635	111.5	111	C1	C1
20	E	.00071	.000735	103	108	C1	C2
18	JTO	.00055	.000635	115	111	C1	C1
42	HP	.00070	.00081	116	111	C1	C1
30	E	.000645	.00081	125	125	A2	A2
37	JTO	.00078	.00081	104	100	D	D
56	JTO	.000650	.000635	98	100	D	D
43	JTO	.000850	.000895	105	108	C1	C2
52	E	.000665	.000804	121	121	B1	B1
33	E	.000675	.000804	119	116	B2	B2
48	JTO	.00068	.000804	118	119	B1	B2
58	E	.00082	.000804	98	91	E1	E1
44	JTO	.00056	.000725	130	125	A2	A2
37	JTO	.000575	.00059	102	105	C2	C2
42	HP	.000684	.00072	105	108	C1	C2
38	JTO	.000730	.00072	99	100	D	D
42	WD	.000635	.00072	113	111	C1	C1
4	WD	.000542	.000635	117	123	A2	B1
17	E	.000605	.000593	98	95	E1	D
20	WD	.000568	.000593	104	105	C2	C2
5	WD	.000460	.000593	129	128	A1	A1
5	PF	.0005	.000635	127	128	A1	A1
20	WD	.00065	.000635	98	100	D	D
20	PF	.00077	.000764	99	100	D	D
4	WD	.000521	.000680	130	128	A1	A1
4	E	.00051	.000680	133	128	A1	A1
60	JTO	.00609	.000600	99	100	D	D

ADDITIONAL TESTS

An interesting study was made which involved a time formula developed from the methods-time data, similar to the one described in Chapter 27. The class of work involved was punch-press work done on small bench punch presses. Twenty-one different operators were included in the study. Six different time-study men participated.

A time value was first established on a given operation from the time formula. The operation was then time studied and the performance of the operator was rated and recorded. The time value determined from the formula was then divided by the average elapsed time determined by time study to establish the actual performance of the operator. This figure was compared with the leveling factor as determined from the performance rating. The agreement, as may be seen from the tabulation opposite, was quite close and seems to indicate that the time formula, the methods-time data on which it is based, and the leveling procedure are all accurate within practical limits.

Although these findings are all highly favorable, it is recommended that they be accepted as evidence that the development of methods-time data has been progressing in the right direction rather than that the development work has been completed. Further research on the part of many other investigators will be desirable before conclusions should be accepted as final.

PART III

APPLICATION PROCEDURE

CHAPTER 16

ELEMENTS OF METHODS-TIME MEASUREMENT

A number of uses of the methods-time measurement procedure have already been pointed out in Chapter 2. In general, they fall into two classes: (1) the determination of the time required to perform an operation by direct observation of the motions used to do the job, and (2) the determination of the time required to perform an operation by mentally visualizing the motions when there is no opportunity for direct observation. In both cases, the basic methods-time data are used to establish the time after the motions have been determined.

The two approaches utilize somewhat different application procedures. It is the purpose of this section of the book to describe the application procedures, (1) when the methods-time measurement procedure is used to take the place of time study and (2) when it is used for estimating purposes.

ELEMENTS OF METHODS-TIME MEASUREMENT

The various elements of the methods-time measurement procedure when applied as the result of direct observation are shown by Fig. 72. This chart assumes that the methods analysis and the development of the method have either already been done or will be done after the existing method has been thoroughly studied. If the methods-time measurement procedure is to be applied to drawings or samples of the part, as described in Chapter 19, the elements of choice of operator, approach to operator, and performance rating will be omitted.

CHOICE OF OPERATOR

When the methods-time measurement procedure has been applied, the result yielded is the time which will be required to do the operation by an operator working with average skill and effort who uses the method on which the allowed time is based. If the allowed time is to be used for wage incentive purposes or in any other connection where accuracy is important, it is essential that it be based on a good acceptable method.

Hence, in choosing the operator who is to be observed, it is necessary to select one who knows and uses the proper method for doing the job.

The detailed analysis required by the methods-time measurement procedure frequently brings to light ideas for improving the method. The methods engineer will find it desirable to have these ideas tried out

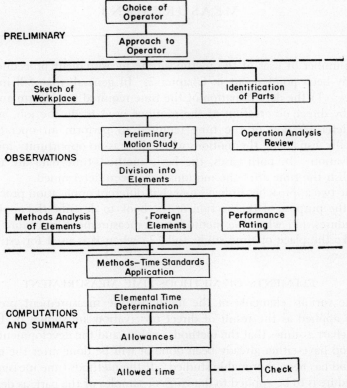

Fig. 72.— Graphic analysis of the elements of methods-time measurement.

while they are still fresh in his mind. Therefore, he will wish to choose an operator for study who is cooperative and who will be willing to try out improved methods without undue reluctance. An operator who is interested enough in the work to offer ideas himself is particularly desirable.

The performance given by the operator during study is not particularly important unless it is exceptionally good or extremely poor, for the leveling procedure will adjust satisfactorily for variations in speed of motions within the range of performance levels ordinarily encountered in the shop. During the research work which accompanied the development of the methods-time data, some evidence was discovered to the effect that the very fast and the very slow operators use quite different methods than the operators working in the fair-to-excellent performance range. The superior operators overlap and combine motions in a way that may quite possibly be beyond the abilities of the normal workers, while the poor operators perform each and every motion separately so that even normal overlap does not occur. A methods engineer skilled in the application of the methods-time measurement procedure can perhaps adjust his observed data obtained on very good or very poor operators to represent the method that would be used by the majority of workers. Until this skill has been developed by the use of the methods-time measurement procedure over a long period of time, it is better for the methods engineer not to include in his studies operators who give unusually good or unusually poor performances.

APPROACH TO OPERATOR

Operators who have been accustomed to being time studied with the aid of a stop watch usually are keenly interested in a procedure that does not use the watch. The methods engineer should make it a point to discuss their questions freely and to tell them as much about the procedure as they are interested in knowing. At the beginning of the study, the methods engineer should let it be known that he wishes to make a study and a record of the motions the operator is using to do the work. Often this leads to a friendly discussion of the motions and the reasons for making them. The methods engineer will promote good relations if he shows respect for the operator's superior knowledge of the details of the job and if he commends any skillful motion sequences the operator may have developed.

The methods-time measurement procedure which arrives at an allowed time by assigning motion-time standards of known accuracy to the method which the operator is using quickly gains the confidence and respect of all fair-minded workers. When the methods-time measurement procedure becomes generally understood, the methods engineer need only observe the usual amenities of human relations in his approach to the worker.

SKETCH OF WORKPLACE

In beginning to make observations, it is helpful to start with a sketch of the workplace. The sketch should identify the locations of tools, fix-

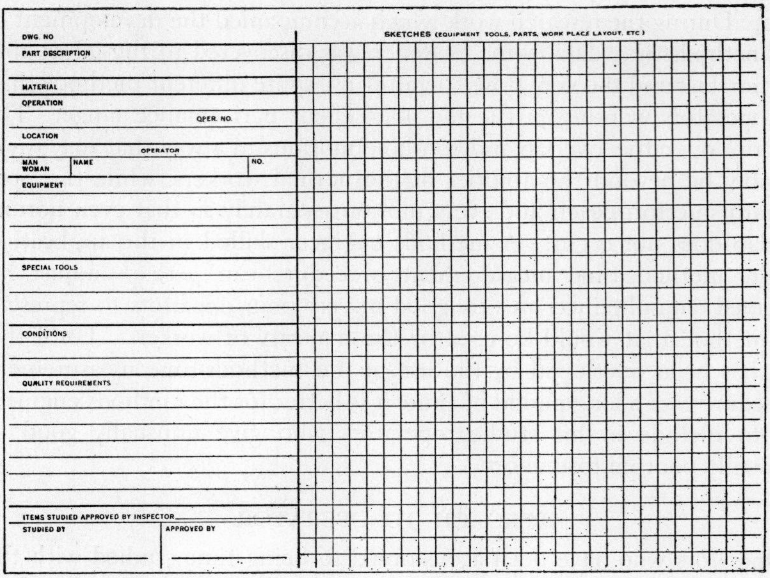

DWG. NO

PART DESCRIPTION

MATERIAL

OPERATION

OPER. NO.

LOCATION

OPERATOR

MAN / WOMAN | NAME | NO.

EQUIPMENT

SPECIAL TOOLS

CONDITIONS

QUALITY REQUIREMENTS

ITEMS STUDIED APPROVED BY INSPECTOR

STUDIED BY | APPROVED BY

SKETCHES (EQUIPMENT TOOLS, PARTS, WORK PLACE LAYOUT, ETC.)

Fig. 73.— Back of methods-time measurement observation sheet.

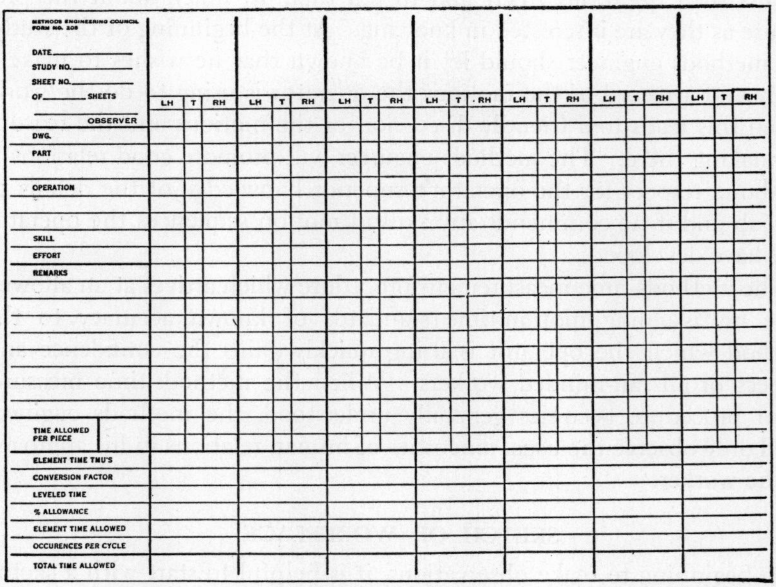

METHODS ENGINEERING COUNCIL
FORM NO. 208

DATE

STUDY NO.

SHEET NO.

OF ______ SHEETS

OBSERVER

	LH	T	RH	LH	T	RH	LH	T	RH	LH	T	RH	LH	T	RH	LH	T	RH	LH	T	RH
DWG.																					
PART																					
OPERATION																					
SKILL																					
EFFORT																					
REMARKS																					
TIME ALLOWED PER PIECE																					
ELEMENT TIME TMU'S																					
CONVERSION FACTOR																					
LEVELED TIME																					
% ALLOWANCE																					
ELEMENT TIME ALLOWED																					
OCCURENCES PER CYCLE																					
TOTAL TIME ALLOWED																					

Fig. 74.— Face of methods-time measurement observation sheet.

tures, and materials, both raw and finished. It should also show all dimensions that may be helpful in judging the length of motions. This latter point is important, for experience has shown that most people are poor judges of the length of motions until they have had considerable training and practice and that even then they may make occasional errors of serious magnitude. Sketches may be made on the methods-time measurement sheet in the space provided for the purpose. The back of the observation sheet on which information about the job is recorded is shown by Fig. 73. The face of the observation sheet is shown by Fig. 74.

IDENTIFICATION OF PARTS

The part, or parts, being worked upon should be listed on the observation sheet and preferably should be sketched. This step is often left to the last in conventional time study with the result that the observer sometimes has only a hazy knowledge of the exact form of the parts being handled. The methods-time measurement procedure requires a thorough knowledge of the nature of the part, or parts, before observations begin, for as the methods engineer begins to list and classify the motions used, he must know whether the parts are large or small, symmetrical or nonsymmetrical, easy or difficult to handle so that he can identify the motions properly. It is well that this intimate knowledge of the parts is necessary before the study proper is begun, for it enables the methods engineer better to judge the adequacy of the methods which he observes.

PRELIMINARY MOTION STUDY

The identification and listing of the motions used to perform the operations is a detailed and time-consuming task. Therefore the methods engineer should assure himself in at least a preliminary manner that the method being used is sufficiently good to make its recording worth while. To do this, he should review the written operation analysis of the job if one has been made, or at least should make a rough mental operation analysis to make sure that no glaring inefficiencies exist.

Following this, he should watch the operation for a few moments while reviewing the principles of motion economy in his mind. He should particularly look for ineffective basic elements, such as idle periods or one hand holding the part while the other performs work on it. It will also prove desirable to review the laws of motion economy and their corollaries to determine whether the method conforms to them sufficiently to justify its acceptance for study. The principles of motion economy are discussed in Chapter 20.

If the method is acceptable, the study should be continued. If not, the method should be revised before proceeding.

DIVISION INTO ELEMENTS

In order to facilitate study and analysis, the operation should next be divided into a series of elements. The principles followed in doing this should in general be the same as those followed in time-study work. The division can be finer however, if desired, for the problem of timing very short elements does not enter in.

The descriptions of the elements which are recorded on the observation sheet should be more complete than is usually the case on time studies. Emphasis is on method throughout the methods-time measurement procedure, and the element descriptions should be complete enough to convey a good understanding of the method employed.

In dividing the operation into elements, care should be taken to separate the constant and the variable elements, for the occasion may arise later on of using the study for time-formula-derivation purposes. A constant element is an element for which the performance time is constant regardless of the characteristics of the part being worked upon. A variable element is one for which the time varies with variations in such characteristics as size, shape, weight, and the like.

METHODS ANALYSIS OF ELEMENTS

With the operation divided into elements, the next step is to determine by close observation the method employed in performing each element. The methods engineer will watch the first element until he feels that he understands how it or at least part of it is performed. He will then record the classification of the limiting motions on his observation sheet as R10B, G1a, M12C, and so on, showing whether it is the right or the left hand that performs each motion. He then observes another element or part of an element. When he has decided upon the motions employed, he records them. The process is repeated until the motions used to perform all elements have been recorded on the observation sheet.

Many motions are made so quickly that they are difficult to detect with the unaided eye. It is, therefore, essential that the methods engineer should have had thorough training in methods analysis with motion-picture films so that he will have the intimate knowledge of typical motion patterns which is a necessary background to the correct observation of motions in the shop.

When the regular elements of the operation have been analyzed, the methods engineer will turn his attention to any other elements that are necessary to the performance of the operation. These are of two general types.

1. Elements regularly necessary.
2. Elements necessary because of an unusual condition.

Regular elements which are always necessary for the performance of the operation, but which do not occur in every cycle, consist of such acts as "replenish material supply," "remove finished parts," and "wind bobbin." The method of performing such elements should be studied as above, and the number of occurrences per cycle should be determined and recorded.

Occasionally elements will be encountered which are not a regular part of the job but which must be performed because of some unusual condition. It may be necessary to remove a heavy burr from a number of parts to get them into a jig, because an operator on a preceding operation has allowed his tool to become dull. When the condition has been corrected, the element will disappear, but time must be allowed for performing it. Such elements can be observed and recorded in the same manner as other elements, but a note should be made that they are not a regular part of the job.

FOREIGN ELEMENTS

Elements that are unnecessary to the job, even though they may be unavoidable, are classed as foreign elements. In this classification are such things as personal requirements, breaking a tool, a slight injury, and unnecessary work. Elements of this type that are necessary are usually covered by the allowance for fatigue and personal and unavoidable delays. Such allowances are determined by all-day time studies and not by the methods-time measurement procedure. Hence, when such elements occur during a methods-time study, they need not be analyzed or recorded.

PERFORMANCE RATING

During the period that the observations are being made, the methods engineer will observe the performance given by the operator. He will judge skill and effort in accordance with the leveling method of rating performance,[1] and will record his conclusions on the observation sheet. Usually, an over-all performance rating for the study will suffice. If, however, the performance of the operator is better on some elements than on others, this fact and the proper ratings should be recorded.

It is useful to have a record of the performance given by the operator in the event that it becomes necessary to investigate the reasons underlying any element for which the performance time may appear out of line with other studies. As pointed out before, when very good or very poor performances are given, the method used is often different from the method employed in the fair-to-excellent performance range. Thus information about the performance given by the operator may provide the clue to understanding the reason underlying an unusually high or low elemental time.

METHODS-TIME STANDARDS APPLICATION

When all observations have been completed, the working up of the study or the computations and summary is a simple matter. The first step is to assign the proper time standard to each motion recorded on the observation sheet. This is done by referring to the tables shown in Chapter 4. Speed may be gained in performing this step of the study at a slight sacrifice of accuracy by using the simplified methods-time data described in Chapter 24. The basic data do not include any allowance for fatigue and personal and unavoidable delays. Therefore proper allowances must be added. The simplified data include a 15 per cent allowance. Therefore, no further computations are necessary if a 15 per cent allowance is considered correct for the type of work being studied. An adjustment must be made, however, if an allowance of other than 15 per cent is to be used.

ELEMENTAL TIME DETERMINATION

The time for each element is determined by adding together the times assigned to the motions used to perform the element. The result is recorded on the first line of the summary on the observation sheet.

ALLOWANCES

The basic methods-time standards represent the time required by a normal operator working with average skill and effort to make the

[1] LOWRY, MAYNARD, and STEGEMERTEN, "Time and Motion Study and Formulas for Wage Incentives," Chapt. XIX, McGraw-Hill Book Company, Inc., 1940.

motions. To this time must be added an allowance to compensate for the time lost during the course of the working day due to fatigue and personal and unavoidable delays if a true production standard is to be obtained. Allowances are determined by making all-day time studies of the delays encountered on representative working days. The method of doing this has been described elsewhere.[1] The methods-time measurement procedure makes use of these allowances in determining the allowed time.

ALLOWED TIME

The time allowed for each element is multiplied by the number of times the element occurs per cycle. In the majority of cases, the number of occurrences per cycle will be one. Some elements on some jobs may occur more than once per cycle. Others may occur once every second or tenth or fiftieth cycle, in which case the multiplier will be a fraction. When the element times per cycle have been determined for all elements, they are added together to give the final allowed time. This represents the time which an operator of average skill would require, when giving an average effort under average working conditions, and when experiencing the retarding effects of fatigue, unavoidable delays, and the like, to perform the operation when using the method upon which the allowed time is based.

CHECKING

Opportunities for errors exist in the methods-time measurement procedure just as in any other computational process. Errors in observing, errors in applying the methods-time standards, and errors in additions and multiplications are all possible. Therefore the allowed time should be carefully checked in order to ascertain if any very serious errors have been made.

RECORDS AND FILING

All observation sheets and related data should be carefully filed, for they provide not only a record of the allowed time but also a complete detailed record of the method upon which the allowed time was based. One of the major problems of wage incentive administration has been that time allowances have tended to get more and more liberal as time passes. Everyone recognizes that this is because methods changes are made from time to time, which, although of minor magnitude indi-

[1] *Ibid.*, Chapt. XX.

vidually, cumulatively become sufficient to cause the allowed time to become considerably out of line. It is also recognized that it is not only right but essential if consistency is to be maintained to adjust time values when methods change. When many minor methods changes are made over a long period of time, however, it is very difficult under conventional time-study practices to prove conclusively that methods have changed. No ethical management wishes to engage in unjustified rate cutting, so the tendency is to do nothing about time values that have gotten out of line because of minor methods changes. The resulting inconsistent standards often become a major problem, however.

The methods-time measurement procedure provides an accurate record of the method upon which the time value was based. If a question about the accuracy of the time value arises in the future, it is necessary merely to reapply the methods-time measurement procedure. If the method has not changed, the same motion sequence will be recorded. If it has changed, the exact nature of the changes will be readily apparent. Thus the methods engineer by carefully preserving his records of the application of the methods-time measurement procedure is in a position to answer any questions that may arise about his time values.

CHAPTER 17

INFORMATION AND OBSERVATIONS

There are two basic steps to be followed in applying the methods-time measurement procedure to operations that are already being performed.

1. Secure complete and detailed information concerning task, equipment, and method.
2. Analyze, classify, and record at the workplace every necessary motion required to perform the job properly.

Neither step can be considered more important than the other. If the information is not recorded in detail, difficulty will be encountered in quickly and accurately classifying the motions during the observation period. In addition, if the occasion arises in which the study is to be used later in constructing a time formula, insufficient information will make it difficult if not impossible to interpret the study. The necessity for careful and accurate observations need not be labored, for it is obvious that if the observations are not correctly made and recorded, the time value derived will be inaccurate.

This entire chapter is devoted to a discussion of the procedure to be followed in applying the methods-time measurement procedure to operations already in existence. It should be stressed that these techniques should be followed in detail, for only in this way can accurate and economical application be made.

INFORMATION

Before application of the methods-time measurement procedure is made, complete information in regard to tools, workplace layout, processing information, operation and material identification, and working conditions should be recorded. Three purposes are served by the compilation of this complete set of information.

1. An increased understanding of the general method is obtained, which contributes to the accuracy of the study and minimizes errors and doubts about the proper motion patterns and classifications when the operation is later observed in detail.

2. The conditions and methods in use when the time value is established are made available for reference if a question as to the validity of the time value is raised later on.
3. The construction of time formulas from the data is simplified and their accuracy is increased, because every condition affecting the method is known.

Every item of information that will clarify the method and add to the future value of the study should be carefully recorded. Figure 75

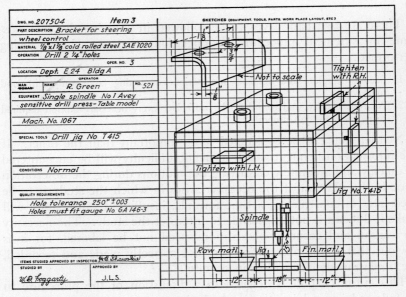

Fig. 75.— Model study showing manner in which information is recorded.

shows the type of information that should be recorded on the methods-time measurement observation sheet before the detailed study of a job is begun.

OPERATION

The operation should be clearly identified by a short and descriptive name, using the terminology in common use in the plant. Although the identifying name should be concise, it should be complete enough to be descriptive. "Mill" conveys only a very general idea of the nature of the operation. "Mill slot" is considerably more meaningful. "Mill ½- × ¾-inch slot for stub shaft" is a positive identification of the operation to anyone who is familiar with the apparatus being manufactured.

Further examples of operation names from various types of industries are "make ½- × 1½-inch bolthole cores," "mold ¼-hp. motor brackets," "shirr right and left sleeves," "weld 4 corners, 66-inch sink top," and "tenon both ends of short cross brace."

In plants that follow the practice of identifying operations by number as well as by name, the operation number should also be recorded.

LOCATION

The location at which the operation was performed should be recorded, for this sometimes has an effect on the method followed. The description of the location should be complete enough to permit any interested person to determine exactly where the study was taken. The department name and number will fix the general location. Where machines that are permanently fastened to the floor are involved, the machine number will determine the exact location. In the case of work done on a bench or on the shop floor, exact location identification is more difficult. If the plant has the practice of numbering columns, the column numbers in conjunction with a sketch will serve to locate the workplace. If not, then the nearest piece of identifiable permanent equipment may be used.

OPERATOR

In identifying the operator, it is usually sufficient to record clock number and name and whether the operator is a man or a woman. Because the previous experience of the operator often has an important bearing on the method used, it is sometimes desirable to ascertain and record the amount of experience previously had by the operator on the operation under study or on similar work.

PART

To identify the part, or parts, involved in the operation, identifying numbers and names, supplemented by sketches, should be used. Practically every plant uses numbers to identify its products. If the components are not numbered, the completed product usually is. The parts of a dress, for example, are not commonly identified by number, although the completed dress is. Thus, a certain part might be identified as "right front skirt gore, Style 705, Size 16, black." In industries of a more mechanical nature, each component is usually identified by number, as "part number," "drawing and item numbers," "pattern number," or "catalogue number."

In recording the name of the part, care should be taken to use the same name that appears on the drawing or other identifying operation. Considerable needless confusion will be caused if a given part is called a bracket on the drawing, a brace on the study, and a support on the shop order, yet such instances occur with sufficient frequency to justify the caution against them.

Sketches usually prove to be the most satisfactory means of part identification. Even a rough freehand sketch will show at a glance the general appearance of the part. The cross-sectional area is provided on the back of the observation sheet for convenience in making sketches.

MATERIAL

Material should be identified completely so that its characteristics are ascertainable later on. Here again, concise but complete descriptions are better than one-word identifications—"20-gauge hot-rolled steel" is a better description than merely "steel." Complete material specifications can often be obtained from the bill of material or other manufacturing information.

Where different kinds of cloth are used, as in the needle-trades industries, a satisfactory way of identifying material is to attach to the observation sheet a small piece of the material itself.

In addition to the material of which the part is made, any other materials which enter into the operation should be identified. If the condition of the principal material or of the other materials is abnormal in any respect, this fact should be duly recorded. The quality of the thread used for sewing, for example, will have a very definite influence on the satisfactory performance of the operation. If the material used while the study is being made is different from the material that will subsequently be used, a record of this fact should be made.

EQUIPMENT

The equipment used to perform the operation has a major influence on method. Therefore it should be clearly identified. Here again, sketches as well as identifying names and numbers are useful if the equipment is at all out of the ordinary. Any auxiliary devices that are used in conjunction with the major piece of equipment, such as jib cranes or special material racks or trays, should also be described.

The condition of the equipment often has an important effect on the operation. Therefore the condition should be investigated, and any departures from normal should be noted.

QUALITY REQUIREMENTS

Although it is constantly stressed that the quality requirements of any operation should be thoroughly understood before the study is begun, this important point is overlooked sufficiently often to justify calling for a description of quality requirements on the observation sheet. In addition, because of the important influence of quality requirements on methods, it is desirable to have a record of the requirements that were in force when the study was made. Then if the requirements are changed later on, it will be possible to determine whether or not a change in time allowance is justified. It is usually best to ascertain quality requirements from the one who is directly responsible for judging the acceptability of the work. This is usually the inspector, but it may be the foreman, the engineer, or even, in the small plant, the owner. In describing the quality requirements on the observation sheet, the methods engineer should keep in mind that the ultimate purpose is to make it clear to anyone who may be interested at any future time just what the quality requirements were at the time the study was made. This is often not easy to accomplish, but with sufficient care in wording the description, the objective may be approached.

TOOL AND PART SKETCHES

A complete and clear sketch of the parts to be processed and the design of any tools, dies, or holding means that affect the motions required to perform the job should be drawn in the cross-sectional area of the observation sheet. These sketches should indicate the conditions affecting positioning, and, when necessary, the hand that must perform the motions. Thus, when sketching the tools and parts, sound opinions are formed, which later simplify the observation procedure.

WORKPLACE LAYOUTS

A sketch of the workplace layout must always be drawn before application of the methods-time measurement procedure. Because the location of the materials and tools and the construction of the parts and tools largely determine the motion pattern used, the sketch will crystallize in the observer's mind the general motion pattern that will be used on the job.

The sketch should be drawn roughly to scale. The location of the parts should be identified by name or style number; tools and fixtures should be indicated; and any object that may hinder free movements of the hands should be included in the sketch. Other pertinent information that it may be desirable to include, such as the type of container, can be sketched rather than recorded in writing if desired. Because the sketch will be a useful source of information when the study is made, as well as later when reference is made to the motion breakdown, it is recommended that the workplace layout be sketched in as much detail as is practical.

CONDITIONS

It is important that a record be made of the working conditions existing at the time of the study. If conditions are normal, this fact should be noted. Any abnormal conditions should, of course, be described. Unsatisfactory working conditions may lower the effectiveness of the operator and may make it difficult for him to attain the standard. Recording such conditions brings them to light and makes the necessity for correcting them more evident.

OBSERVATIONS

The term "observations," as used here, covers the identifying and recording of the motions necessary to perform the operation that is being studied in order to make possible the application of the methods-time data. It includes breaking the job into its proper elements, listing them in their proper sequence, and then breaking down each element into the motions required to perform it.

GENERAL OBSERVATION PROCEDURE

Observation and application of the methods-time measurement procedure to existing methods follow in general the accepted procedure for making and recording stop-watch time studies. An outline of the procedure is presented below step by step.

1. Assume a position in which all motions required to perform the method are clearly visible.
2. Determine the elemental breakdown.
   a. Separate constant and variable elements mentally.
   b. Determine the proper sequence of elements.
3. Describe each element in detail, and record its description in its proper sequence at the top of the spaces at the top of the observation sheet.
4. Observe each element of the operation individually and in detail, and record the motions performed in the columns provided for the left and the right hands.
   a. Record only the limiting motions and simultaneous motions, unless it is felt that a record of some or all of the nonlimiting motions will increase understanding of the method employed. If nonlimiting motions are recorded, draw a circle around them to distinguish them from the limiting motions.

b. Record foot, leg, or body motions in the column headed RH.

c. Observe only one element at a time. Complete the observation of one element before moving to the next element, except on long-cycle operations.

d. Record the motions used by means of the conventions described in Chapter 4.

5. When the study has been completed, check the motion sequences for errors in observing or recording.

6. Before leaving the job, rate the skill and effort exhibited by the operator during the observation.

7. Sign and date the study.

POSITION OF THE OBSERVER

The methods engineer making the observation should assume a position from which all motions necessary for the performance of the operation can be easily observed. It is especially important that all actions of the hands and arms be seen. If it is impossible, because of the nature of the workplace, to assume a position from which every motion can be clearly seen and analyzed, the observer should take the best possible vantage point from which the greater part of the operation can be seen, complete the study as far as possible, and then move to a location from which the rest of the motions can be observed. Movements of the observer about the workplace, however, should be kept at a minimum, for they may disturb and confuse the operator.

The observer should assume a position that will cause the least distraction to the workers. Generally, it is better to assume a position similar to that of the person being studied—i.e., if the person being studied is standing, the observer should stand, and if the operator is seated, the observer should sit down.

DIVIDING THE OPERATION INTO ELEMENTS

In dividing the operation into elements, the general procedure used in making a time study should be followed. Constants and variables should be recorded separately for observation. Elements should be kept as short as possible to enable the observer to identify more clearly and quickly the motions used in performing them.

This latter point is important. To gain speed and accuracy in applying the methods-time measurement procedure, it is imperative that the observer be able mentally to reconstruct each element after it has been witnessed once or twice. If the element is of long duration and made up of a great many motions, the observer's mind may become confused when trying to recall all the motions and their order of occurrence. Thus the element will have to be observed many more times in order to record accurately the motions used. This is time consuming and may result in inaccuracies. If the elements are kept short, with the number of motions required for their performance not exceeding 20 per element, this difficulty will not be encountered.

The importance of clearly describing each element should be emphasized. The description should indicate the method by which the element was performed. The description should be written in such a

METHODS ENGINEERING COUNCIL FORM NO. 20B	Get part with LH from totepan, transfer to RH and place in jig			Tighten 2 locators simultaneously close jig cover with LH, and tighten thumb screw with RH			Reach to spindle lever RH, lower spindle and position jig under drill			Drill 1/4" hole 1/8" deep			Raise spindle RH move to second hole LH, lower spindle and position jig under drill			Raise spindle RH loosen 2 locators simultaneously loosen thumbnut RH and open cover LH			Remove part from jig RH and toss aside in totepan on right		
DATE 2-15-47 STUDY NO. 3 SHEET NO. 1 OF 1 SHEETS																					
	LH	T	RH	LH	T	RH	LH	T	RH	LH	T	RH	LH	T	RH	LH	T	RH	LH	T	RH
OBSERVER																					
DWG 207504 Item 3																					
PART Bracket																					
OPERATION Drill 2 1/4" holes																					
SKILL																					
EFFORT																					
REMARKS																					
TIME ALLOWED PER PIECE																					
ELEMENT TIME TMU'S																					
CONVERSION FACTOR																					
LEVELED TIME																					
% ALLOWANCE																					
ELEMENT TIME ALLOWED																					
OCCURRENCES PER CYCLE																					
TOTAL TIME ALLOWED																					

FIG. 76.— Model study showing elemental breakdown completed.

manner that an engineer unfamiliar with the method described, but with an understanding of the methods-time measurement procedure, can, by reading the element description and the recorded motion sequence, accurately reconstruct the method followed in performing the operation.

A detailed sketch of the workplace layout and tools used makes it possible to shorten element descriptions. For example, distances recorded on the sketch may be omitted from the element description. When the sketch shows the location of parts and materials, the hand used in reaching for them is usually obvious.

Figure 76 shows the model study with the elemental breakdown recorded. The elements include rather more motions than would be desirable if the study is to be used for formula-derivation purposes, but this is necessary to show the complete operation on one form. It is interesting to note, however, how easy it is to subdivide the operation further when the methods-time measurement procedure is used, if this is necessary later on.

RECORDING MOTIONS

With all sketches drawn, all necessary information recorded properly on the back of the observation sheet, and with the elemental break-down determined and recorded, the detailed observations may be begun.

The observer should begin by watching carefully one or two cycles of the operation. During this time, if he is familiar with the methods-time measurement procedure, he can obtain a fairly complete mental picture of the motions required to perform the entire operation. The study of the workplace, tools, and setup made before the observations began will assist greatly in obtaining this preliminary mental picture of the motions required.

Each regular element of the operation should then be studied in order of occurrence, and the motions required to perform it should be recorded. One or two observations of the element may be necessary to determine with exactness the way it is performed, especially if the motions required are complex in nature. Each motion should be recorded in either the column headed Left Hand or Right Hand under the element column in the order of its occurrence. Motions performed by the left hand are listed in the column headed Left Hand, and those performed by the right hand are listed in the column headed Right Hand. The motions used are indicated by the conventions for describing motions in abbreviated form, which are given in Chapter 4. Figure 77 shows the model study with the observations completed.

The limiting motions only should be recorded. The element descriptions, if properly written, should preclude any possibility of a later misinterpretation of the method used, even though the motions which are not limiting are not recorded on the observation sheet. If for any reason it is desired to record the nonlimiting motions, they may be recorded in the same manner as the limiting motions, but the descriptions should be circled to indicate they have no bearing on time allowed. On line 5, column 1, Fig. 77, the motion M6C is circled to show that it is not limiting. Several other nonlimiting motions are shown on the model study.

Foot, leg, and body motions should be recorded in the columns headed Right Hand in all instances. If the hands and arms are performing nonlimiting motions simultaneously with the motion of the leg, the motions may be recorded if desired on the line immediately above the line on which the leg motion is recorded. The descriptions should be circled to show that they are nonlimiting.

Form header: METHODS ENGINEERING COUNCIL, FORM NO. 208 — DATE 2-15-47 — STUDY NO. 3 — SHEET NO. 1 — OF 1 SHEETS

Element descriptions:
- E1: Get part with LH from totepan, transfer to RH and place in jig
- E2: Tighten 2 locators simultaneously close jig cover with LH, and tighten thumb screw with RH
- E3: Reach to spindle lever RH lower spindle and position jig under drill
- E4: Drill 1/4" hole 1/8" deep
- E5: (blank)
- E6: Raise spindle RH move to second hole LH, lower spindle and position jig under drill
- E7: Raise spindle RH loosen 2 locators simultaneously loosen thumbnut RH and open cover LH
- E8: Remove part from jig RH and toss aside in totepan on right

Drill data (E4, written vertically): Speed = 70 F.P.M. = 1070 R.P.M.; Feed = .0025" per revolution; Lead of drill = .025"; Thickness of material = $\frac{1}{25}$"

Label	E1 LH	E1 T	E1 RH	E2 LH	E2 T	E2 RH	E3 LH	E3 T	E3 RH	E6 LH	E6 T	E6 RH	E7 LH	E7 T	E7 RH	E8 LH	E8 RH
OBSERVER	R10c			R6B		R6B			R15A	M12E	(MBB)	M22A					R4B
DWG 207504 Item 3	G4			G1a		G1a			G1a	MIC				(RLI)	RLI		G1c
PART Bracket	M15B			T90		T90			M12B	P2SD	(M2B)	(R6B)			R15B		D2D
		G3		RLI		RLI	P2SD			M6A			G1a		G1a		M10D
OPERATION Drill	R8B	(M6C)		T90		T90			M6A		G3		AP		AP		RLI
2 1/4" holes	G1a			G1a		G1a			G1a				T90		T90		
		P2NSD		T90		T90							RLI		RLI		
SKILL C-1	RLI		RLI	AP		AP							T90		T90		
EFFORT C-2				RLI		RLI							G1a		G1a		
REMARKS Operator				R6B									T90		T90		
has had 6 months				G1a											RLI		
experience on				M10a											R4B		
this class of						R4B									G1a		
work						G1a									T90		
						T90									RLI		
						RLI									R4E		
														M10A			

TIME ALLOWED PER PIECE		
ELEMENT TIME TMU'S		
CONVERSION FACTOR		
LEVELED TIME		
% ALLOWANCE		
ELEMENT TIME ALLOWED		
OCCURENCES PER CYCLE		
TOTAL TIME ALLOWED		

FIG. 77.— Model study showing observations completed.

Although it is desirable if possible, to study elements in the order of their occurrence, it is not always practicable. On long jobs, considerable time could be spent by the engineer in waiting for a given element to occur in the work cycle. In cases of this sort, the engineer may direct his attention to another element in another part of the cycle and continue his recordings.

Elements which are necessary but which are not repeated on every cycle should be observed and recorded on the observation sheet in the same manner as the repetitive elements. A notation should be made on the next to the last line of the observation sheet of the number of times they occur per cycle, and whether the necessity for performing them is temporary or permanent. If they are a permanent part of the operation, such as gauging every fifth part, replenishing supply of material in bins, etc., they must be included as a part of the final time value.

FOREIGN ELEMENTS

Foreign elements are those elements which are not necessary for the performance of the operation. They include such items as dropping a part, personal delays, minor machine troubles, etc.

The time for unavoidable foreign elements is not included in the final time value as a distinct elemental time, but is covered by the allowance for fatigue and unavoidable and personal delays, which is added to the leveled time.

The skill and effort exhibited by the operator during the study should be recorded before leaving the job. This may be of assistance in judging the effectiveness of the method, as was explained in the preceding chapter. The study should then be signed and dated.

CHAPTER 18

COMPUTATIONS AND SUMMARY

With the observations and information recorded, the remainder of the work necessary to complete the study and to determine the allowed time consists of calculations and mathematical procedure. Most of the work is routine and can be delegated to a clerk, although it must be borne in mind that accuracy is essential.

APPLYING METHODS-TIME DATA

The column for each element headed Time will appear blank on the observation sheet at this point. In the columns headed Left Hand and Right Hand will appear the descriptions of the motions used in performing the element. The first step in working up the study is to determine from the methods-time data tables the leveled time in TMU for each motion and to record it in the Time column. Descriptions that are circled should be disregarded and only the time values for the limiting motions recorded. The time values should be recorded in ink to ensure permanency and to make it possible to distinguish them from the penciled descriptions.

When all time values for each element have been determined and recorded in the Time column, they should be added and the sum recorded on the line headed Element Time, TMU at the bottom of the form. This sum is the time in TMU required to perform the element when a normal performance is given, exclusive of allowances for delays and fatigue. This value must then be converted into hours, minutes, or seconds to coincide with the procedure used in the plant. The conversion factors have already been given in Chapter 4. The proper factor should be recorded on the line headed Conversion Factor. The product of this factor and the element time in TMU is then determined and recorded on the line headed Leveled Time. It is usually wise to indicate the units in which the leveled time is expressed—namely, hours, minutes, or seconds—in order to avoid any possibility of future confusion.

ALLOWANCES

During the course of the working day, there are a number of occurrences that prevent the operator from working continuously. Many minor delays occur that are unavoidable no matter how much the operator tries to escape them. He must stop work from time to time to receive instructions from the foreman, to answer legitimate questions asked him by staff people, to make minor repairs to tools and equipment, to pick up dropped materials, and for a number of other reasons, all of them justified. Such interruptions are known as "unavoidable delays."

In addition, the operator will find it necessary to stop work from time to time for personal reasons such as getting a drink of water, making a trip to the lavatory, etc. Finally, as the working day progresses, the operator will experience in increasing amount the retarding effects of fatigue.

Allowances must be made for these retarding factors if the operator who works at the average performance level is to be able to meet the time allowed for doing the work throughout the full day. These allowances are determined by the all-day time-study procedure described elsewhere.[1] Each element should be considered separately and the appropriate allowance recorded on the next to the last line in terms of a percentage by which the standard time is to be increased. If the same allowance is to be used for all elements, it need be recorded only once.

OCCURRENCES PER PIECE AND ALLOWED TIME

In the next to the last line at the bottom of the observation sheet, the number of times each element occurs for each piece is recorded. If every fifth piece produced is gauged, the allowed element time divided by five would determine the amount of time that should be allotted to each part. Similarly, if chips are brushed from a drill-press table every tenth piece, the allowed elemental time for brushing chips divided by 10 would be the time allowed per piece for brushing chips. If two identical parts were contained in a jig, the element time for "move to drill-press spindle" would be divided by two to determine the time allowed per piece.

When the number of occurrences per piece has been recorded, the total time allowed for each element should be determined and recorded on the last line of the observation sheet. The total times allowed for

[1] Lowry, Maynard, and Stegemerten, "Time and Motion Study and Formulas for Wage Incentives," Chapt. XX, McGraw-Hill Book Company, Inc., 1940.

each element are then added to determine the time allowed per piece. This is recorded in the space provided on the left side of the observation sheet.

	Get part with LH from tote pan, transfer to RH and place in jig			Tighten 2 locators simultaneously, close jig cover with LH, and tighten thumb screw with RH			Reach to spindle lever RH, lower spindle and position jig under drill			Drill 1/4" hole 1/8" deep			Raise spindle RH move to second hole LH, lower spindle and position jig under drill			Raise spindle RH simultaneously loosen 2 locators loosen thumbnut RH and open cover LH			Remove part from jig RH and toss aside in tote pan on right		
METHODS ENGINEERING COUNCIL FORM NO. 208	LH	T	RH	LH	T	RH	LH	T	RH	LH	T	RH	LH	T	RH	LH	T	RH	LH	T	RH
DATE 2-15-47 / STUDY NO. 3 / SHEET NO. 1 / OF 1 SHEETS	R10c	12.9		R6B	8.6	R6B		11.0	R15A					13.4	M12E	(M8B)	20.9	M22A		7.1	R4B
W. B. Fogarty OBSERVER	G4	8.7		G1a	1.7	G1a		1.7	G1a				MIC	1.7		(RL1)	1.7	RL1		8.7	G1c
DWG. 207504 Item 3	M15B	15.2		T90	5.4	T90		13.4	M12B				P2SD	19.6	(M2B)	(R6B)	15.1	R15B		11.8	D2D
PART Bracket		5.6	G3	RL1	1.7	RL1	P2SD	19.6						8.1	M6A	G1a	1.7	G1a		8.6	M10D
OPERATION Drill	R8B	10.1	(MEC)	T90	5.4	T90		8.7	M6A					5.6	G3	AP	16.2	AP		1.7	RL1
2 1/4" holes	G1a	1.7		G1a	1.7	G1a		1.7	G1a							T90	5.4	T90			
		22.2	P2NSD	T90	5.4	T90										RL1	1.7	RL1			
SKILL C-1	RL1	1.7	RL1	AP	16.2	AP										T90	5.4	T90			
EFFORT C-2				RL1	1.7	RL1										G1a	1.7	G1a			
REMARKS Operator				R6B	8.6											T90	5.4	T90			
has had 6 months				G1a	1.7												1.7	RL1			
experience on				M10a	11.3												7.1	R4B			
this class of					7.1	R4B											1.7	G1a			
work					1.7	G1a											5.4	T90			
					5.4	T90											1.7	RL1			
					1.7	RL1											6.8	R4E			
																M10A	11.3				
TIME ALLOWED PER PIECE .00774 hrs										Speed = 70 F.P.M. / Feed = .0025" per revolution / Lead of drill = .025" / Thickness of material = .25" / Drilling time / R.P.M. = 1070 / .075 + .125 .067 = .00125 hrs / .025 x 1070											
ELEMENT TIME THU'S	83.1			85.3			56.1						48.4			110.8			37.9		
CONVERSION FACTOR	.00001																				
LEVELED TIME hrs	.000831			.000853			.000561			.00125			.000484			.001108			.000379		
% ALLOWANCE	15%																				
ELEMENT TIME ALLOWED	.00096			.00098			.00065			.00144			.00056			.00127			.00044		
OCCURENCES PER CYCLE	1			1			1			2			1			1			1		
TOTAL TIME ALLOWED	.00096			.00098			.00065			.00288			.00056			.00127			.00044		

FIG. 78.— Model study showing computations and summary completed.

Reference to Fig. 78 will make clear all the steps performed in making the computations and summary.

CHAPTER 19

ESTIMATING FROM DRAWINGS
AND SAMPLES

There are frequent occasions when it is desired to have an accurate estimate of the time required to produce a given part. If a drawing or a sample of the part is available, it is possible for a trained methods engineer who is thoroughly familiar with both the working methods prevailing in the shop and the methods-time measurement procedure to arrive at estimates that are extremely accurate. It is easy to go astray in estimating, however, and the less experienced estimator is likely to make sizable errors unless he uses every precaution to avoid them.

ESTIMATING PROCEDURE

The estimating procedure itself is quite simple. The methods engineer first studies the drawing or sample of the part and determines the operations that will be required to produce it. He then visualizes the method that will be used to perform each operation and subdivides the operation into its elements. Finally he establishes the motions that will be required to perform each element and assigns methods-time standards to them. If he has done his work properly, the resulting time values will be accurate.

SEQUENCE OF OPERATIONS

The operations required to produce the part and their sequence are determined by the methods engineer based upon his knowledge of good manufacturing practices and the available equipment in the shop. As the operations are determined, they may be recorded for record and reference purposes on a form. The Master Card form shown by Fig. 79 has been found satisfactory for this use.

If the product is an assembly made up of several parts, one Master Card should be used for each part. When two or more parts come together to form an assembly, a new Master Card should be used to show the assembly operations. The Master Cards for the individual parts may be identified by using drawing and item numbers or part num-

bers as they appear on the drawing or bill of material. The assembly
Master Card, if no item or part number has been assigned to the assembly
on the drawing, may be identified by using the drawing number of the
principal part and an arbitrarily assigned item number in a high series
such as 50. If two subassemblies come together to make a major assembly, the subassemblies may be identified as items 50 and 51, and the
major assembly as item 52. By using a simple but systematic identification system of this sort, confusion is avoided as paper work begins to
accumulate.

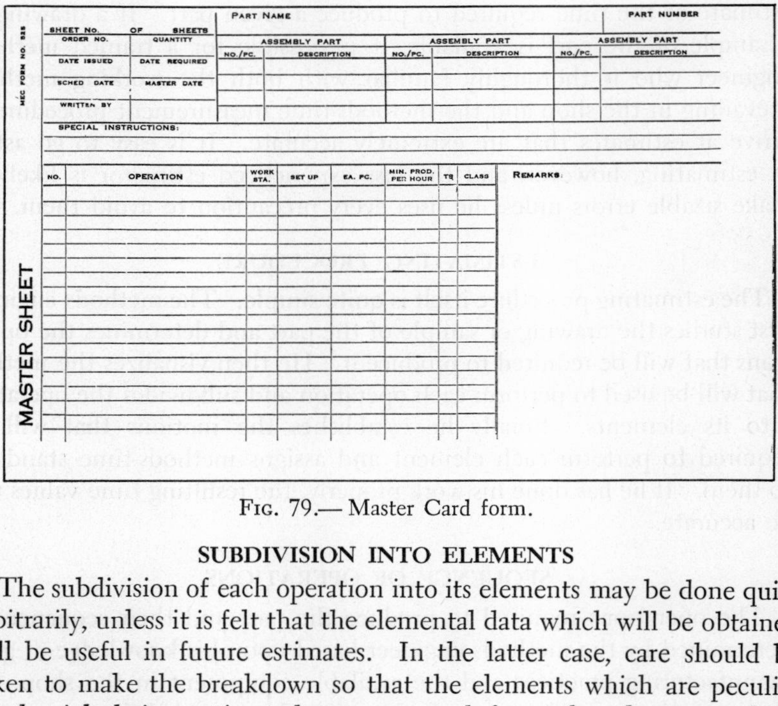

FIG. 79.— Master Card form.

SUBDIVISION INTO ELEMENTS

The subdivision of each operation into its elements may be done quite
arbitrarily, unless it is felt that the elemental data which will be obtained
will be useful in future estimates. In the latter case, care should be
taken to make the breakdown so that the elements which are peculiar
to the job being estimated are separated from the elements which
might be used on other jobs.

The major purpose of subdividing the operation into elements is to
simplify the task of visualizing the motions that will be used to do the
work. It is easier and less confusing to determine the motions used to
perform a short operation than a long operation. Thus by subdividing
an operation into short elements, the methods engineer finds it easier
to do the detailed work of motion determination without becoming lost

or confused part way through the motion sequence. With this in mind, the subdivision should be made into elements which are short enough to be visualized readily, but not so short that the orienting aid which they give during estimating is lost. Usually elements of from .0004 to .0025 hour duration will prove most satisfactory, although shorter or longer elements can be set up if there is anything to be gained by so doing.

The element descriptions may be recorded in the column headings on the observation sheet form No. 205, if this form is to be used as the work sheet for estimating, or on the Methods Analysis Chart form No. 117.

METHODS ANALYSIS

Figure 80 shows the Methods Analysis Chart form that has been found useful for methods analysis work. It provides more room for giving a description of the acts accomplished by the right and left hands than form No. 205 does, and hence provides a better record. In using this form, it is the practice first to record in a few words in the extreme right- and left-hand columns the motions made by the right and left hands, respectively. The motion which is limiting is then indicated by placing a check mark in the proper column headed with a check mark ($\sqrt{}$). Next the classification of the limiting motion is recorded in the column headed Class, using the abbreviation conventions shown in Chapter 4. The proper methods-time standards may then be recorded in the column headed TMU, or this may be postponed until the descriptions of all motions of the element or operation have been recorded.

The form should be filled out on the top two lines with identifying information before anything else is done to avoid the confusion that inevitably results if work sheets are not clearly identified. If the operation has been subdivided into elements, the element name is next recorded on the first line of the body of the form in capital letters or in colored pencil in order to distinguish it from other information. The motions used by each hand to perform the element are then listed and the limiting motions are identified and classified. If a given motion is used more than once, the number of occurrences may be recorded in the column headed No. This practice saves considerable writing on some types of operations.

At any convenient time, values from the tables of methods-time data are assigned to each limiting motion and are recorded in the column headed TMU. At the end of the element, a line is drawn horizontally below the last value recorded. The values for all motions included in the element are then added, and the total is recorded on the next blank line. The result is the time in TMU that will be required by an operator giving an average performance to do the job. This figure should then be converted to decimal hours and the result recorded in the column headed

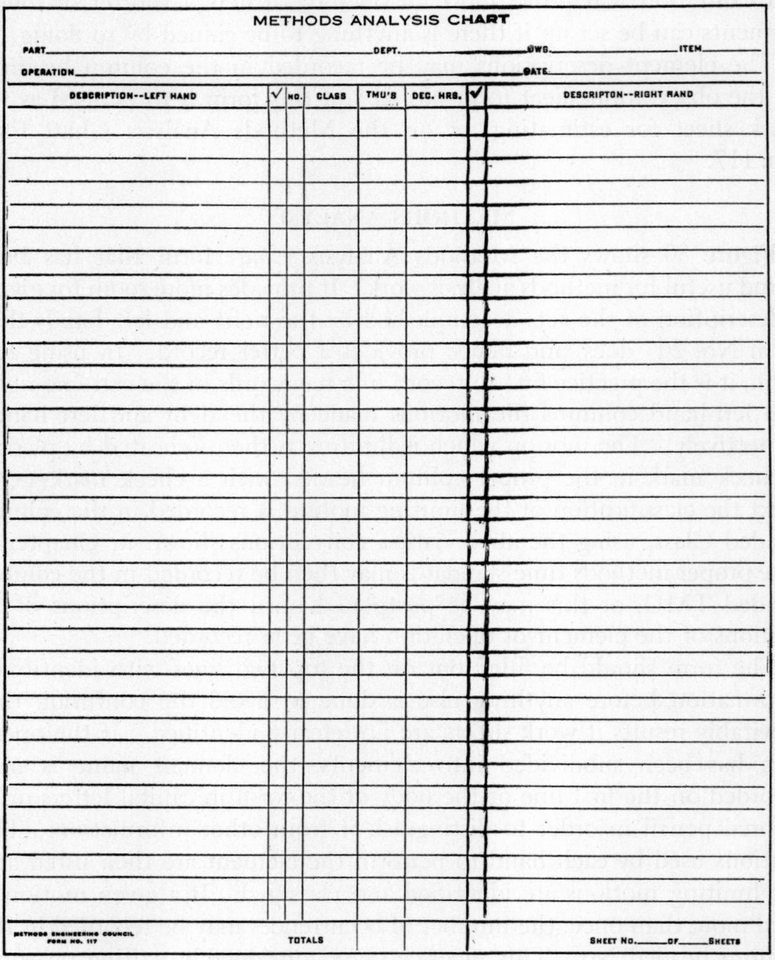
METHODS ANALYSIS CHART

PART ____ DEPT. ____ DWG. ____ ITEM ____

OPERATION ____ DATE ____

DESCRIPTION--LEFT HAND	✓	NO.	CLASS	TMU'S	DEC. HRS.	✓	DESCRIPTON--RIGHT HAND

METHODS ENGINEERING COUNCIL FORM NO. 117 — TOTALS — SHEET NO. ____ OF ____ SHEETS

FIG. 80.— Methods Analysis Chart.

Dec. Hrs. If an allowance for fatigue and personal and unavoidable delays is included, a note to this effect should be made at the head of the column. It is usually desirable to show the time in decimal hours for the complete element only, rather than for each individual motion.

AVOIDING INACCURACIES IN ESTIMATING

The methods-time data give the methods engineer an exceptionally accurate tool to use in estimating if properly used. Because the methods-time standards are themselves correct, it follows that the only chance of error lies in estimating the method itself incorrectly. This, however, can be a major factor. If it is assumed that a certain operation can be done with half the motions that are actually required, then the resulting time value will be in the order of 50 per cent of the time actually required to do the job in the shop. If orders are accepted on the basis of that kind of estimating, the company cannot expect to remain in business for any length of time.

It is essential, therefore, that the one who is to do the estimating should take every precaution to avoid errors. First of all, he should be thoroughly familiar with the methods-time measurement procedure and should have done enough film-analysis work during his training to have learned what motions are most likely to be employed to accomplish a given result. For example, assume that an operation consists of tightening a screw cap on a small bottle. The cap is already in place and the purpose of the operation is to make sure that it is tight. The method visualized might be that the operator would pick up the bottle by the cap with the left hand, grasp the bottle with the right hand, and tighten the cap with the left hand. The inexperienced analyst might assume that as soon as the bottle was grasped by the right hand, the next limiting motion would be Apply Pressure with the left hand. There will be a Regrasp with the left hand, however, before the Apply Pressure occurs, a fact that anyone can demonstrate by going through the motions himself with a small bottle or even a fountain pen. The estimator must learn such things through training, so that he does not leave out motions which must be made. It is probably more common in estimating to omit necessary motions than it is to include unnecessary motions.

The second precaution the estimator must take is to become thoroughly familiar with the operating methods used on the equipment in his shop. Otherwise he is again likely to make incorrect assumptions. For example, an estimator after considering the motions required to engage the feed on a milling machine arrived at a value of approximately .0002 hour. On checking over a recent time study, he found that this element had consumed .0005 hour. Being reasonably sure that the same beginning and ending points for the element had been used in each case, he was unable to account for the discrepancy. He therefore went to the shop and observed the machine in operation. The reason for the

168 METHODS-TIME MEASUREMENT

difference was at once clear. In his estimating, he had assumed that the feed lever would be engaged with a single M6A motion after it had been grasped. Actually the operator found it difficult to engage the feed

METHODS ANALYSIS CHART

PART _Terminal Block_ DEPT. _Assembly_ DWG. _SK49A1_ ITEM _50_
OPERATION _Solder Terminal to Block_ DATE _April 24_

DESCRIPTION—LEFT HAND	✓	NO.	CLASS	TMU'S	DEC. HRS. + 15%	✓	DESCRIPTON—RIGHT HAND
GET PART FROM CONVEYOR							
Reach to base on conveyor	✓		R25B	22.2			Idle
Grasp base	✓		G1a	1.7			
Move base to RH above fixture	✓		M20B	18.2			Reach to point above fixture
							and contact grasp
Move base to fixture	✓		M6C	9.7		✓	Move base to fixture
Position base to fixture	✓		P1NSE	10.8		✓	Position base to fixture
Turn base to lock in fixture	✓		T30S	2.8		✓	Turn base to lock in fixture
Release	✓		RL1	1.7		✓	Release
				67.1	.000771		
ASSEMBLE TERMINAL TO BASE							
Idle			R10C	12.9		✓	Reach for terminal
			G4	8.7		✓	Grasp terminal
			M10B	12.2		✓	Move terminal to left hand
Receive terminal from RH	✓		G3	5.6		✓	Transfer to LH
Turn terminal to position	✓		T30S	2.8			Idle
Return terminal to RH	✓		G3	5.6		✓	Receive terminal from LH
Idle			M3C	5.7		✓	Move terminal to base
			P1NSD	16.3		✓	Position terminal on base
			RL1	1.7		✓	Release
				71.5	.000822		
SOLDER TERMINAL							
Place hand on pivoted solder-							
ing torch			R8B	10.1		✓	Reach for solder
			G1a	1.7		✓	Grasp solder
Swing torch in position			M8C	11.8		✓	Move solder to terminal
			Est.	24.3			Solder
Release torch			RL1	1.7		✓	Release solder
				49.6	.000570		
LAY PART ASIDE IN TOTEPAN							
Idle			R3B	5.9		✓	Reach to part
			G1a	1.7		✓	Grasp part
			T30S	2.8		✓	Turn 30° to unlock
			D1D	5.7		✓	Disengage from fixture
			M18C	20.4		✓	Move to totepan
			RL1	1.7		✓	Release
METHODS ENGINEERING COUNCIL FORM NO. 117			TOTALS	38.2	.000442 .002605		SHEET NO. 1 OF 1 SHEETS

FIG. 81.—Methods Analysis Chart of operation "solder terminal to base."

and had to move the lever back and forth several times before it would go into the engaged position. The methods engineer saw at once that he would either have to get the machine repaired or allow more time for this element.

It might be pointed out that the fact the machine was out of repair was not noticed during time study. An element of .0005 hour is too short to permit much time for observing the method used. When the time taken was compared with the time that should have been taken as determined by methods-time measurement, however, attention was directed to the element. It then took only a moment's observation to discover the difficulty.

It may be seen that the estimator who would use methods-time data for estimating must be more familiar with detailed methods than if he were to do conventional over-all estimating. When he has gained this familiarity, however, his estimates will be much more exact. Figure 81 shows a Methods Analysis Chart made to obtain an estimate of the time required to solder a terminal to a base. Element 2 is Assemble Terminal to Base. One who was not too familiar with detailed methods might assume that the operator could pick up the terminal with the right hand and place it directly on the base. The terminal is nonsymmetrical, however. Therefore it must be pre-positioned in the hand before it is placed on the base. To accomplish this, the operator would pick the terminal up with the right hand, transfer it to the left, pre-position it with the left hand by turning it an average of 30°, and transfer it back to the right hand. Once the fact is understood that this is what occurs in a situation of this kind, estimating presents no particular difficulty. Until it is understood, however, the estimator can easily go astray. It is for this reason that the need for thorough training is so frequently stressed not only in this chapter but throughout the book. The methods-time measurement approach offers a highly satisfactory answer to accurate estimating, but only if it is properly applied.

PART IV

METHODS DEVELOPMENT PROCEDURE

CHAPTER 20

PRINCIPLES OF MOTION ECONOMY

One of the most valuable uses of the methods-time measurement procedure is in connection with the development of improved methods of doing work. When an existing operation has been analyzed in the detail required by the procedure, the inefficient portions of it are clearly revealed. By correcting these portions where possible and by making them conform to the principles of motion economy, worth-while improvements can be effected.

Although the principles of motion economy have been discussed in detail elsewhere,[1] it will be worth while to review these principles in this section of this book which is devoted to a discussion of the methods development procedure based on methods-time measurement. Not only will this make motion economy information available here for ready reference, but in addition the opportunity will be afforded of pointing out some of the changes in former concepts which have come about as the result of the information gained during the research work which has more recently been undertaken.

GILBRETH BASIC ELEMENTS

The technique of motion study rests on the concept originally advanced by Frank and Lillian Gilbreth that all work is performed by using a relatively few basic operations in varying combinations and sequence. These Gilbreth Basic Elements have also been called "therbligs" and "basic divisions of accomplishment."

The original list of the Gilbreths contained 17 basic elements. This has been varied from time to time by other workers in the field as additional information was gained or new theories formed. The latest researches in the field of methods-time measurement indicate the necessity for certain other revisions, which are included in this discussion.

The basic elements at present recognized may be listed as follows:

[1] LOWRY, MAYNARD, and STEGEMERTEN, "Time and Motion Study and Formulas for Wage Incentives," Chaps. VII and VIII, McGraw-Hill Book Company, Inc., 1940.

GROUP A

Reach	R
Move	M
Grasp	G
Position	P
Disengage	D
Release	RL

GROUP B

Hold	H
Do	DO
Examine	E
Change Direction	CD
Pre-position	PP
Search	S
Select	SE
Plan	PL
Avoidable Delay	AD
Unavoidable Delay	UD
Rest to Overcome Fatigue	F
Balancing Delay	BL

The first group has already been defined in the chapters devoted to a discussion of their characteristics. Methods-time standards have been developed for each of these basic elements. Methods-time standards have also been developed for Turn and Apply Pressure, but these are not considered here to be true basic elements. Turn appears to be merely a special case of Reach, Move, or Pre-position. Apply Pressure, although lumped in with the values for the other acts which go to make up Position, also is encountered frequently by itself. There seems to be some justification for considering it as a basic element, but it will probably be wisest to wait until more investigators have studied it before deciding on whether or not it should be added to the list of basic elements.

The following are definitions of the basic elements included in group B:

Hold is the basic element employed to maintain static control of an object with the hand while work is performed upon the object and is of such a nature that the substitution of a holding device will not impair the performance of the work. Hold is never a limiting operation, and therefore no time values need be assigned to it. If it is desired to ascertain the time for any Hold operation, it can be done by determining the time for the acts that are performed by the other hand and/or the feet during the duration of the Hold.

Do is the basic element that accomplishes in full or in part the purpose of the operation. It may sometimes be expressed in terms of other basic elements. Do replaces the former basic elements Use and Assemble. The time for Do, when mechanically controlled, must be determined by time study, tables of feeds and speeds, etc. When manually performed, the time may usually, although not always, be determined from the methods-time data. Do, manually performed, is a combination of Reaches, Moves, Turns, Apply Pressures, Grasps, Positions, Disengages, and Releases, for all of which time standards have been derived.

Examine is the basic element employed to compare the quality of an object with a standard by means of any of the senses. It was formerly called "Inspect," but the name has been changed to get away from the confusion frequently encountered in the minds of those untrained in motion study with factory inspection operations, many of which do not include the basic element of Examine. No time standards have as yet been developed for Examine. A visual inspection value of 7.3 TMU has been encountered several times. It may be used with judgment until more complete data have been collected.

Change Direction is the basic operation employed to change the line or plane along which a Reach or Move is made. The only instance in which its effect was measurable in the investigations made to date was in the case A Reach. Here the Change Direction was found to slow the Reach down until the time coincided with that of a standard case B Reach. The only value in retaining Change Direction in the basic element list is that it provides the explanation for the slowness of certain case A Reaches and also calls attention to the possibility of shortening motion paths by eliminating the obstacle which causes the Change Direction.

Pre-position is the basic element which prepares either the transporting device or the object transported for the next basic element which is usually Position. In the majority of cases in which it is encountered, it is overlapped by the Reach or Move which is performed at the same time so that no time need be computed for it. When performed as a separate act, it is usually a Turn, a series of Regrasps, or Regrasps and Turns, for all of which time standards are available.

Search is the basic operation employed to locate any object. Select is the basic element of choosing among several items, which have been found as the result of searching. In practice, even when analyzing a motion-picture film, it is impossible to tell where Search stops and Select begins. They show up in the increased time that they cause for the Reach and the ensuing Grasp. The time is covered by the case C Reach and the G4 Grasp.

Plan is a delay or hesitation in order to decide upon the method to be followed. Plan seldom if ever is encountered when studying repetitive operations where the performance of the operator is average or better. Because it is practical to use the methods-time measurement procedure only on repetitive work, the fact that Plan does not lend itself to inclusion with the acts for which time can be predetermined is of no practical importance.

Avoidable Delay is a delay that occurs when the sequence of motions recognizes no delay as being necessary. Because the delay is unnecessary, no predetermined time need be assigned to it. This basic element need not be considered in the methods-time measurement procedure.

Unavoidable Delay, in its most important sense, is a cessation of work because of the arrangement of the motion sequence. In plain shop language, one hand works while the other hand is idle because nothing has been provided for it to do. As in the case of Hold, the duration of an Unavoidable Delay can be determined by ascertaining the time required to perform the acts accomplished by the other hand.

Rest to Overcome Fatigue is a delay allowed the worker for the purpose of recovering from exertion. On most operations, it is not allowed as a definite predetermined period, but is included in the general allowance. For this reason, it poses no problem in methods-time measurement.

Balancing Delay is a delay caused by the fact that it is not always possible to arrange the cycle so that each hand performs motions which require exactly the same length of time. One hand performs the limiting motion while the other works at a reduced speed. The time for the limiting motion determines the time required to make the other motion, including Balancing Delay. The time for a Balancing Delay can be determined by subtracting the time the motion would take if it were limiting from the time of the limiting motion.

GUIDE TO METHODS IMPROVEMENT

For purposes of understanding further the nature of the various basic elements and to provide a clue toward points in the cycle at which improvement is possible, the following groupings may be made:

Group 1	Group 2	Group 3
Reach	Change Direction	Hold
Move	Pre-position	Avoidable Delay
Grasp	Search	Unavoidable Delay
Position	Select	Rest to Overcome Fatigue
Disengage	Plan	
Release	Balancing Delay	
Examine		
Do		

Group 1 may be considered to be the useful group of basic elements, or the ones that accomplish the work. They do not necessarily accomplish it in the most effective way, however, and a study of these elements will often uncover possibilities for improvement.

Group 2 contains the basic elements that tend to retard accomplishment when they are present. In the majority of cases, they do this by slowing down the time required to perform the group 1 basic elements. They should therefore be eliminated wherever possible. This may usually be done in every case but that of Plan by improving the workplace layout.

Group 3 may be considered as the nonaccomplishment group. With the exception of Hold, these basic elements accomplish nothing towards the completion of the task. Hold maintains control of the part, so that in a sense it accomplishes something, but it does it in such an expensive way that its inclusion in the nonaccomplishment group seems justified. The greatest improvements in method usually come from the elimination of the group 3 basic elements from the cycle. This is done by rearranging the motion sequence, by providing mechanical holding fixtures, and by improving the workplace layout in the case of Hold and Unavoidable Delay, the two most important in the group. Avoidable Delays and Rest to Overcome Fatigue are not usually considered to be part of the cycle. The first is eliminated by supervision and sound wage incentives, and the second is eliminated or reduced by removing the causes for fatigue.

To summarize:

Group 1 accomplishes.
Group 2 retards accomplishment.
Group 3 does not accomplish.

PRINCIPLES OF MOTION ECONOMY

Methods improvement may be made on any operation by eliminating insofar as is possible the group 2 and group 3 basic elements and by arranging so that the group 1 basic elements are performed in the shortest reasonable time. In doing this, the so-called Laws of Motion Economy and their corollaries are useful in suggesting what may be done. The Laws of Motion Economy and their corollaries will be restated here, together with some of the findings about them that have come from methods-time measurement research.

LAWS OF MOTION ECONOMY

1. *When both hands begin and complete their motions simultaneously and are not idle except during rest periods, maximum performance is approached.*

When both hands are working, it is desirable that they begin and complete their motions at the same time. In this way, a working rhythm is developed that carries the worker along toward maximum performance. If only one hand is working and the other is idle, only a part of the maximum possible efficiency is obtained. When one hand is working, the idle hand is not relaxed, and it does not rest. In fact, it is usually fatiguing to hold one hand motionless while the other is working. Workers, realizing this instinctively, will introduce balancing and otherwise useless motions to escape this type of fatigue. To recover from fatigue, all work should be stopped, and a rest period should be introduced. The operator can then relax completely and will become rested more quickly. Rest to Overcome Fatigue is the only permissible idle time, although Unavoidable Delay and Balancing Delay idlenesses cannot always be altogether eliminated. The latter two, however, are never useful for overcoming fatigue.

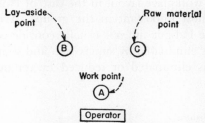

On classes of work where it is not possible to do the same thing with each hand at the same time, idle periods often occur as the operator works first with one hand and then with the other. Part of this idleness can be eliminated by overlapping motions. Assume, for example, that an operator is working at the setup shown by the sketch above and assume that, due to the nature of the mechanical equipment involved, workpoint A, lay-aside point B, and the point where raw material is obtained, C, must be in the relative positions shown. Assume further that the part worked upon, although bulky, can be handled with one hand. One way of laying aside the completed part and of obtaining the next would be as follows:

Description—left hand	√	No.	Class	TMU	Dec. hr.	√	Description—right hand
Idle			G1a	1.7		√	Grasp part
			M16B	15.8		√	Move to point B
			RL1	1.7		√	Release
			R16B	15.6		√	Reach to point C
			G1a	1.7		√	Grasp part
Total				36.5			

This is a complete violation of Law 1. A better method would be the following:

Description—left hand	√	No.	Class	TMU	Dec. hr.	√	Description—right hand
Grasp part	√		G1a	1.7			Idle
Move to point B	√		M16B	15.8			Start to reach to point C
Release	√		RL1	1.7			
			R6Bm	5.9		√	Complete reaching to point C
			G1a	1.7		√	Grasp part
Total				26.8			

Here Law 1 is still violated, but by putting both hands to work and overlapping their motions, the work is accomplished in less time. If the workplace could be rearranged so that the work could be done as follows, Law 1 would be approached closely and maximum accomplishment would result.

Occasionally, even where work is set up for two-handed operation, the operator is found to be violating Law 1 and to be overlapping motions.

Description— left hand	√	No.	Class	TMU	Dec. hr.	√	Description— right hand
Grasp part	√		G1a	1.7			Idle
Move to point B	√		M16B	15.8		√	Reach to point C
Release	√		RL1	1.7		√	Grasp part
Total				19.2			

To the casual observer, the operator may appear to be working continuously with each hand. In reality, however, minor idlenesses occur constantly when working this way, and fatigue increases rapidly because of the necessity of constantly shifting attention from one hand to the other. Usually, as fatigue becomes great, overlapping ceases, and the operator works first with one hand and then with the other. He probably feels that he is working as hard as, or harder than, when he works in conformance with Law 1, as indeed he is, but he is making the common mistake of confusing effort with accomplishment. The methods engineer should explain the reasons why maximum performance cannot be attained under this way of working and encourage the operator to work in accordance with Law 1.

Law 1 can be realized by arranging for the simultaneous performance of motions which require an equal length of time, provided that they are motions which can be performed simultaneously, as discussed in Chapter 14. If they are not the type of motions that can be performed simultaneously or if the workplace layout is such that it discourages simultaneous performance of such motions as grasp, then Law 1 cannot be realized.

2. *When motions of the arms are made simultaneously in opposite directions over symmetrical paths, rhythm and automaticity develop most naturally.*

The principle of two-handed operation is expressed by the second law of motion economy, and its practical application leads to workplace layouts, such as that shown by Fig. 40. Motions of the arms should be made simultaneously if Law 1 is not to be violated. They should be made in opposite directions from the axis of the body, for when this is done, one arm balances the other, and no body movement is necessary. If the arms are moved in the same direction, either to the right or to the left of the body, the whole trunk has to be shifted to balance the weight of the arms. This brings a number of body muscles into play and, on repetitive work, increases fatigue materially. If the arms must be moved in the same direction, they should move away from and toward the body rather than to the right or to the left, as the body can more easily balance a motion of this kind.

Motions should be made over symmetrical paths, or paths of the same shape, because most human beings are so constructed physiologically that one side of the body wants to work in unison with the other doing similar things. If the workplace is laid out so that the right hand must follow a triangular path while the left hand is following a circular path, the operator will have difficulty in working in accordance with Law 1. There will be a tendency for both hands to move either along the triangular path or the circular path. To overcome this, the operator is likely to find himself working first with one hand and then the other. This tendency toward symmetrical movements of the two sides of the body has an important bearing on safety. If unsymmetrical paths must be followed in moving near machinery, care should be taken to see that the tendency to change over into symmetrical paths will not carry the hand into a danger zone.

When motions are symmetrical, and in opposite or easily balanced directions, rhythm and automaticity develop naturally. Rhythm is most important and is attained by coordinating and synchronizing motions with respect to time rather than distance. When an operator works rhythmically, he works without conscious planning or thinking, and hesitation and lost time are eliminated.

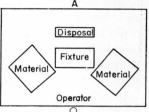

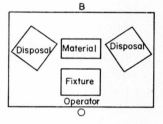

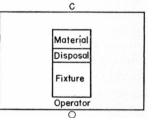

Fig. 82.— Typical workplace layouts. A, material containers outside area of normal vision; B, material container in area of normal vision—disposal points outside area of normal vision but large enough so that simultaneous Releases are practical; C, material container in area or normal vision—disposal point in path of Reach for material.

On large work, it is not always possible to arrange the motion sequence so that both hands work all of the time. In lining up motion sequences on work of this nature, however, the desirability of two-handed performance should be kept in mind, and it should be arranged for wherever possible. For example, large steam turbines are designed to suit each customer's operating conditions and are usually made in quantities of one. It would obviously be impracticable to draw operator process charts showing every move each operator should make, for the turbine would be shipped before the charts could be completed. Each turbine spindle and cylinder, however, takes several hundred blades. The installation of these blades is in the nature of a repetitive operation, and it will be profitable to spend considerable time perfecting an efficient installation procedure.

In attempting to arrange for the making of motions in opposite directions, care should be taken to avoid calling for the performance of certain types of basic elements outside the field of normal vision. A common error in workplace layout design is shown in A, Fig. 82.

Material is placed on either side of a fixture. The right hand goes to the right-hand bin to secure a part while the left hand goes to the left-hand bin. This carries the hand outside the normal area of vision, which is only about 4 inches in diameter at 18 inches. Therefore, in order to see the parts that are to be grasped, the operator must look first toward one bin and then the other. This means that the parts will not be grasped simultaneously, but that first one part will be grasped and then the other, which not only causes a time loss but interferes with rhythm. If disposal points were located where the material containers are shown in sketch A, simultaneous releases could be made, assuming the disposal areas to be large, for an accurate motion is not required. The material could then be placed directly in front of the fixture where a simultaneous grasp with both hands would be possible because both hands would be in the area of normal vision.

The motions in the first case would be as follows:

Description— left hand	√	No.	Class	TMU	Dec. hr.	√	Description— right hand
Reach for part	√		R10B	11.5		√	Reach for part
Idle			G1a	1.7		√	Grasp part
Grasp part	√		G1a	1.7			Idle
Move to fixture, etc.	√		M8C	11.8		√	Move to fixture, etc.
Move to disposal point	√		M6B	8.9		√	Move to disposal point
Release	√		RL1	1.7		√	Release
Total				37.3			

The motions in the second case would be as follows:

Description—left hand	✓	No.	Class	TMU	Dec. hr.	✓	Description—right hand
Reach for part	✓		R8B	10.1		✓	Reach for part
Grasp part	✓		G1a	1.7		✓	Grasp part
Move to fixture, etc.	✓		M6C	9.7		✓	Move to fixture, etc.
Move to disposal point	✓		M10B	12.2		✓	Move to disposal point
Release			RL1	1.7		✓	Release
Total				35.4		✓	

This would be a slight improvement, for idleness has been eliminated. A further improvement and one of greater magnitude can still be made by going to the layout shown by sketch C. The motions in this case would be:

Description—left hand		No.	Class	TMU	Dec. hr.		Description—right hand
Reach for part, dropping finished part on way	✓		R6C	10.1		✓	Reach for part, dropping finished part on way
Grasp part	✓		G1a	1.7		✓	Grasp part
Move to fixture, etc.	✓		M6C	9.7		✓	Move to fixture, etc.
Total				21.5			

3. *The motion sequence which employs the fewest basic elements is the best for performing a given task.*

The example just cited is an illustration of Law 3. It would be possible by lengthening the motions in the third case to increase the time over the second case, which employs more basic elements, but it is hardly conceivable that this would be done in any actual workplace layout.

4. *When motions are confined to the lowest practical classification, maximum performance and minimum fatigue are approached.*

All physical motions have been divided into five classifications, according to the body parts involved in making them. They are

1. Finger motions
2. Finger and wrist motions
3. Finger, wrist, and forearm motions
4. Finger, wrist, forearm, and upper arm motions
5. Finger, wrist, forearm, upper arm, and body motions

The law implies that the lower classes of motions are quicker to make than the higher classes of motions. With the exception of the fifth-class motions, this was not found to be the case in the operations analyzed during the development of the methods-time measurement procedure. As explained in Chapter 3, an investigation was made to find out if there was any difference in the time taken to make the various cases of reach between third- and fourth-class motions. No difference could be found. Later a similar study was made of second-class motions with no differences being found. Although it can be shown experimentally that it is possible to make more third-class motions of a given length than fourth-class motions in a fixed period of time when a maximum effort is exerted, apparently this has no bearing when an operator working with a normal performance is performing an operation requiring an assortment of Reaches, Moves, Grasps, Positionings, etc.

Hence, the chief value in reducing the classification of motions below fourth class now appears to be that the motions will probably be shortened by so doing. Fatigue may be somewhat lessened also, but this has yet to be determined definitely.

5. *When conditions are the same, the time required to perform all basic elements is constant for any given degree of skill and effort.*

The word "conditions" is used to cover all factors that can possibly affect the time required to perform a basic element. It embraces not only such factors as light, heat, ventilation, etc., but also such factors as nature of the part with respect to size, shape, and weight, distance moved, material, inspection and accuracy requirements, etc. For example, among the conditions that affect the time for performing the operation of lifting a weight of 10 pounds a distance of 1 foot (a simple Move operation) are temperature, location of the lift (near the floor, waist-high, overhead), material and condition of surface grasped (rough or slippery), bulk, and many others. But for a given set of conditions, if the skill and effort of two workers are the same, using skill in the limited sense of proficiency at following a given method, they will take the same time to perform the operation. The concept, when grasped, is simple, but it forms the basis for all time allowances. If it were conceivable that an operator working at a given performance level would perform the same operation under the same conditions in a different length of time on one occasion than he would on another occasion, then it would be impossible to establish definite standards. On the contrary, however, it is possible to establish accurate performance standards by eliminating through standardization all, or nearly all, variations in conditions. Any operator can equal the standard performance by meeting the skill and effort requirements upon which it was based, or can exceed it by increasing skill or effort, or both.

The methods-time investigation fully confirms this law. When the conditions applying to a given motion are fully defined, as a Reach 20 inches long to an object that is one of a group, with the hand not in motion at the beginning and end of the movement (an R20C motion), the time required to make the motion varies only with the skill and effort of the operator. The difference caused by differences in skill and effort was found upon investigation to be covered accurately by the leveling factors of the conventional leveling procedure.

Occasionally an exceptional operator is encountered who can perform a job in much less time than the other operators. This is sometimes taken to show that the upper range of the leveling factors is insufficient. In such cases, however, the exceptional operator does not make motions any faster than the other operators working at the same performance level, but rather uses a different motion sequence, which employs fewer motions. This constitutes a difference in method, and the leveling procedure, of course, is not designed to compensate for differences in method.

Corollaries to the Laws of Motion Economy

1. *Hesitation, or temporary and often minute cessation from motion, should be analyzed, studied, and its cause accounted for and, if possible, eliminated.*

The methods-time measurement procedure makes it possible to carry out the recommendations of this corollary with a minimum of effort. As the motions employed for performing a given task are observed, recognized, and recorded, the hesitations are also noted. Some of them appear as idle periods and some as Balancing Delays. Others are included in the methods-time data, as for example, Search and Select in the case C Reach and G4 Grasp. When the factors causing the hesitations are known, their elimination is often relatively simple. Search and Select may be eliminated, in some cases at least, by proper pre-positioning of tools and materials at the time the workplace layout is made. The time for Position may be reduced by devising stops and guides. Unavoidable Delays may be eliminated by rearrangement of the sequence of operations and by setting the job up so that it can be done in conformance with the first and second laws of motion economy. This latter action will also reduce or eliminate the Balancing Delays. It is, of course, not feasible to do all the things suggested on every job studied, but an earnest attempt should be made to do so when methods improvements are desired.

2. *The shortest time taken for each element during the course of the study made on an expert operator should be considered the desired standard; all variations of time from this standard should be analyzed for each element, and the causes should be determined and recorded.*

When studying several cycles of an operation, one will find that the elemental times vary. This is because different sets of motions are used for performing the element. In part, this may be caused by variations in the job itself, such as variations in location of material, variations in the position in which the parts present themselves for grasping, etc. Such variations can often be eliminated by improved workplace layout. Another cause of variation in method from cycle to cycle is the operator himself. For reasons which are as yet obscure, an operator will apparently unconsciously vary his method slightly from time to time to an extent which is hardly visible to casual observation, but which shows up when the motions are analyzed into terms of the methods-time measurement procedure.

By studying the various methods which are employed to perform a given element, the method which requires the shortest time can be determined. Whether or not it is possible to train the operator to use this method consistently is at present debatable. It is also not certain if the method can be taught to others who may not possess the same degree of natural coordination. The corollary, however, serves the useful purpose of calling attention to the fact that different methods are employed for performing the same element and that one method is better than the rest. Thus an ideal goal is established. How closely it can be approached in practice is a matter for further investigation.

3. *The best sequence of motions for any one class of work is useful for suggesting the best sequence for other kinds of work.*

Each study made should not be considered as an entirely new investigation. Operations are made up of various combinations of basic elements. If the best combination has been found for one job, the possibility of applying it to another similar job should be considered. Where more than one methods engineer is working on motion study in the same plant, arrangements should be made for the interchange of ideas through reports, process charts, motion pictures, and discussion groups.

The methods-time measurement procedure makes it possible to determine with accuracy which is the best of several motion sequences which may be under discussion.

4. *Where delay occurs, consideration should be given to the advisability of providing additional work which will permit the utilization of the time of delay, if study indicates that the delay is unnecessary for overcoming fatigue.*

Provision of additional work to utilize periods of delay is an important factor toward cost reduction. The length of the delay period will largely determine the use to which it is put. The most common application of this principle occurs when an operator is given one or more additional machines to run while his first machine is making a cut. Sometimes part of the operation performed on one piece can be done during the idle period occurring on another piece. For example, on a certain shaft turned in an engine lathe, the operator was required to stencil a part number. His practice was to place the shaft in the lathe, take the cut— a power-feed operation during which he was idle—and then stencil on the number while the shaft was still in the lathe centers. A rearrangement of the motion sequence was suggested, and thereafter he removed the shaft from the lathe without marking it, and applied the stencils while the cut was being taken on the next piece. This reduced the over-all time of the operation by the time required for stenciling, without appreciably increasing the fatigue of the operator.

5. *All material and tools should be located within or as near as possible to the normal grasp area.*

The area in which the worker performs his operation should be kept at a minimum. Wherever possible, materials and tools should be so arranged that the operator can perform the operations by moving hands and arms only. The height of the work area should be such that the operator is able to work either seated in a comfortable chair, designed so as to secure a minimum of fatigue with a maximum of freedom of movement, or while standing. Thus he will be able to vary his position from time to time and reduce his fatigue. Where the work is so large or so complicated that it is necessary for the operator to move about in performing it, the distance which it is necessary to move should be reduced as much as possible by the proper arrangement of the workplace.

When the operation can be performed within a limited space, the following principles advanced by the Gilbreths should be kept in mind when laying out the working area. Assume that a worker is comfortably seated at or is standing by his bench or table of proper height. His arms

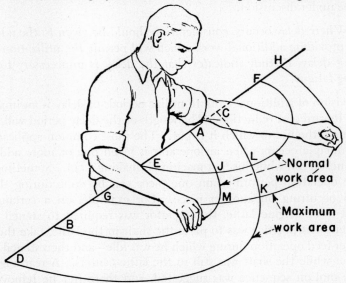

FIG. 83.— Normal and maximum working areas for the hands in the horizontal plane.

hang naturally from the shoulders. Placing his right hand on the near edge of the table approximately opposite his left side, point A, Fig. 83, he can sweep his right hand through the arc AB without any noticeable use of the shoulder muscles and with a normal expenditure of energy. The area included between this arc and the edge of the table represents the normal, or most comfortable, working area for the right hand. With the arm fully extended, the arc CD may be described, which represents the maximum reach of the right hand without change of posture. Likewise the normal EF and maximum GH working areas may be determined for the left hand.

Obviously, work requiring both hands can be most comfortably done in the overlapping area AJE. Second choice will be area CKG, with preference for the portions CLJA and EJMG, where at least one hand may work in its normal area. Right-handed workers may prefer *CLJA*, giving a greater effort to the more dexterous hand, and left-handed workers may prefer *EJMG*. With the nearer areas occupied, the more distant parts of the normal areas may be used for work requiring only one hand, or for tools and material that may be picked up and used or replaced with one hand.

Fig. 84.— Work table with adjustable height and removable top.

The principles of the normal and the maximum working areas are valuable for guiding the layout of workplaces in making setups. The idea of the circular workplace was evolved from this concept. These setups are a great improvement over the older setups, where material and tools were placed either haphazardly or in straight lines, which caused at least part of the material to be located in inconvenient positions.

When a good setup has been worked out, it should be used every time the job is done. If a job is not worked upon continuously, the setup is likely to be torn down when one worker is finished, and when the next order comes through, the setup may not be made as originally worked out by the methods engineer. The methods engineer, of course, will have records showing the proper setup, but arrangements should be made so that it will not be necessary to consult him continuously about setups, once he has worked them out.

FIG. 85.— Rack for storing table tops with material containers and fixtures permanently attached.

One way of accomplishing this is through the use of the worktable shown in Fig. 84. The top is made of masonite or plywood and is removable. The material bins, fixtures, etc., for a given job are properly located by the methods engineer when the workplace layout is originally developed and are permanently attached to the table top. When the job is not being worked on, the top is removed and is stored in a rack, Fig. 85, usually under the control of the tool crib. When the job is to be performed, the whole workplace layout is drawn from the tool crib just as would be the case with any other tool. It is the correct workplace layout, for it is impossible for anyone to change it, at least without considerable difficulty.

It should be noted that the height of the worktable shown by Fig. 84 can be readily adjusted by merely turning a hand crank. This not only makes it possible to set the table at the ideal height for any operator on any job, but also provides a practical way of working alternately sitting and standing, with the workplace always at the correct height.

In the vertical plane, the arc described by the fingers when a third-class

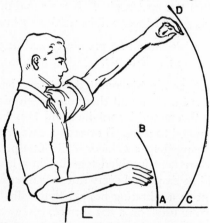

FIG. 86.— Normal and maximum working areas for the hands in the vertical plane.

movement is made is the arc AB of Fig. 86, while the arc CD is the maximum arc employing a fourth-class movement. These arcs determine the efficient placement of materials in the vertical plane.

When positioning tools which are suspended above the work area, care should be taken to locate them within the sphere which would be generated if the arc CD were to be rotated about the body of the operator as an axis. If no other equipment or material interferes, the tools should be located on the surface of the sphere that would be generated by similarly rotating the arc AB. In any case, they should be located so that they can be grasped without the necessity of employing major body movements.

The principles of efficient work areas should be applied to all lines of work, for they are universal. It is customary to think of them in connection with bench operations, but they can and should be applied to the arrangement of tools and materials around machines or on work, such as molding, forging, etc.

6. *Tools and materials should be located so as to permit the following of the proper sequence of motions. The part required at the beginning of the cycle should be next to the point of release of the finished piece of the preceding cycle.*

An operation may be performed within the normal working area and yet be performed very inefficiently because of improper arrangement of tools and materials. In general, one operation of a sequence should end at the same point that the next begins. If tools and materials are not so arrranged, the Reaches and Moves will be needlessly long.

7. *Tools and materials should be pre-positioned in order to eliminate the Search and Select basic elements.*

Search and Select, as already pointed out, are basic elements that retard accomplishment and should therefore be eliminated. The problem is to rearrange the material container and tool holders so that the case C Reach is changed to a case B or even a case A Reach and so that the G4 Grasp is changed to a G1a or a G5 Grasp. For example, if a number of washers are kept jumbled together in a box, a case C Reach and a G4 Grasp will be employed every time a washer is obtained. If the washers can be kept in a vibrating hopper that will shake them out, at about the rate they are used, on a flat surface, somewhat separated from one another, each washer can be obtained with a case B Reach and, if the washer can be slid into position, with a G5 Grasp. If the washers are stacked in a device like a coin changer, the Reach will become case A. The grasping motions will depend upon the design of the device.

8. *Hands should be relieved of all work which can be done with the feet or other parts of the body, provided that there is other work which the hands can do at the same time.*

Any time that an operation can be performed by parts of the body other than the hands, it should be so done, if there is other work which the hands can perform at the same time. In this way, the hands are relieved of performing certain motions, and time is saved in accordance with Law 3. The foot-operated drill press is an illustration of this principle. The operator works the drill spindle by a foot pedal, leaving both hands free to place drilled parts aside and to get other parts to be drilled.

CONCLUSION

The principles of motion economy set forth in this chapter are fundamental and provide a valuable guide to follow in developing improved methods. They require a detailed motion-by-motion knowledge of the job before they can be applied, but this is just what the methods-time measurement procedure provides. Thus the principles of motion economy and the methods-time measurement procedure together provide a tool for the methods engineer of the utmost usefulness.

CHAPTER 21

METHODS ANALYSIS AND DEVELOPMENT

Armed with an understanding of the principles of motion economy and the methods-time measurement procedure, the methods engineer is in a position to develop methods improvements for practically any job he studies. The procedure requires time to apply, however, so that care should be taken to make sure that the savings resulting from the improvements, when developed, will exceed the cost of making the study. There is also another pitfall to be avoided. The methods-time measurement procedure is a detailed procedure, and in applying it, there is the danger that the methods engineer will "get so close to the trees that he cannot see the forest." In other words, he may become so engrossed in the study of detailed motions that he will overlook something as obvious as the fact that the operation he is improving may be entirely unnecessary. These pitfalls can be avoided by making a proper approach to the study and improvement of the job.

METHODS ANALYSIS AND DEVELOPMENT PROCEDURE

The steps that should be taken to develop effective and practical methods with the aid of the methods-time measurement procedure are as follows:

1. Ascertain the expected yearly activity of the job, and determine the yearly labor cost per .0001 hour.
2. Apply the operation analysis procedure, at least mentally.
3. Consider all of the methods which appear to have possibilities, and determine machine equipment, tooling, and labor costs. This latter step involves the application of the methods-time measurement procedure.
4. Determine the best method to adopt by applying the principle of the most economical method.

The procedure is portrayed graphically in Fig. 87. The first three steps are discussed briefly in this chapter. The principle of the most economical method is described in the following chapter.

ESTABLISHING ECONOMIC JUSTIFICATION FOR STUDY

Experience has demonstrated that if sufficient analysis and study are devoted to any given job, the method for doing it can usually be improved, at least until the point of fully automatic operation is reached. In order to be profitable, however, the cost of the study must not exceed

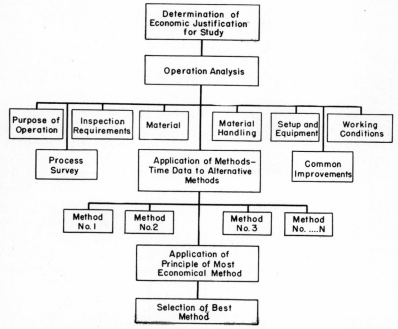

Fig. 87.— Graphic representation of the methods-analysis and development procedure.

the savings that result. Therefore, it is important for the methods engineer to regulate his work so that, as nearly as possible, he devotes sufficient time to any study to obtain as great savings as possible, and yet not so much time that there is no net saving after the cost of making the study has been defrayed.

An excellent guide to the amount of study that is economically justified is the index—the yearly labor cost per .0001 hour. This is computed from the equation

Yearly activity $\times$ labor rate $\times$ .0001 = yearly labor cost per .0001 hour

The yearly activity in the case of jobs that are already in production may be determined by referring to past activity records of the production

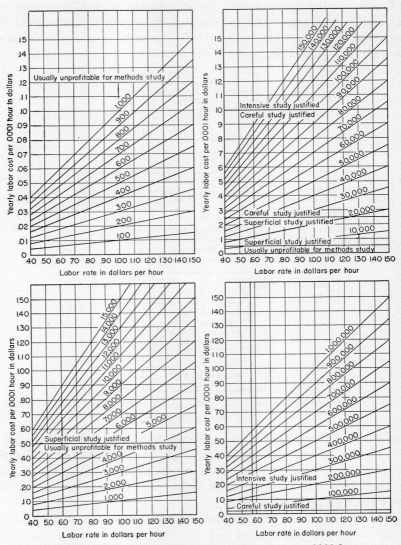

FIG. 88.— Charts for computing yearly labor cost per .0001 hour.

or stores departments, if such records are maintained, and then checking with the engineering and sales representatives to determine if it is expected that this activity will increase, decrease, or be maintained. In the case of new jobs, estimated expected activities must be obtained from the engineering and sales representatives.

The yearly labor cost per .0001 hour for activities ranging from 100 to 1,000,000 pieces and labor rates ranging from 40 cents to $1.50 per hour may be quickly determined from the charts A to D, Fig. 88. These charts may be quite easily used for activities or hourly rates outside their range. For example, assume an activity of 1,000,000 pieces and a labor rate of $1.80 per hour. This labor rate is beyond the range of the charts, but by determining from the chart the yearly labor cost per .0001 for the 1,000,000 activity and one-half the labor rate, or 90 cents per hour, and then multiplying the result by two, the desired answer will be readily obtained.

The yearly labor cost per .0001 hour gives a quick indication of the amount of study justified on any job. In general, it may be said that any job with a yearly labor cost per .0001 hour lower than 50 cents is unprofitable to study insofar as the method is concerned. Unless a major improvement can be made without any expenditure, it will usually prove most economical to establish a time value based upon good standard practice and leave it to the operator or his group leader to devise a method that will meet the standard. It might be possible by studying the job more carefully, by providing better tools, and by following through with operator instruction to reduce the time for doing the job considerably, but even if a job which could be done without methods improvement for .0100 hour were improved to the point where it could be done for .0040 hour, if the yearly labor cost per .0001 hour were 25 cents, the total gross saving would be only $15, an amount which would quickly be surpassed by the expenditure necessary to obtain it.

When the yearly labor cost per .0001 hour ranges between 50 cents and $2.50, it will usually pay to give the job at least superficial study. The methods engineer should make an operation analysis and then on the basis of his experience should mentally work out the best setup for doing the job. It may or may not pay to consider additional methods possibilities.

If the yearly labor cost per .0001 hour is between $2.50 and $10, it will probably pay to apply the methods-time measurement procedure in its entirety, for the savings begin to be really worth while in this range.

Above a yearly labor cost per .0001 hour of $10, the job should be subjected to intensive study. As this index figure gets larger, it becomes more and more worth while to consider specially designed fixtures, special hoppers and chutes, devices for automatic ejection, etc. It will even pay in many cases, after the best method which the methods engineer can conceive has been put into effect, to restudy the operation as it is being performed in the shop in an attempt to make still further refinements.

It should be kept in mind that the yearly labor cost per .0001 hour is an index and a guide only and that it should not be used blindly. In determining the amount of study effort to apply, the total yearly labor expenditure must also be considered. A given operation might have a yearly labor cost per .0001 hour of $5, but if the total allowed time is only .0005, the total yearly labor expenditure will be only $25. Even if the method is improved to the extent that the operation can be performed in half the time, the yearly saving will be only $12.50, which is not enough to justify much expenditure of either time or money.

OPERATION ANALYSIS

The operation analysis procedure has been described in detail elsewhere.[1] Briefly, it is the procedure employed to study the major factors that affect the general method employed to perform a given operation. The study is made by approaching the job with an open mind and asking either oneself or others questions that are likely to lead to methods-improving ideas.

The nine major points that the operation analysis procedure considers are as follows:

1. Purpose of operation
2. Complete survey of all operations performed on part
3. Inspection requirements
4. Material
5. Material handling
6. Setup and tool equipment
7. Common possibilities for job improvement
8. Working conditions
9. Method

A tenth factor that might well appear in the No. 3 position on the list is "design." If the job is highly repetitive, a study of the design of the part may lead to suggestions for changes that will reduce operating costs.

Items 6, 7, and 9 on the above list overlap the area covered by the

[1] MAYNARD, H. B., and G. J. STEGEMERTEN, "Operation Analysis," McGraw-Hill Book Company, Inc., 1939.

methods-time measurement procedure. There is no conflict, however. During operation analysis, these factors are given only broad general consideration. They are then studied in detail as the motions required are worked out during the application of the methods-time measurement procedure. Operation analysis, for example, might indicate the desirability of a holding fixture and a gravity-feed chute. Methods-time measurement analysis would fix their exact design and location at the workplace.

The details of the operation analysis procedure need not be discussed here, for this information is already available. It will be sufficient merely to point out that by going through the steps of operation analysis before plunging into the details of methods-time measurement, the methods engineer will gain perspective about the operation and will remain properly oriented with reality.

METHODS DEVELOPMENT PROCEDURE

After it has been determined by checking the yearly labor cost per .0001 hour that a detailed study of methods will be profitable and after the operation analysis procedure has been applied, the methods engineer is ready to develop the best method of performing the operation under existing conditions that his ingenuity and experience will permit. The procedure for doing this consists of visualizing one or more methods for doing the job and then determining which method is the most economical.

The first step in visualizing a method is to decide upon the machine or other equipment with which the job might be done. Then with a given machine in mind, the method of getting the material to and from the machine should be visualized. Next the setup of the machine, feeds and speeds to be used, and like information should be considered and recorded if variables exist.

The next and usually one of the most important steps on many kinds of work is to determine the most economical holding means to use for the method that is being visualized. Both the cost of the holding means and the time required to manipulate it must be considered.

With the method fully visualized, the motions that must be employed to follow it should be decided upon and recorded on the Methods Analysis Chart. The method first recorded should be carefully studied in detail in the light of the principles of motion economy, and refinements should be made until no further improvement possibilities can be discovered. The allowed time for the method may then be established by means of the methods-time data.

Usually the methods engineer will desire to consider several different methods of doing the operation. The methods may involve the use of different machines, different tools, or different motion sequences. Every method that appears to offer possibilities should be studied in detail, and equipment, tooling, and labor costs should be determined. Often a study of two or more methods after they have been worked out will suggest combining parts of the methods into still another method.

When at length the methods engineer has developed all the different methods that his judgment indicates should be considered, he is ready to select the best method. This he can do by applying the principle of the most economical method, which is described in the following chapter.

CHAPTER 22

PRINCIPLE OF THE MOST ECONOMICAL METHOD

In order to produce any manufactured product economically, it is essential that effective manufacturing methods be used. There are usually a number of different ways in which a given job can be done. For example, assume that it is desired to have a hole in a given casting. Because size and finish are relatively unimportant, the hole may be produced by coring or by drilling. In the first instance, there are a number of different ways of producing the core and setting it in the mold. The core may be made by hand in a core box producing one or more cores at a time. It may be made on a coremaking machine. Variations in the design of the print ends of the cores are possible.

If the hole is to be drilled by machine it may be drilled on a lathe, a profiler, a jig borer, or on one of a number of types of drilling machines. On a given machine, the part may be clamped and held for drilling by a number of different devices. There are a great many ways in which the workplace can be laid out. In fact, the variables which enter into the method which may be used to produce the hole in the casting are so numerous that it is difficult, if not impossible, to select the best method by judgment alone.

PRINCIPLE OF MOST ECONOMICAL METHOD

In order to determine which method of all of those available is the most economical, three major factors must be taken into consideration. These are

1. Machine cost
2. Tool cost
3. Labor cost

Other factors also enter in, such as floor space occupied, power consumed, material used, etc. In most cases, however, they are so similar for different methods that they may be neglected. If in special cases they differ enough to justify inclusion in the analysis, they may be included in the formula for the determination of the most economical method.

The principle of the most economical method may be stated as follows:

The most economical method is attained when machine cost + tool cost + labor cost is a minimum.

It is assumed, of course, that any method tested by this formula will yield the necessary quality with no more than a normal amount of scrap. If there is a difference in the amount of scrap that would be produced from the various methods under consideration, the factor of scrap cost may also be added to the above expression.

FORMULA FOR DETERMINING THE MOST ECONOMICAL METHOD

In order to arrive at the most economical method for doing a given job, all the various methods that appear to have possibilities for economical production should be considered by the analyst. For each different method, the machine cost, the tool cost, and the labor cost should then be determined. By substituting these data in the following formula and solving it, the total yearly cost will be determined. The formula expression is

$$\frac{\text{Cost of machine}}{\begin{array}{c}\text{Number of years for}\\\text{machine amortization}\end{array}} \times \frac{\begin{array}{c}\text{each-piece time} \times \text{yearly}\\\text{activity}\end{array}}{\begin{array}{c}\text{number of hours per year}\\\text{machine normally}\\\text{operates}\end{array}} + \frac{\text{tool cost}}{\begin{array}{c}\text{number of years}\\\text{for tool}\\\text{amortization}\end{array}}$$

$$+ \text{each-piece time} \times \text{yearly activity} \times \text{labor rate per hour}$$

or

$$\frac{M}{A_m} \times \frac{TA \times R}{C} + \frac{T}{A_t} + TA \times R \times L \qquad (1)$$

or

$$\frac{T}{A_t} + TA \times R\left(L + \frac{M}{A_m \times C}\right) \qquad (2)$$

where

A_m = number of years allowed by accounting department for machine amortization

A_t = number of years allowed by accounting department for tool and fixture amortization

C = number of hours per year that machine normally operates

L = labor rate in dollars per hour

M = cost of machine including motors and installation

R = yearly activity of part

T = cost of special tooling and of jigs and fixtures

TA = each-piece time allowed in hours for method contemplated

When either formula (1) or (2) is solved for each method conceived of for doing a given operation, the method that gives the lowest total result will be the best method to use. For benchwork, the term $M \div A_m C$ is usually considered to equal zero and thus drops out of the formula.

MACHINE COST

The reasoning behind the first term of formula (1) is as follows: When a given machine tool is purchased, it is the usual practice to try to distribute the cost of the machine over the various jobs done on it in proportion to the amount of time required to produce each job. In general factory cost work, this is accomplished by including the item of depreciation in the overhead, or burden. It is not satisfactory, however, to use any general overhead figure for the purpose of determining the most economical method, because the depreciation of all machine tools in a given area is usually lumped together with a number of other items to give a single percentage figure. This single figure would not reflect the difference in cost between different types of machines, and hence the computation required by the first term in the formula must be made.

Accounting practices vary among different plants, and the formula should be worked out in conformance with existing procedures. In many plants, the cost of the machine includes the cost of motors and installation. This is logical, for the cost of machine, motors, and installation represents the total amount of money that must be spent to provide the facilities needed for doing the job. Amortization practices vary, but the attempt is usually made to charge off the cost of the machine within a reasonable time.

If a certain machine cost is $1,000 and the number of years for machine amortization is 10, the cost per year for that machine may be taken as $1,000 ÷ 10, or $100. This cost must then be apportioned to individual jobs. This is done by determining the percentage of normal operating time that is consumed by the job under study. The each-piece allowed time for the job under study may be determined from the methods-time data. The allowed time multiplied by the expected yearly activity of the job will give the number of hours the machine will be tied up on this job. This figure divided by the number of hours the machine normally operates per year will give the proportion of operating time chargeable to the job under study. The actual number of hours a given machine operates in any year is likely to fluctuate considerably. In making computations of this sort, it is good practice to be on the conservative side.

Assume that the job under study has an each-piece allowed time of .0500 hour. It is expected that 10,000 pieces will be made per year. The machine tool on which the job is to be done ordinarily runs steadily throughout the year for one 8-hour shift. If the machine cost is $1,000 and the number of years for machine amortization is 10, then the machine cost chargeable to the job is

$$\frac{1,000}{10} \times \frac{.0500 \times 10,000}{2,000} = \$25$$

TOOL COST

The cost of special tooling which can be used only on the job which is under a study must also be taken into consideration in determining the most economical method. This is covered by the second term of formula (1). The most common practice is to charge off the cost of special tooling in 1 year. Therefore, A_t, the number of years allowed by the accounting department for tool and fixture amortization, usually equals 1. On short-life jobs, or jobs where there is likelihood of frequent design changes, the period allowed for tool amortization may be shortened. One plant faced with imminent cancellation of certain special contracts made the ruling that the cost of all special tooling would have to be absorbed through savings within 30 days to justify making the expenditures.

The opposite condition occurs on stable products where the anticipated life without change is long. In such cases, it may be permissible to allow a period longer than 1 year for the absorption of the cost of special tooling.

LABOR COST

The yearly labor cost for performing any operation is covered by the third term of formula (1). It is determined by multiplying the each-piece allowed time by the yearly activity and by the labor rate.

The each-piece allowed time for the various methods being compared is derived as the result of the application of the methods-time data. Each method considered must be analyzed into its limiting motions. Then the proper time is applied to each motion. The total time of the motions is the each-piece time for the operation.

Formula (2) is a simplification of formula (1). It may be used to facilitate computations if a number of them must be made. Formula (1), although slightly more cumbersome to handle, possesses the advantage of presenting machine cost, tool cost, and labor cost separately so that their relative importance is clear throughout. This may be an important aid to the analysis and may help to prevent the common tendency to concentrate too much on labor cost while considering the other two items only superficially, if at all.

CHAPTER 23

INSTALLATION OF IMPROVED METHOD

When, as the result of analysis and study, a method of performing a given job has at length been developed, certain definite actions are necessary on the part of the methods engineer to transform the method from a written description on paper to an actual practical reality in the shop. It is the purpose of this chapter to describe briefly the steps that are necessary to accomplish this.

PRACTICABILITY OF METHOD

There is always the possibility that a method which is worked out on paper may not prove successful when it is tried out in the shop. It is sometimes impossible to foresee certain conditions or factors that will cause failure of a contemplated procedure. In making dresses, for example, the operators on certain sewing operations where two parts are to be joined together ordinarily locate the parts by notches and small punched holes which are put into the cloth at the time of cutting in the cutting room. Ordinarily no difficulty is experienced with this method of locating parts, and the methods man would be justified in assuming that this was an entirely practical method to specify. In the case of a certain style, however, the method proved to be impractical because the material contained a very small, variegated, multicolored pattern that made it almost impossible to see the small punched locating holes. So much time was lost trying to find them that a bottleneck developed, which was relieved only when an entirely new and hitherto unused locating method was developed.

Thus before any method is accepted for use, it should be checked to determine its practicability. An actual tryout is the best method of checking, of course. Where a methods laboratory is available, the tryout may be made there. If the tryout must be carried on in the shop, conditions will dictate the best procedure to follow. A simple job would be given to the operator who is to perform it with the necessary instructions, and the tryout would consist of watching him briefly in order to make sure that he could follow the specified method properly. On the

205

other hand, to try out methods on an elaborate progressive manufacturing line involving several hundred people, it might be deemed advisable first to set up a pilot line in another location where the method to be used at each work station could be tested.

In departments handling miscellaneous work on a variety of machine tools, the available capacity of the machine selected for a given job should be checked so that one or two particularly effective machine tools in the department are not overloaded. The time required to tool up a job in comparison with delivery requirements must be considered in certain instances, so that the proper balance between cost and delivery is maintained. For instance, it may work out that the most economical method of drilling a hole in a small part calls for the use of a certain drill press with a dial feed. If the dial feed mechanism cannot be obtained and installed for 3 months, and if the parts are needed in 30 days, then the method is impractical from an over-all viewpoint in spite of the low cost.

Another point to consider before the method is accepted on certain classes of work is the possibility of modifying a contemplated holding device, or special tool, so that something already in existence can be used.

The factors of this sort that should be given consideration will vary with the nature of the work being performed. The point to be stressed is that the factors which apply in any given situation should be checked before going ahead with the planned method.

INSTALLING THE METHOD

When the practicability of the method has been checked, the necessary action for putting it into effect must be taken. The method in all its details, at this point, is usually clear only in the mind of one man, the methods engineer. Therefore care must be taken to translate the plan into an actual reality by seeing that the necessary information is furnished to everyone who may be connected with the job.

Those responsible for routing the operation must be informed of the machine selected for the job. A clear description of the desired tooling and jig or fixture must be furnished to the tool designer so that the finished design will correspond with the contemplated design. As an added precaution, arrangements should be made for the analyst to check and approve the tool designs before the work is begun of making the tools. If there is anything new or unusual about the contemplated method, the foreman who is to supervise the work should be made familiar with it before the job reaches the shop.

Finally, the problems of the operator who is to do the work should be considered. If there is nothing particularly unusual about the new method, it probably is unnecessary to discuss it with the operator until the material and tools are at hand and the job is ready to be started. On the other hand, if a new method completely revolutionizes an established procedure, it may be well to pave the way for it by advance discussions not only with the operator involved but also with his steward if a union is involved. The quickest way of eliminating the distrust with which anything new is almost always regarded is to keep everyone informed who is likely to be affected. Thus when the new device, method, or procedure eventually comes along, it is regarded as something that has been known about for some time.

Once again, it should be pointed out that the exact manner in which the introductory steps are taken will vary with the conditions, procedures, and personalities involved. The way in which they are to be handled will therefore have to be determined in each situation in which the methods development procedure herein described is used.

INSTRUCTION SHEET

The final step in putting a new method into effect consists of instructing the operator with respect to what is required of him. The desirability of reducing instructions about methods to writing has long been recognized by industry, even though in practice this step is all too often neglected. If an operator is to be expected to follow the method which has been worked out by the methods engineer assisted by his data and specialized knowledge of effective working methods, some means must be provided for telling the operator about the method. Verbal instructions are of only partial effectiveness and are undeniably impermanent. Written instructions are better; for they provide a permanent record of the method which is useful not only when new operators must be trained or when the memories of all concerned must be refreshed concerning the method after a protracted shutdown, but which also provides a basis for determining at a future period whether or not a method has been changed, and if so, to what extent.

Motion pictures provide the best instruction medium of all. They give a record of the method and surrounding conditions. They are easy to understand when used for training purposes. Finally, they may be used to show beyond question whether methods have changed or not whenever the question arises. Motion pictures are somewhat difficult to catalogue, store, and protect, and therefore many organizations hesitate to use them. The concern that is willing to take the trouble necessary to use motion pictures for methods-record purposes, however, will usually find itself well repaid through the control it gains over the methods-change problem.

Returning to the discussion of written instruction sheets, the perennial problem is how complete to make them. Instruction sheets which are complete enough to describe every detail of every element of a job are usually so lengthy and involved that most shop men will not read them. Briefer records are more readable but are likely to leave unanswered questions that may arise in the future. Brief instruction sheets, however,

```
                    INSTRUCTION CARD
                         FOR
          SHOULDERING OR JOINING SHOULDERS
                 OF DRESS STYLE P 81

        Pick up the back with your left hand and place it face up on the
machine table near the presser foot.  Then pick up a pair of right fronts
with your right hand.  Place the fronts on the back, being sure to keep
the face sides together.  Match the parts carefully at the armhole seam.
Then raise the presser foot with your right knee and place the back and
the fronts under the foot.  Lower the presser foot with your right knee.
Match the seams at the neckline so they are even, holding the parts at
the armhole with your left hand and at the neckline with your right hand.
Sew the parts together.  Repeat the operation with the left fronts.  Then
trim all threads and slide the finished work to the girl on your left.
```

FIG. 89.— Instruction card prepared in simple narrative form.

are far better than no instruction sheets at all, and they usually prove to be the most practical.

An instruction card with instructions given in simple narrative form is shown by Fig. 89. This follows good practice in writing for understanding by using short sentences, short words, and personal references. It should be readily understood by anyone with a sixth-grade education.

To increase ease of understanding, illustrations, drawings, or cartoons are sometimes used on instruction sheets on the theory that "one picture is worth 10,000 words." They are effective but require someone with special talent to prepare. For this reason, they are not much used.

A more formal type of instruction sheet, which has been used successfully in machine-shop work of a more or less jobbing nature for a number of years, is shown by Fig. 90. This form gives a brief descrip-

MEC FORM 133

INSTRUCTION CARD

ORDER NO. M - 18736 OPER. NO. 1

PART Sleeve | DRAWING B - 4732-3

OPERATION Turn, drill, Cbr, & cut off | PATT. Bar stock

FIXTURE 9/16 collet | MACH. NO. 514 QUANTITY 200

TOOLS Stop, box tool, A1 center drill, #29 drill, #7 flat bottom drill, cutoff tool & file

SKETCH

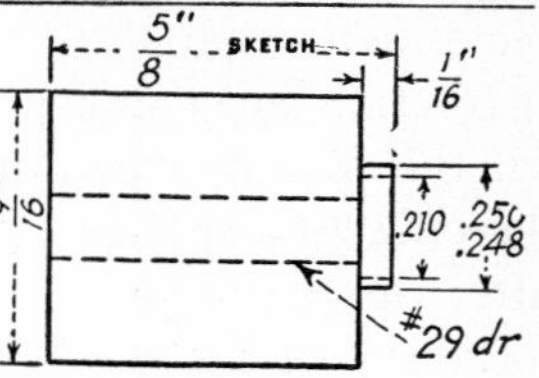

INSPECTION 10 % operator Patrol by Inspector

NO.	OPERATION DESCRIPTION	TOOL	SPEED R.P.M.	FEED
1	Set stock to length	Stop		
2	Turn turret			
3	Turn .248-.250 dia. 1/16" long	Box tool	1500	Hand
2	Turn turret			
4	Center drill	A1 C.D.	1500	Hand
2	Turn turret			
5	Drill 11/16" deep	#29 drill	1500	Hand
2	Turn turret			
6	Cbr. .210 dia. 1/16" deep	#7 F.B. drill	1500	Hand
7	Turn turret & set crosslide			
8	File & cut off	Cutoff	1500	Hand
9	Piece aside			
10	Check 1 piece in 10			

DATE	APPROVED	SET UP	HRS. PER PC.
2-28-47	W.A.	.57	.015

FIG. 90.— Instruction sheet used for jobbing machine work.

tion of the setup, lists the elements of the operation in the order in which they are to be performed, and gives specific information about feeds and speeds. A qualified machine operator can read over the instruction sheet and then proceed to do the job, following in general the method which it describes. No two operators would be likely to do the job exactly the same, motion by motion, from this type of instructions. On fairly low activity work, however, it is impractical to seek this degree of perfection.

The instruction sheet shown by Fig. 91 is a more detailed type, desirable when the repetitiveness of the work is sufficient to warrant more exact adherence to a specified method. The form shown was designed for use after the development, by means of the methods-time measurement procedure, of the method for doing a given job on a six-spindle sensitive drill press. It gives exact information about the setup, including table height and distance of tool points from table. The method is described in narrative form, using simple informal language. Where the repetitiveness of the work is sufficient to justify the use of the methods-time measurement procedure, this is a practical instruction sheet form to use.

Still another type of instruction sheet is shown by Fig. 92. The work is broken down to show the steps by which the operation is performed. This step-by-step procedure is listed on the left-hand side of the instruction sheet. The key points, or techniques, that the operator must know, in order to perform the job successfully, are listed on the right-hand side of the sheet. This type of instruction sheet has been widely and successfully used in training operators to perform repetitive operations.

Regardless of the exact type of form used, the instruction sheet should be made out by the methods engineer before the job goes to the shop and should carry complete instructions and the allowed time, but no signatures. As soon as the job goes in work for the first time, it should be thoroughly checked—if this was not done at a previous tryout—to see that the setup will operate as contemplated and that the method as written up is correct. The instruction sheet should then be signed by all concerned to indicate acceptance of the method and of the time allowance.

The form shown in Fig. 91 carries the note: "Time value applies to method described above and is guaranteed until method is changed. Cash awards paid for suggestions leading to improvements in this method if submitted through Shop Suggestion Plan." This represents excellent

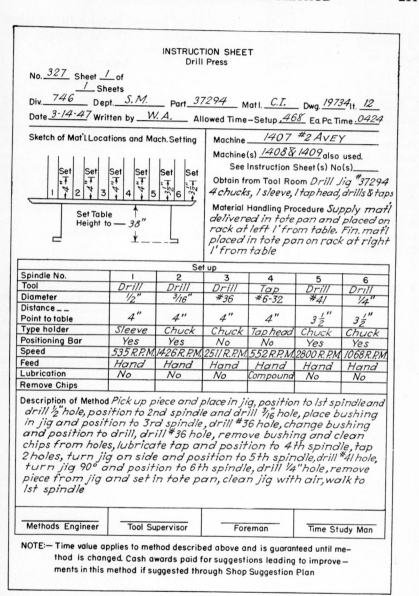

INSTRUCTION SHEET
Drill Press

No. *327* Sheet *1* of
____ *1* ____ Sheets

Div. *746* Dept. *S.M.* Part *37294* Mat'l. *C.I.* Dwg. *19734* It. *12*

Date *3-14-47* Written by *W.A.* Allowed Time—Setup *.468* Ea. Pc. Time *.0424*

Sketch of Mat'l Locations and Mach. Setting	
	Machine *1407 #2 AVEY*
	Machine(s) *1408 & 1409* also used.
	See Instruction Sheet(s) No(s) ____
	Obtain from Tool Room *Drill Jig #37294*
	4 chucks, 1 sleeve, 1 tap head, drills & taps
	Material Handling Procedure *Supply mat'l delivered in tote pan and placed on rack at left 1' from table. Fin. mat'l placed in tote pan on rack at right 1' from table*

Set Table Height to — *38"*

Set up

Spindle No.	1	2	3	4	5	6
Tool	Drill	Drill	Drill	Tap	Drill	Drill
Diameter	1/2"	3/16"	#36	#6-32	#41	1/4"
Distance — Point to table	4"	4"	4"	4"	$3\frac{1}{2}"$	$3\frac{1}{2}"$
Type holder	Sleeve	Chuck	Chuck	Tap head	Chuck	Chuck
Positioning Bar	Yes	Yes	No	No	Yes	Yes
Speed	535 R.P.M.	1426 R.P.M.	2511 R.P.M.	552 R.P.M.	2800 R.P.M.	1068 R.P.M.
Feed	Hand	Hand	Hand	Hand	Hand	Hand
Lubrication	No	No	No	Compound	No	No
Remove Chips						

Description of Method *Pick up piece and place in jig, position to 1st spindle and drill 1/2" hole, position to 2nd spindle and drill 3/16 hole, place bushing in jig and position to 3rd spindle, drill #36 hole, change bushing and position to drill, drill #36 hole, remove bushing and clean chips from holes, lubricate tap and position to 4th spindle, tap 2 holes, turn jig on side and position to 5th spindle, drill #41 hole, turn jig 90° and position to 6th spindle, drill 1/4" hole, remove piece from jig and set in tote pan, clean jig with air, walk to 1st spindle*

Methods Engineer	Tool Supervisor	Foreman	Time Study Man

NOTE:— Time value applies to method described above and is guaranteed until method is changed. Cash awards paid for suggestions leading to improvements in this method if suggested through Shop Suggestion Plan

FIG. 91.— Instruction sheet for six-spindle drill-press work.

practice and is recommended as a means of helping to solve the problem of keeping time standards in correspondence with the methods currently used in the shop.

INSTRUCTION SHEET FOR BLINDSTITCHING OR BASTING

This operation is used on the bottom hem of a skirt and/or around the neck and sleeves of a dress.

The machine is equipped with a curved needle that does not penetrate completely through the material. It does not have a bobbin and therefore the stitch is not locked as with the plain stitcher.

A folding attachment, which can be adjusted for a 2- or 3-inch hem, is used to turn the material while sewing. The operation of the machine is similar to a plain stitcher.

Procedure	Techniques
1. Pick up.	1. Both hands and fold ¼ inch at bottom.
2. Lower feed.	2. Press right pedal.
3. Position in machine.	3. Fill entire width of folder. Place seam near needle.
4. Release right pedal.	4. Remove foot from pedal.
5. Sew.	5. Press treadle, left foot—open seams with left hand—right hand holds bottom of material slightly tighter than top—bottom feeds faster than top. Sew approximately 1 inch beyond start of stitches to lock basting.
6. Remove and lay aside.	6. Press folder release with right hand, then with both hands remove and lay over bar for next operation.

FIG. 92.— Instruction sheet for repetitive work.

PART V

APPLICATION OF METHODS-TIME MEASUREMENT

CHAPTER 24

SIMPLIFIED METHODS-TIME DATA—USE AND LIMITATIONS

Tests of the accuracy of the methods-time data, as originally developed, show it to be highly accurate when properly applied, which was pointed out in Chapter 15. An experienced analyst can apply the procedure quite rapidly and, on short-cycle operations at least, can develop an accurate time standard more quickly than by the use of the conventional stop-watch time-study procedure.

At the same time, the desirability of making the procedure even simpler and easier to apply is self-evident. Not only is application time saved, but the easier the procedure is to apply, the more it will be used by methods engineers, tool designers, and others who may have the occasion to determine how long it will take to perform a given task.

In studying this problem, it was found that the methods-time data could be greatly simplified with a loss of accuracy of not more than 5 per cent on the great majority of operations tested. The simplified data are so much easier to handle than the more complete data that they have considerable value to the methods engineer in spite of the slight loss in accuracy.

REACH AND MOVE

One of the most time-consuming factors in the application of the methods-time data is the necessity for classifying each Reach and Move motion as case A, B, C, D, or E. When the data are plotted on one composite curve sheet, as shown by Fig. 93, it is seen that the curves for the various cases of Reach and Move group fairly closely together with the exception of the case A Reach. An average curve drawn through the Reach and Move curves, with the exception of the case A Reach, will give values that do not differ more than a few per cent from the values determined from the individual curves for a given length of motion. When it is recognized that in practically every cycle there are a variety of different cases of Reach and Move, it is seen that the use of the average curve for Reach and Move will give values which will not vary greatly in total from the values taken from the individual curves.

One of the problems of simplification is to set up values that can be remembered easily.   After some experimentation, the curve AA, Fig. 93, was drawn to represent the average curve.   It includes a 15 per cent allow-

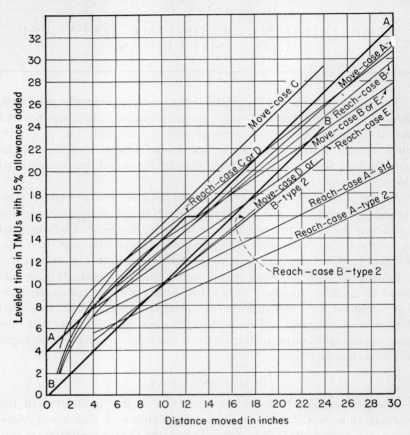

Fig. 93.— Composite curves of all cases of Reach and Move.

ance factor, and it is so drawn that the time for any Reach and Move in decimal hours up to and including 12 inches is equal to

$$(4 + \text{length of motion in inches}) \times .00001$$

Above 12 inches the formula is

$$(3 + \text{length of motion in inches}) \times .00001$$

Thus the time for a 10-inch Reach is $(4 + 10) \times .00001 = .00014$. The time for a 16-inch Move is $(3 + 16) \times .00001 = .00019$.   In application, it is easier to work with whole numbers and not to perform the multiplication by .00001 until values in whole numbers have been assigned to all motions.

Description of motion	Time values			Difference between basic and simplified values	
	From basic data		From simplified data		
	TMU	Dec. hr. +15 per cent	Dec. hr.	Dec. hr.	Per cent
R6E	8.0	.00009	.00010	+.00001	+11.1
R8B	10.1	.00012	.00012		
R8D	11.5	.00013	.00012	−.00001	− 7.7
R10C	12.9	.00015	.00014	−.00001	− 6.7
R12B	12.9	.00015	.00016	+.00001	+ 6.7
R14E	13.0	.00015	.00017	+.00002	+13.3
R16C	17.0	.00020	.00019	−.00001	− 5.0
R18D	18.4	.00021	.00021		
R20B	18.6	.00021	.00023	+.00002	+ 9.5
R22B	20.1	.00023	.00025	+.00002	+ 8.7
R24D	22.5	.00026	.00027	+.00001	+ 3.8
R26C	23.9	.00026	.00029	+.00003	+11.5
M4E	6.9	.00008	.00008		
M6C	9.7	.00011	.00010	−.00001	− 9.1
M8C	11.8	.00014	.00012	−.00002	−14.3
M10B	12.2	.00014	.00014		
M10C	13.5	.00016	.00014	−.00002	−12.5
M12B	13.4	.00015	.00016	+.00001	+ 6.7
M14B	14.6	.00017	.00017		
M16C	18.7	.00022	.00019	−.00003	−13.6
M20E	18.2	.00021	.00023	+.00002	+ 9.5
M24B	20.6	.00024	.00027	+.00003	+12.5
Total	328.5	.00378	.00385	+.00007	+ 1.85

FIG. 94.—Comparison of basic and simplified methods-time data for a number of cases of Reach and Move.

The accuracy of the simplified data as compared with the more exact data may be checked by jotting down a number of cases of Reaches and Moves at random, avoiding the case A Reach. Figure 94 shows such a check. Although the difference of the individual times as determined by the original methods-time data and the times determined by the simplified data varies from −14.3 per cent to +13.3 per cent, the difference in the totals of the two columns is only 1.85 per cent. This is close enough for most purposes.

To determine the time for any Reach and Move where the hand is in motion at the beginning or end of the motion the formula is merely

$$\text{Length of motion in inches} \times .00001$$

This is represented by the curve *BB* on Fig. 93.

TURN

The time for any Turn has arbitrarily been selected as $6 \times .00001$, or .00006 hour. This is high for all turns up to 90°, but is somewhat compensated for in other portions of the simplified data.

The value assigned to Apply Pressure is $20 \times .00001 = .0002$. This compares with an original value of 16.2 TMU, or .000186 hour with 15 per cent added.

GRASP

To simplify the Grasp data, three values have been selected, 2, 6, and 10, multiplied by .00001 hour. The lowest value, 2, may be applied to all simple Grasps. These would be Cases G1a and G1b in the original data. The value of 6 is applied to Regrasps and Transfer Grasps, or G2 and G3, respectively. The value of 10 is used for complex Grasps such as G1c and G4. No time is allowed for a Contact, Sliding, or Hook Grasp, G5.

POSITION

Considerable simplification may be made of the Position data for ease of application, although somewhat at the expense of accuracy if the less common types of Position occur. For all semisymmetrical and non-symmetrical positionings, the values of 15 for a loose fit, 25 for a close fit, and 55 for an exact fit, all multiplied by .00001, may be used. For the positioning of symmetrical parts, the values are 5 less than given above, or 10 for a loose fit, 20 for a close fit, and 50 for an exact fit.

DISENGAGE

Disengage values may similarly be simplified. The values are 5 for a loose fit, 10 for a close fit, and 30 for an exact fit.

RELEASE

The Release basic element may be disregarded altogether in the simplified methods-time data. By omitting it from consideration, not only is the task of application simplified, but the high values assigned to Turn and Apply Pressure are, in part at least, compensated for.

TABLE OF SIMPLIFIED METHODS-TIME DATA

For convenient reference, all the values given above may be condensed into the following table:

Reach	4 + Length of motion*	1–12 inches inclusive
Move	3 + Length of motion*	Over 12 inches

* Use length of motion only, if hand is in motion at beginning or end of movement.

Turn—AP		Grasp		Position			Disengage	
					Sym-metrical	Other		
Turn	6	Simple	2	Loose	10	15	Loose	5
Pressure	20	Regrasp or Transfer Grasp	6	Close	20	25	Close	10
		Complex	10	Exact	50	55	Exact	30

NOTE: Above values multiplied by .00001 give leveled time in decimal hours +15 per cent.

FIG. 95.— Simplified methods-time data.

APPLICATION PROCEDURE FOR SIMPLIFIED METHODS-TIME DATA

The procedure used for applying the simplified methods-time data is similar to that followed in applying the more complete data which is shown by the chart, illustrated in Fig. 72. It is exactly the same down to and including Subdivision into Elements. In the methods analysis of the elements, however, there are some differences. It is not necessary to determine the case of each Reach or Move that is employed but merely to determine the length of motion used and whether or not the hand is in motion at the beginning or the end of the movement. The degrees turned during a Turn movement need not be noted, but merely the fact that a Turn is made. In observing Grasp, no distinctions need be made between easily grasped single objects and very small objects or parts lying close against a flat surface. Insofar as Position is concerned, only the class of fit and whether or not the part is symmetrical need be determined. Disengage is classified as to fit only and Release is not considered at all.

When methods-time standards are applied, the values shown in the simplified table (Fig. 95) are used. Because these are few and are easily remembered, it is seldom necessary to refer to the table after it has been

used a few times. The allowance factor need be considered only if an
allowance of other than 15 per cent is to be used. In such cases, the
table values should be totaled and multiplied by

$$\frac{\text{Per cent allowance to be applied} + 100}{115}$$

The allowed time is determined by multiplying the sum of the simplified methods-time standards, adjusted only if an allowance of other
than 15 per cent is to be used, by .00001. The result is the allowed time
in decimal hours. In all other respects the application procedure is the
same as that described in Chapter 16.

USE AND LIMITATIONS OF SIMPLIFIED METHODS-TIME STANDARDS

The simplified methods-time standards may be used wherever the
more complete data are used if small inaccuracies in the final results are
not objectionable. The magnitude of the inaccuracies ordinarily encountered may be demonstrated as follows: Methods Analysis Sheets are
reproduced throughout the book as Figs. 81, 97, 98, 99, 100, 103, 104, 106,
and 107. The complete methods-time data were applied in all these
examples. The difference in results that would have been obtained had
the simplified data been applied is shown in the following tabulation.

Figure	Total Time		Determined from simplified data	Difference original to simplified data, per cent
	Determined from original data			
	TMU	Dec. hr. +15 per cent	Dec. hr.	
81	226.4	.00261	.00257	−1.5
97	118.7	.00137	.00132	−3.6
98	103.7	.00119	.00112	−5.9
99	34.5	.00039	.00040	+2.6
100	32.8	.00038	.00040	+5.3
103	1,084.1	.01248	.01298	+4.0
104	955.0	.01098	.01130	+2.9
106	35.9	.00041	.00042	+2.4
107	45.3	.00052	.00048	−7.7
Total	2,636.4	.03033	.03099	+2.2

FIG. 96.— Comparison of time allowances established with basic and simplified
methods-time data.

These differences are not serious in many situations in which the methods-time measurement procedure is used. The very real saving in application time that the simplified procedure brings about makes its use most attractive.

CHAPTER 25

APPLICATION OF METHODS-TIME STANDARDS TO TOOL DESIGN

The tool designer on numerous occasions is confronted with a choice of several different designs of tool- or work-holding devices he might utilize to accomplish a given purpose. If all designs will be equally satisfactory from a functioning standpoint, there is a tendency to be governed by first cost in making the choice. If this is done, a very important factor is overlooked, namely, the cost of manipulating the various designs when they are in use in the shop. Probably one reason that more attention is not given to manipulation time by many tool designers is that they have no good means of determining how much this time is. They must obtain an estimate from the methods engineer—who may be difficult to locate—or they must estimate the time themselves, which usually they are not well equipped to do. Where the difference in manipulation time is slight, it is difficult for one who has not analyzed such problems carefully to realize that a saving of even a few seconds in time can result in worth-while total savings if the repetitiveness of the work is great. For all these reasons, a consideration of differences in manipulation time is likely to be slighted.

With the advent of methods-time data, however, the tool designer has a new and easily used means of determining for himself with a high degree of accuracy what the manipulation time will be for any device he may consider. After a period of training, he can learn to use the procedure to help him to improve the over-all effectiveness of his work.

The paragraphs that follow show how the tool designer can use the methods-time measurement procedure to assist him in arriving at sound decisions on two typical design problems. The first covers a decision with regard to the best type of clamping device to use on a box drill jig. The second covers the study of the best design of a completely new jig. Both problems are worked out by using the basic methods-time data, for the sake of illustrating how the more accurate procedure is used. They could have been worked out almost equally well, and certainly a good deal more quickly, by using the simplified methods-time data.

HOLDING DEVICE FOR DRILL JIG

For the purposes of this illustration, it will be assumed that a certain drill-press job has an anticipated yearly activity of 150,000 pieces and that the labor rate paid for this class of work is $1 per hour. The yearly labor cost per .0001 hour of work done on this part is therefore

$$150,000 \times 1 \times .0001 = \$15$$

With this fact established, the tool designer is ready to consider the best design of drill jig to specify. On the assumption that current shop practice is such that a box jig is considered desirable, the tool designer at length comes to the point of providing some kind of a clamping device to hold the part securely during drilling. He decides that the clamping device should be located in the side of the jig and then considers what type it should be. He thinks first of a standard Allen Head setscrew as an economical form of clamping device. Then it occurs to him that a quick-acting cam clamp could be provided which would be somewhat quicker to use.

He next studies past cost records, makes a few rough computations, and decides that it will cost about $40 more to provide the quick-acting clamp than the Allen Head setscrew. Although this increases the first cost of the jig materially, he is experienced enough to realize the importance of little savings on high-activity jobs. Therefore he decides to use his knowledge of methods-time measurement to determine whether or not the quick-acting clamp is justified.

His first step is to visualize the motions that will be required to tighten the Allen Head setscrew. He assumes in his mind a practical workplace layout, and then as he visualizes the motion sequence, he records it in terms of the methods-time measurement procedure on a Methods Analysis Chart. When this step is completed, it will appear as in Fig. 97.

Next he visualizes the motions required to unclamp the part after the drilling has been completed. On a second Methods Analysis Chart, Fig. 98, he records the method and determines the time. As a result of his computations up to this point, he has determined that it will require .00155 hour to tighten the setscrew and .00119 to loosen it again, or a total of .00274 hour to manipulate it.

He next repeats the procedure for the quick-acting clamp. He visualizes the motions required to tighten the clamp and records them, as on Fig. 99. The loosening motions that he decides are necessary are shown on Fig. 100. In making these assumptions, he tries to stay on the conservative side, for he sees that his computations are coming out greatly in favor of the quick-acting clamp. He knows that a good operator after working at the job for a while will tend to reach for the clamp lever with a case A motion, for with his left hand resting on the jig, he would

METHODS ANALYSIS CHART

PART___Left Front Latch Lever___ DEPT.Small Machining___ DWG. B 10462___ ITEM __2__

OPERATION_Clamp Lever in jig with Allen Head set screw___ DATE _October 4, 1946_

DESCRIPTION – LEFT HAND	√	NO.	CLASS	TMU'S	DEC. HRS. *.15%	√	DESCRIPTION – RIGHT HAND
Hold jig			R8B	10.1		√	Reach to Allen Head set screw
			G1a	1.7		√	Grasp set screw
			T90°	5.4		√	Preliminary tighten screw
			RL1	1.7		√	Release
			R12B	12.9		√	Reach to set screw wrench
			G1b	3.5		√	Grasp wrench
			M12C	15.2		√	Move to set screw
			P2SSD	25.5		√	Position wrench in set screw
			AP	16.2		√	Press Wrench in set screw head
			T45S	3.5		√	Turn set screw
			AP	16.2		√	Final tighten
			G2	5.6		√	Regrasp
			D1D	5.7		√	Remove wrench from set screw
			M12D	10.0		√	Move wrench aside
			RL1	1.7		√	Release
		TOTALS		134.9	.00155		SHEET NO. 1 OF 2 SHEETS

FIG. 97.— Methods Analysis Chart—"clamp part in jig with Allen Head set screw."

quickly learn to reach for the lever without looking for it. Furthermore, a complete grasp of the clamp lever might not be necessary, for a Contact Grasp would probably be sufficient. Finally, he believes that if he provides a smoothly operating cam, Apply Pressure may not be necessary to give it a final tightening. By visualizing the most unfavorable conditions, he feels that he is allowing a factor of safety. He thus decides that

METHODS ANALYSIS CHART

PART Left Front Latch Lever   DEPT Small Machining   DWG. B 10462   ITEM 2

OPERATION Unclamp Allen Head set screw   DATE October 4, 1946

DESCRIPTION--LEFT HAND	✓	NO.	CLASS	TMU'S	DEC. HRS. $\pm 15\%$	✓	DESCRIPTON--RIGHT HAND
Hold jig			R12B	12.9		✓	Reach for set screw wrench
			G1b	3.5		✓	Grasp
			M12C	15.2		✓	Move to set screw
			P2SSD	25.5		✓	Position wrench in set screw
			AP	16.2		✓	Start screw
			T135S	7.4		✓	Turn screw
			G2	5.6		✓	Regrasp wrench
			D1D	5.7		✓	Remove wrench from set screw
			M12D	10.0		✓	Move wrench aside
			RL1	1.7		✓	Release

METHODS ENGINEERING COUNCIL FORM NO. 117   TOTALS 103.7 | .00119   SHEET NO. 1 OF 1 SHEETS

Fig. 98.— Methods Analysis Chart—"unclamp part in jig—Allen Head set screw."

a total manipulation time of .00039 + .00038, or .00077 hour, is a fair value to use.

He is now in a position to decide whether or not the quick-acting clamp is justified. It will save .00274 — .00077, or .00197 hour. Each .0001 hour saved represents a yearly saving of $15. Therefore the saving to be realized from the quick-acting clamp is $19.7 \times 15.00 = \$295.50$. Because the quick-acting clamp will add only $40 to the cost of the jig, it is

METHODS ANALYSIS CHART

PART___Left Front Latch Lever_____DEPT. Small Machining_DWG. B 10462_____ITEM__2___

OPERATION___Clamp lever in jig with quick-acting clamp_____DATE October 4, 1946

DESCRIPTION--LEFT HAND	✓	NO.	CLASS	TMU'S	DEC. HRS. ÷.13%	✓	DESCRIPTION--RIGHT HAND
Hold jig			R8B	10.1		✓	Reach for clamp lever
			G1a	1.7		✓	Grasp
			T75S	4.8		✓	Tighten clamp
			AP	16.2		✓	Final tighten
			RL1	1.7		✓	Release
METHODS ENGINEERING COUNCIL FORM NO. 117			TOTALS	34.5	.00039		SHEET NO._1__OF__1__SHEETS

Fig. 99.— Methods Analysis Chart—"clamp part in jig—quick-acting clamp."

obviously well worth while to use it, for the first year's net savings will amount to $255.50. The tool designer therefore proceeds to specify the quick-acting clamp with the full knowledge that he is acting wisely.

DESIGNING AN EFFECTIVE DRILL JIG

The same process of testing out contemplated designs may be used on more complicated problems. The general procedure, however, is the

METHODS ANALYSIS CHART						
PART Left Front Latch Lever			DEPT. Small Machining DWG. B 10462 ITEM 2			
OPERATION Unclamp lever in jig with quick-acting clamp					DATE October 4, 1946	
DESCRIPTION--LEFT HAND	✓	NO.	CLASS	TMU'S	DEC. HRS.	✓ DESCRIPTON--RIGHT HAND
Hold jig			R8B	10.1		✓ Reach for clamp lever
			G1a	1.7		✓ Grasp
			AP	16.2		✓ Loosen
			T75S	4.8		✓ Turn clamp
			RL2	0		✓ Release
METHODS ENGINEERING COUNCIL FORM NO. 117			TOTALS	32.8	.00038	SHEET NO. 1 OF 1 SHEETS

FIG. 100.— Methods Analysis Chart—"unclamp part in jig—quick-acting clamp."

same. The contemplated tool is either sketched or mentally designed. Next, the motions required to manipulate it are visualized and the methods-time measurement procedure is applied. Finally, a cost study is made to determine which of several possibilities is the best.

The procedure is one of cutting and trying. The number of trials made and the closeness with which the method which is finally selected approaches the best which can be devised will depend largely upon the experience of the analyst. After one has applied the procedure a number of times, he should be able to arrive at good methods fairly rapidly.

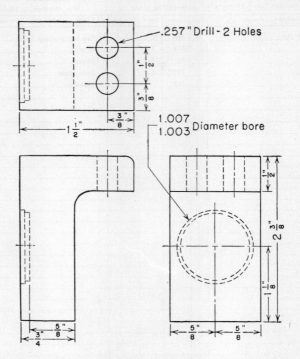

FIG. 101.— Small copper part for which drill jig is to be designed.

The procedure may be demonstrated by showing the steps that a tool designer went through to design a drill jig for drilling and burring the small copper part shown in Fig. 101. The part had an anticipated yearly activity of 24,000 pieces. At a labor rate of $1 per hour, the yearly labor cost was $2.40 per .0001 hour.

The designer sketched and analyzed four different jigs before he selected the one to build. It was not necessarily the best one which could be designed but was considerably better than the first one which was considered.

The tool designer first thought of a box jig holding one piece. He visualized boring the large hole on the second spindle of a No. 3 Avey sensitive drill press, the only machine available. The two small holes would be drilled on the first spindle. He mentally placed a positioning bar at the rear of the drill-press table to help locate the jig under the first two spindles. The jig was to be a box jig with a cover held down by a thumb nut. Two locators would be necessary to hold the part securely

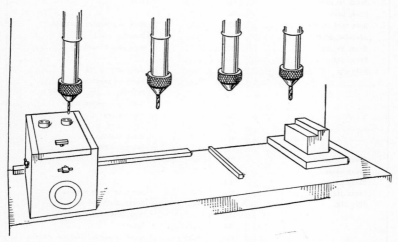

Fig. 102.— Sketch of contemplated drilling setup for part shown in Fig. 101.

in the jig; these would be thumbscrews tightened by hand. The burring operation, he thought, could best be done outside the jig. He visualized a special block clamped permanently under the fourth spindle of the drill press on which the part could be held by hand while burring.

As the tool designer developed this method in his mind, he roughly sketched it on paper. His finished sketch is shown by Fig. 102. With the general setup visualized, he next proceeded to think through the method, which he recorded on Methods Analysis Chart, Fig. 103. The methods-time data provided time standards for everything but machine time, which he obtained from drill-press data charts furnished him by the methods department. His computations and estimates at length showed him that by spending $100 for tooling, the job could be done for an each-piece time of .0125 hour.

After studying over his figures and his Methods Analysis Charts briefly, it occurred to the tool designer that a jig designed to hold two parts might prove more economical to handle than a jig holding only one

METHODS ANALYSIS CHART						
PART Copper Block DEPT. 181 - A DWG. 623402 ITEM 1						
OPERATION Bore, drill and burr - 1st Method DATE August 6, 1946						
DESCRIPTION--LEFT HAND	✓	NO.	CLASS	TMU'S	DEC. HRS. ÷ 100	✓	DESCRIPTION--RIGHT HAND
PLACE PART IN JIG AND SECURE						
Reach to part	✓		R24C	22.5		Idle
Grasp part	✓		G4	8.7		
Move part to right hand	✓		M24B	20.6		Move to grasping position
Transfer grasp	✓		G3	5.6	✓	Transfer grasp
Reach to jig	✓		R8B	10.1		Move part toward jig
Grasp jig	✓		G1a	1.7		
Hold jig			M4C	7.3	✓	Move part to jig
			P2NSD	27.2	✓	Position part in jig
			RL1	1.7	✓	Release
			R4A	6.1	✓	Reach to locator screw
			G1a	1.7	✓	Grasp screw
			T90S	5.4	✓	Turn screw
			AP	16.2	✓	Final tighten
			RL1	1.7	✓	Release screw
Reach to cover	✓		R3A	5.6		Idle
Grasp cover	✓		G5	0		
Close cover	✓		M6A	8.1		
Grasp jig			R4A	6.1	✓	Reach to thumb nut
Hold jig			G1a	1.7	✓	Grasp thumb nut
			T90S	5.4	✓	Turn thumb nut
			RL1	1.7	✓	Release
			R4A	6.1	✓	Reach to second locator screw
			G1a	1.7	✓	Grasp screw
			T90S	5.4	✓	Turn screw
			AP	16.2	✓	Final tighten
			RL1	1.7	✓	Release screw
METHODS ENGINEERING COUNCIL FORM NO. 117			TOTALS	196.2	.00227	SHEET NO. 1 OF 5 SHEETS

FIG. 103.— Methods Analysis Chart—"bore, drill, and burr small copper part—first method."

part. He could visualize such a jig clearly without sketching, for it would be only an enlargement of his first design with two cavities and four locating screws. The Methods Analysis Chart that he drew up,

Fig. 104, showed that he was progressing in the right direction, for, although the tooling cost was increased to $130, the each-piece time was reduced to .0091 hour.

METHODS ANALYSIS CHART

PART Copper Block

OPERATION Bore, drill and burr - 1st Method

DEPT. 181 - A   DWG. 623402   ITEM 1

DATE August 6, 1946

DESCRIPTION--LEFT HAND	√	NO.	CLASS	TMU'S	DEC. HRS. + 15%	√	DESCRIPTON--RIGHT HAND
LUBRICATE DRILL AND COUNTERBORE							
Idle							
			R18B	17.2		√	Reach to brush in lubricant
							container
			G1a	1.7		√	Grasp brush
		1	M16E	15.8		√	Scrape off surplus lubricant
							(4" motion)
			M12B	13.4		√	Move to first spindle
			M4E	6.9		√	Apply lubricant
			M14B	14.6		√	Move to second spindle
			M4E	6.9		√	Apply lubricant
			M16B	15.8		√	Move brush to container
			RL1	1.7		√	Release brush
				94.0	.00108		
DRILL 2 .257" HOLES							
Move jig under spindle 10"			R24B	21.5		√	Reach to spindle lever
			G5	0		√	Grasp
			M18B	17.0		√	Lower spindle
Position jig under drill	√		P2SE	13.3			Hold spindle
Hole jig			M4C	7.3		√	Lower spindle
			G2	5.6		√	Regrasp spindle lever
				34.7		√	Drill
Move jig ½"			M12E	13.4		√	Raise spindle
			M4B	6.9		√	Lower spindle
Position jig under drill	√		P2SE	13.3			
Hold jig			M4C	7.3		√	Lower spindle
			G2	5.6		√	Regrasp spindle lever
				34.7		√	Drill
			M26A	24.0		√	Raise spindle
			RL1	1.7		√	Release
			R24A	14.9		√	Reach to jig
				221.2	.00254		

1
The motion of scraping surplus lubricant off brush is performed more slowly than a normal
Move. Therefore, although the motion is only 4" in length, time for a 16" motion is
allowed.

METHODS ENGINEERING COUNCIL
FORM NO. 117

TOTALS

SHEET NO. 2 of 5 SHEETS

FIG. 103. (Continued)—Methods Analysis Chart—"bore, drill, and burr small copper part—first method."

Some searching study of the second method showed that an improvement might result if two fixtures with quick-acting clamps were provided, one under each of the first two spindles. This would eliminate the movable drill jig and might reduce handling time. The idea was investigated with the aid of a Methods Analysis Chart, which is not here reproduced. It was found that no gain in time had been made, for the

DESCRIPTION--LEFT HAND	√	NO.	CLASS	TMU'S	DEC. HRS. + 15%	√	DESCRIPTION--RIGHT HAND
METHODS ANALYSIS CHART							
PART Copper Block DEPT. 181 - A DWG. 623402 ITEM 1							
OPERATION Bore, drill and burr - 1st Method DATE August 6, 1946							
TURN JIG, MOVE TO SECOND							
SPINDLE, AND COUNTERBORE							
			G1a	1.7		√	Grasp jig
Turn jig 90°			T90S	5.4		√	Turn jig 90°
Grasp jig			RL1	1.7		√	Release
Slide jig to second spindle			R24B	21.5		√	Reach to second spindle lever
			G5	0		√	Grasp
			M18B	17.0		√	Lower spindle
Position jig under counter-			P2SE	13.3			Hold spindle
bore							
Hold jig			M4C	7.3		√	Lower spindle
			G2	5.6		√	Regrasp
				43.3		√	Counterbore
			M20A	19.2		√	Raise spindle
Release			RL1	1.7		√	Release
Reach to locator screw			R24A	14.9		√	Reach to jig
				152.6	.001756		
REMOVE PART FROM JIG AND LAY							
ASIDE							
Grasp locator screw			G1a	1.7			Grasp thumb nut
Apply Pressure			AP	16.2			
Turn locator screw			T90S	5.4		√	Turn thumb nut
Release			RL1	1.7		√	Release
Reach to cover	√		R6B	8.6			
Grasp cover	√		G1a	1.7			'
Open cover	√		M6A	8.1			Reach to second locator screw
Hold jig by cover			G1a	1.7		√	Grasp screw
			AP	16.2		√	Apply Pressure
			T90S	5.4		√	Turn locator screw
			RL1	1.7		√	Release
			R6B	8.6		√	Reach to part in jig
			G1a	1.7		√	Grasp
			D1E	4.0		√	Disengage part from jig
			M18D	14.2		√	Move part aside
				96.9	.001114		
METHODS ENGINEERING COUNCIL FORM NO. 117			TOTALS				SHEET NO. 3 OF 5 SHEETS

FIG. 103. (Continued)—Methods Analysis Chart—"bore, drill, and burr small copper part—first method."

each-piece time was the same as for method 2, or .0091 hour. The tool cost, however, was reduced to an estimated $100, which was an improvement over the second method.

The quick-acting clamps on the fixtures suggested the possibility of improving the clamping means used in the box jig. An improved box jig holding two pieces was therefore sketched. It was also thought that

METHODS ANALYSIS CHART

PART Copper Block   **DEPT.** 181 - A   **DWG.** 623402   **ITEM** 1

OPERATION Bore, drill and burr - 1st Method   **DATE** August 6, 1946

DESCRIPTION--LEFT HAND	✓	NO.	CLASS	TMU'S	DEC. HRS. ± 13%	✓	DESCRIPTON--RIGHT HAND
BRUSH CHIPS FROM TABLE							
Slide jig to first spindle			R18B	17.2		✓	Reach for brush
			G1a	1.7		✓	Grasp brush
		5	M12E	67.0		✓	Brush chips from table
			M24B	20.6		✓	Move brush aside
			RL1	1.7			Release brush
				108.2	.00124		
Note: This completes drill and counterbore cycle. When a number of drilled parts have been							
accumulated, operator moves to 4th spindle and burrs both sides of the two .257" holes.							
PICK UP PART							
Reach to part	✓		R6C	10.1			Hold spindle lever
Grasp part	✓		G4	8.7			
Move toward burring block	✓		M8E	10.6			
Regrasp	✓		G2	5.6			
Turn	✓		T90S	5.4			
Regrasp	✓		G2	5.6			
Move to burring block	✓		M4C	7.3			
Position on burring block	✓		P1NSE	10.8			
				64.1	.000738		

METHODS ENGINEERING COUNCIL FORM NO. 117   **TOTALS**   SHEET NO. 4 OF 5 SHEETS

FIG. 103. (*Continued*)—Methods Analysis Chart—"bore, drill, and burr small copper part—first method."

it might be quicker to burr the parts while they were still in the jig rather than to handle them a second time. Provision for this was made accordingly in the jig design. When the fourth method was analyzed,

it was found that an each-piece time of .0075 hour had been achieved
for a total cost of $130.

METHODS ANALYSIS CHART

PART... Copper Block   DEPT... 181 - A   DWG. 623402   ITEM 1
OPERATION Bore, drill and burr - 1st Method   DATE   August 6, 1946

DESCRIPTION--LEFT HAND	✓	NO.	CLASS	TMU'S	DEC. HRS. + 15%	✓	DESCRIPTION--RIGHT HAND
BURR TWO HOLES BOTH SIDES							
AND LAY ASIDE							
		2	M4C	14.6		✓	Lower spindle
Position part under spindle	✓	2	P1SE	11.2			
		2		6.9		✓	Burr
		2	M4E	13.8		✓	Raise spindle
Move part ¼"		2	M4C	14.6		✓	Lower spindle
Position part under spindle	✓	2	P1SE	11.2			
		2		6.9			Burr
		2	M4E	13.8		✓	Raise spindle
Move part away from block	✓		M4E	6.9			Hold spindle
Regrasp	✓		G2	5.6			
Turn	✓		T180S	9.4			
Regrasp	✓		G2	5.6			
Move part to burring block	✓		M4C	7.3			
Position on burring block	✓		P1NSE	10.8			
Move part aside	✓		M8B	10.6			
Release	✓		RL1	1.7			
				150.9	.001738		

METHODS ENGINEERING COUNCIL
FORM NO. 117   TOTALS   SHEET NO. 5 OF 5 SHEETS

FIG. 103. *(Continued)*—Methods Analysis Chart—"bore, drill, and burr small copper
part—first method."

With each suggested improvement showing successively smaller
returns, it was decided to stop at this point and to select the best of the
four methods to use. As pointed out above, this does not mean that the
ultimate had been achieved, but merely that the tool designer at that

time had no additional ideas which he felt were worthy of further consideration.

METHODS ANALYSIS CHART

PART __Copper Block__   DEPT. __181 - A__   DWG. __623402__   ITEM __1__
OPERATION __Bore, drill and burr - 2nd Method__   DATE   __August 6, 1946__

DESCRIPTION--LEFT HAND	√	NO.	CLASS	TMU'S	DEC. HRS. + 15%	√	DESCRIPTON--RIGHT HAND
PLACE 2 PARTS IN JIG AND							
SECURE							
Reach to parts			R30C	26.7		√	Reach to parts
Grasp part	√		G4	8.7		√	Grasp part
Move part to jig	√		M24C	25.5		√	Move part to jig
Position part in jig	√	2	P2NSD	54.4		√	Position part in jig
Release	√		RL1	1.7		√	Release
Reach to locator screw	√		R6B	8.6		√	Reach to locator screw
Grasp screw	√		G1a	1.7		√	Grasp screw
Turn screw	√		T90S	5.4		√	Turn screw
Final tighten	√		AP	16.2		√	Final tighten
Release screw	√		RL1	1.7		√	Release screw
Reach to cover	√		R6B	8.6			Idle
Grasp cover	√		G5	0			
Close cover	√		M6C	9.7			
Grasp jig			R4A	6.1		√	Reach to thumb nut
Hold jig			G1a	1.7		√	Grasp thumb nut
			T90S	5.4		√	Turn thumb nut
Release jig			RL1	1.7		√	Release
Reach to second locator	√		R4B	7.1		√	Reach to second locator screw
screw							
Grasp screw	√		G1a	1.7		√	Grasp screw
Turn screw	√		T90S	5.4		√	Turn screw
Final tighten	√		AP	16.2		√	Final tighten
Release screw	√		RL1	1.7		√	Release screw
				215.9	.00248		
LUBRICATE DRILL AND COUNTER-							
BORE							
Same as Method #1							
METHODS ENGINEERING COUNCIL FORM NO. 117		TOTALS					SHEET NO. 1 OF 3 SHEETS

Fig. 104.— Methods Analysis Chart—"bore, drill, and burr small copper part—second method."

SUMMARY OF FINDINGS

With tool costs, each-piece time, and yearly labor cost per .0001 hour known, a simple summary of these figures serves to indicate the best method to use since all methods contemplate using the same machine. The summary is as follows:

Method	Tool cost	Each-piece time	Yearly labor cost	Total tool and yearly labor cost
1	$100	.0125	$300.00	$400.00
2	130	.0091	218.40	348.40
3	100	.0091	218.40	318.40
4	130	.0075	180.00	310.00

METHODS ANALYSIS CHART

PART Copper Block   DEPT. 181 - A   DWG. 623402   ITEM 1

OPERATION Bore, drill and burr - 2nd Method   DATE August 6, 1946

DESCRIPTION--LEFT HAND	√	NO.	CLASS	TMU'S	DEC. HRS.	√	DESCRIPTION--RIGHT HAND
DRILL 4 .257" HOLES							
Move jig under spindle			R24B	21.5		√	Reach to spindle lever
			G5	0		√	Grasp
			M18B	17.0		√	Lower spindle
Position jig under drill	√	4	P2SE	53.2			Hold spindle
Hold jig		4	M4C	29.2		√	Lower spindle
		4	G2	22.4		√	Regrasp spindle lever
		4		138.8		√	Drill
Move jig ½"		3	M12E	40.2		√	Raise spindle
		3	M4B	20.7		√	Lower spindle
			M26A	24.0		√	Raise spindle
			RL1	1.7		√	Release
			R24A	14.9			Reach to jig
				383.6	.00441		
TURN JIG, MOVE TO SECOND							
SPINDLE, AND COUNTERBORE							
2 HOLES							
			G1a	1.7		√	Grasp jig
Turn jig 90°			T90S	5.4		√	Turn jig 90°
Grasp jig			RL1	1.7		√	Release
Slide jig to second spindle			R24B	21.5		√	Reach to second spindle lever
			G5	0		√	Grasp
			M18B	17.0		√	Lower spindle
Position jig under							
counterbore	√	2	P2SE	26.6			Hold spindle
		2	M4C	14.6		√	Lower spindle
		2	G2	11.2		√	Regrasp
		2		86.8			Counterbore
Move jig 3"			M8E	10.6		√	Raise spindle
			M4B	6.9		√	Lower spindle
			M20A	19.2		√	Raise spindle
Release			RL1	1.7		√	Release
Reach to locator screw			R24A	14.9		√	Reach to jig
				239.8	.00276		

METHODS ENGINEERING COUNCIL FORM NO. 117   TOTALS   SHEET NO. 2 OF 3 SHEETS

FIG. 104. (*Continued*)—Methods Analysis Chart—"bore, drill, and burr small copper part—second method."

SELECTION OF METHOD

There are several factors which must be considered before the method which is to be used is selected. Method 4 gives the lowest total yearly

---

METHODS ANALYSIS CHART

PART __Copper Block__ DEPT. __181 - A__ DWG. __623402__ ITEM __1__

OPERATION __Bore, drill and burr - 2nd Method__ DATE __August 6, 1946__

DESCRIPTION--LEFT HAND	√	NO.	CLASS	TMU'S	DEC. HRS. ÷ 1.25%	√	DESCRIPTION--RIGHT HAND
REMOVE PARTS FROM JIG AND							
LAY ASIDE							
Grasp locator screw	√		G1a	1.7		√	Grasp locator screw
Apply pressure	√		AP	16.2		√	Apply pressure
Turn locator screw	√		T90S	5.4		√	Turn locator screw
Release	√		RL1	1.7		√	Release
Move to jig cover			R6B	8.6		√	Reach to thumb nut
Grasp cover			G1a	1.7		√	Grasp thumb nut
			T90S	5.4		√	Turn thumb nut
			RL1	1.7		√	Release
Open cover	√		M6A	8.1			
Release cover	√		RL1	1.7			
Reach to second locator screw	√		R6B	8.6			Reach to second locator screw
Grasp locator screw	√		G1a	1.7		√	Grasp locator screw
Apply pressure	√		AP	16.2		√	Apply pressure
Turn locator screw	√		T90S	5.4		√	Turn locator screw
Release	√		RL1	1.7		√	Release
Reach to part in jig	√		R6B	8.6		√	Reach to part in jig
Grasp	√		G1a	1.7		√	Grasp
Disengage part from jig	√		D1E	4.0		√	Disengage part from jig
Move part aside	√		M20D	15.6			Move part aside
				115.7	.00133		
BRUSH CHIPS FROM TABLE							
Same as Method #1							
PICK UP PART,							
BURR TWO HOLES BOTH SIDES							
AND LAY ASIDE							
Same as Method #1							

METHODS ENGINEERING COUNCIL FORM NO. 117   TOTALS   SHEET NO. __3__ OF __3__ SHEETS

FIG. 104. (*Continued*)—Methods Analysis Chart—"bore, drill, and burr small copper part—second method."

labor cost. If it is fairly certain that the job will continue for a year or more at the activity figure used, then this method should be selected. If, however, design changes are a possibility, then the method that involves the lowest tool cost would probably be preferable. Method 3 costs only a total of $8.40 more than method 4 if the job lasts a year, and if it runs out sooner, the lower tool cost would be in its favor. On the other hand, if the job lasts more than a year, the lower each-piece cost definitely favors method 4, since after tool costs have been amortized, the each-piece cost is greatly in favor of this method.

In some cases, the number of pieces produced per hour will be important. This is particularly true in progressive manufacturing setups that run continuously. If a production of 100 pieces per hour is required and the least expensive method yields a production of only 90 pieces per hour, it will probably be better from an over-all standpoint to provide more costly tooling to obtain the 100 pieces rather than to call for two machines that would then run only part time. In any event, it should be recognized that all the factors surrounding the operation should be considered before the selection is made.

APPLICATION OF THE PRINCIPLE OF THE MOST ECONOMICAL METHOD

Because the same machine would be used for all four methods considered, a simple summary of findings as given above is sufficient to determine which is the best method. If different machines were used, it would be necessary to use the formula developed in Chapter 22 to determine which method was the best, all costs being considered.

It is interesting to note how the figures change in the case just discussed when the full formula is applied. The complete factors to be taken into account are as follows:

Number of years allowed by accounting department for machine cost amortization	A_m	13.5
Number of years allowed by accounting department for tool and fixture amortization	A_t	1
Number of hours per year that machine normally operates	C	1,600
Labor cost in dollars per hour	L	$1
Cost of machine including motors and installation	M	$1,650
Yearly activity of part	R	24,000
Cost of tooling, jigs, and fixtures specially required for operation	$T1$	$100
	$T2$	$130
	$T3$	$100
	$T4$	$130
Each-piece time allowed for method contemplated	$TA\,1$	.0125
	$TA\,2$	.0091
	$TA\,3$	.0091
	$TA\,4$	.0075

Substituting these figures in the formula

$$\frac{T}{A_t} + TA \times R\left(L + \frac{M}{A_m C}\right)$$

for each of the four methods, the following total yearly costs are obtained:

Method 1	$422.50
Method 2	365.00
Method 3	335.00
Method 4	323.75

Thus it may be seen that when machine cost is considered as well as tool and labor cost, the savings which result from reducing the each-piece time become greater. This is because the number of hours needed to do the job are reduced, and hence machine cost chargeable to the job is reduced, assuming of course that other work will be provided for the machine to do.

CHAPTER 26

APPLICATION OF METHODS-TIME
STANDARDS TO OFFICE METHODS

Methods development and the improvement of office procedures, although recognized as being worth while from both a cost and a service standpoint, have generally been neglected in favor of the more obvious improvements that can be made on shop operations. Furthermore, time study and wage incentives have been infrequently applied to office work, and hence time values with which a comparison of costs of various methods can be made are lacking. Because of the fact that it is unusual, it is often difficult to obtain permission to take time studies of office personnel.

Many opportunities for improving office methods exist, however, which can be realized when the objections to stop-watch time study are avoided by the use of the methods-time measurement procedure. The following cases are typical of those which lend themselves to improvement when analyzed with the aid of the methods-time data.

OFFICE AND DESK ARRANGEMENTS

The methods-time measurement procedure has been used successfully for determining the most effective desk arrangement for a given set of conditions. A typical case occurred in a large concern, which had undertaken a program of office methods improvement. It was noted during the program that key personnel were often interrupted by the ringing of the telephone. Upon answering, they frequently found the call was for another person seated at an adjacent desk with no telephone facilities. The person called was then forced to arise, walk to the phone, complete the call, and return to the desk. The work and train of thought of two individuals were interrupted until the call was completed.

The first step in seeking improvement was to make a layout of five possible combinations into which four desks, with one telephone, could be arranged, four being the maximum number of persons and desks serviced by one telephone. The five layouts are shown by Fig. 105.

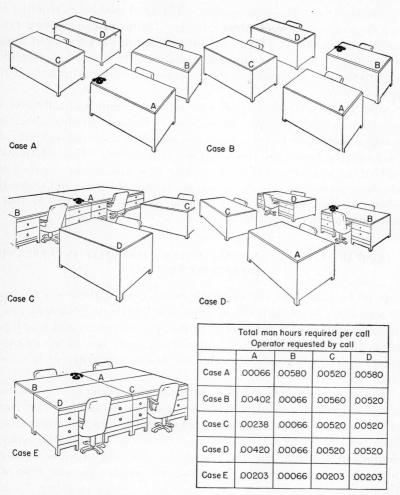

	Total man hours required per call Operator requested by call			
	A	B	C	D
Case A	.00066	.00580	.00520	.00580
Case B	.00402	.00066	.00560	.00520
Case C	.00238	.00066	.00520	.00520
Case D	.00420	.00066	.00520	.00520
Case E	.00203	.00066	.00203	.00203

FIG. 105.— Alternative layouts of four desks and one telephone.

A motion-by-motion breakdown was made of the operations performed by all people involved when an incoming call was received, and the methods-time data were applied. The total man-hours required for each type of call for each arrangement, exclusive of conversation time, was thus determined. The results are recorded in the lower right corner of Fig. 105. The vertical columns contain the time in hours expended by both the person called and the person who answered for each of the layouts.

After the table was developed, a record of the number of calls received by each individual was kept. By multiplying the number of calls received in a given period by the man-hours consumed for each call, as shown by the table, the total time consumed was determined. This information enabled the analyst to determine on what desk and in what location the telephone should be placed, who should occupy the desk, and where the others involved in using the telephone should be located so that a minimum of time would be consumed by telephone calls.

COMPARING DIAL AND MANUALLY OPERATED INTERPLANT TELEPHONE SYSTEMS

In all types of work and especially in office work, there is a tendency to accept as a permanent fixture upon which little improvement can be made equipment which has been in use for many years and which performs its functions satisfactorily. This is especially true of service equipment, such as filing cabinets, reference books, typewriter desks, chairs, etc.

The case of the telephone is an interesting example. It has been accepted for years (and rightly so) as one of the quickest and best means of communicating between two locations. Little thought, however, may have been given to determining the differences between the types of equipment available and the savings in time and in money and the increased service that may be gained by supplanting one type with the other.

In an office which was very methods conscious, a comparison between a manually operated system where each interplant call was made through a switchboard operator and a dial system where the number desired could be obtained directly by dialing was made by use of the methods-time measurement procedure. The time required from the start of the call to the moment the phone of the person called begins to ring was worked out for the manually operated system as follows:

ACTIVITY DESCRIPTION

Get telephone, request number, and await completion of call.

Caller activity, description	Operator activity, description	Symbol	Time, TMU
Reach for telephone 28 inches		$R28B$	24.4
Grasp telephone		$G1a$	1.7
Move receiver 28 inches to ear		$M28C$	29.0
Position receiver to ear		$P1SE$	5.6
Await operator's response — idle			
	Hear buzzer and see light on switchboard	Est.	17.3
	Reach 16 inches to plug with right hand	$R16C$	17.0
	Grasp plug	$G4$	8.7
	Raise plug 16 inches	$M16E$	15.8
	Regrasp plug	$G2$	5.6
	Move plug to answering jack	$M10C$	13.5
	Position to jack	$P2SE$	13.3
	Turn key to answering position left hand	$T90$	5.4
	Request number verbally	Est.	17.3
Give number	Await number	Est.	17.3
Idle	Acknowledge number	Est.	17.3
	Reach 16 inches for associated plug right hand	$R16C$	17.0
	Grasp plug	$G4$	8.7
	Raise plug 16 inches	$M16E$	15.8
	Regrasp plug	$G2$	5.6
	Move plug to jack of called station	$M10C$	13.5
	Position to jack	$P2SE$	13.3
	Turn ringing key three times left hand	$T90 \times 3$	16.2
Total			299.3

	Time, TMU
Caller	299.3
Operator	238.6
Total	537.9

The time to make the call on a dial phone was computed as follows:

ACTIVITY DESCRIPTION

Dial three-number telephone station.

Motion description	Symbol	Time, TMU
Reach for telephone 28 inches with right hand as left hand reaches to dial	R28B	24.4
Grasp telephone	G1a	1.7
Move telephone 28 inches to ear	M28C	29.0
Position to ear	P1SE	5.6
Hear dial signal	Est.	17.3
Insert finger in dial number 3	P1SE	5.6
Dial number 3	M2A	3.6
Move finger 3 inches to release dial	R3E	6.3
Reach 4 inches to dial number 6	R5C	9.4
Insert finger in dial	P1SE	5.6
Dial number 6	M5A	7.3
Move finger 3 inches to release dial	R3E	6.3
Move finger to number 9	R5C	9.4
Insert finger in dial	P1SE	5.6
Dial number 9	M7A	8.9
Move finger 3 inches to release dial	R3E	6.3
Await electric connection to ring called station	Est.	48.6
Total		200.9

When these time values were applied to the volume of calls being made in the business where this study was conducted, the following reduction in man-hours per week was found to be possible as the result of installing a dial system.

SUMMARY

	Time required manual system, hours	Time required dial system, hours	Savings per 1,000 calls, hours
Elapsed time per call	.0030	.0020	1.0
Man-hours expended per call	.0054	.0020	3.4

Number of stations... 46
Average number of weekly calls per station........................ 150
Average number of calls made weekly.............................. 6,900
Weekly savings in man-hours expected............................. 23.46

COST COMPARISON OF FILING SYSTEMS

The methods-time measurement procedure may be used to determine whether the purchase and use of new office equipment will result in savings sufficient to cover the cost of such equipment.

A case of this sort involved the operation of filing and referring to tool-control records. It was suggested that the existing form which was kept in a drawer-type filing cabinet might be abandoned in favor of a small card that could be filed in a small drawer file to be kept on the clerk's desk. The form was prepared and found satisfactory. A thought was expressed, however, that the cost of retyping the existing records would more than offset the savings to be gained by reducing the time for filing and referring to the new form. To determine whether or not the proposed change was justified, the times consumed by the existing method and the proposed method of filing and referring were determined by the methods-time measurement procedure. Tabulations of the number of records filed and the number of references made to the file during a week were made, and the time saved by the new method was determined. The time for retyping the complete file was similarly determined and an accurate comparison was made, based on yearly activity. The results showed that it would be well worth while to make the contemplated change.

CHAPTER 27

TIME-FORMULA DERIVATION FROM METHODS-TIME STANDARDS

Where it is necessary to establish a large number of time standards on a variety of similar jobs in a given class of work, time-study men have long found it desirable to compile standard data or time formulas. With the aid of time formulas, it is possible to establish accurate and consistent time standards in from 1 to 15 minutes, whereas it would require from half an hour to several days to establish time values on the same jobs by individual time study. The time-formula derivation procedure has been fully described elsewhere.[1] It will be assumed, therefore, that the reader has an understanding of the derivation and use of time formulas and recognizes their very real value as a means of handling the standards-setting problem.

ADVANTAGES OF TIME-FORMULA DERIVATION FROM METHODS-TIME STANDARDS

The conventional method of deriving a time formula is by the use of time-study data. Time studies are made of representative jobs scattered through the range of jobs to be covered by the formula. Each job is divided into elements for study purposes, and an attempt is made to use the same division points on all time studies. The elemental data thus obtained are then posted on a Master Table of Detail Time Studies. Constant and variable elements are identified and the time for performing them is determined. Elements are combined where possible, and finally a formula expression is developed that expresses the time required to do a given job in a given class of work in terms of the variable characteristics of the work, such as size, shape, or weight of part, etc. To make the steps followed in the derivation of the formula and the manner in which it is to be applied a matter of record, a formula report is prepared which gives this information. The whole process requires from

[1] LOWRY, MAYNARD, and STEGEMERTEN, "Time and Motion Study and Formulas for Wage Incentives," Chaps. XXIV–XXXV, McGraw-Hill Book Company, Inc., 1940.

246

a few days to several months, depending upon the nature and the complexity of the work.

The methods-time measurement procedure offers a somewhat easier way of developing time-formula data than the method just described. Instead of determining element times by time study and building up a time formula from them, the element times can be determined with much greater emphasis on method from the methods-time data. The emphasis on method is important, for in the formula-derivation procedure based on time study, it is often found that the time data collected for a given element are unexplainably inconsistent. If the same beginning and ending points were used in timing the element on all jobs and if the leveling procedure for making adjustments for differences in performance was properly applied, then the inconsistent data can only be attributed to differences in method. Because no really complete record of method is usually made during conventional time study, it cannot be known just what the differences in method were. Hence, it is difficult to come to sound conclusions as to what time values should and should not be admitted for use in the derivation of the formula.

When the methods-time measurement approach is used, a complete record of the method of performing each element must be made before the allowed time can be derived. This not only serves to ensure that elemental data will be developed consistently, but it does much to prevent formulas from getting out of line as conditions change. By revising the time for elements as methods and conditions change—something which can be done easily and quickly with the methods-time data—the accuracy of time formulas can be readily maintained.

TIME-FORMULA DERIVATION PROCEDURE USING METHODS-TIME DATA

The procedure for deriving a time formula by the use of methods-time data will be described and illustrated by presenting a typical example. The example covers the operation of small punch presses. A methods engineer, observing the wide variety of work done in the small punch-press department of a certain plant, decided that it would be useful to have a time formula covering the work. He decided to derive the formula from methods-time data instead of time studies.

His first step was to observe the work and to subdivide the operation into logical elements. He noted first of all that there were two types of presses, bench presses with a stroke of $1\frac{1}{2}$ inches and floor presses with a stroke of $1\frac{1}{2}$ to 4 inches. The time for making a stroke on each type of machine he checked with a stop watch, for the methods-time data, of course, do not cover mechanically controlled operations.

On either type of press, there were two general types of operations, one where the ejection of the completed part was automatic and the other where the completed part was removed by hand. The methods engineer then listed the elements which occurred on each type of operation, classified them as constants or variables after observation of the methods employed, and listed the factors which seemed to affect the variable elements. The information that he compiled was as follows:

AUTOMATIC EJECTION

Element description	Classification	Influencing factor
Move part to die	Constant	
Place part in die	Variable	Symmetry
Withdraw hand	Constant	
Trip press (get part from left hand while press is operating)	Variable	Machine
Discard occasional bad part	Variable	Number of occurrences depends upon nature of part

HAND DISPOSAL

Element description	Classification	Influencing factor
Reach to part in left hand	Constant	
Grasp part	Constant	
Move part to die	Constant	
Place part in die	Variable	Symmetry
Withdraw hand	Constant	
Trip press	Variable	Machine
Reach to part in die	Constant	
Remove part from die	Variable	Fit of part in die
Toss part aside	Constant	
Discard occasional bad part	Variable	Number of occurrences depends upon nature of part

While these observations were being made, the methods engineer noticed several two-position dies which necessitated the performance of the following elements after the first tripping of the press, whether automatic ejection or hand disposal was used to dispose of the completed part.

Element description	Classification	Influencing factor
Move to part in die	Constant	
Remove part from die	Variable	Fit of part in die
Turn part	Constant	
Place in second position in die	Variable	Symmetry
Withdraw hand	Constant	
Trip press	Variable	Machine

The methods engineer made some sketches of typical workplace layouts, measured accurately the distances covered by typical Reaches and Moves, and jotted down the motion sequences in terms of the methods-time measurement procedure for several typical jobs. He then had all the data needed to derive his formula. It required slightly less than 1 day to obtain this information.

On the second day at his desk, the methods engineer completed the derivation of his formula. First he developed his formula expression for the case of automatic ejection. The variable elements he decided to handle by tables with the exception of "discard occasional bad part." Since the frequency with which this occurred depended on a host of factors, including kind of material, condition of material, nature of part, and condition of die, he felt this could be handled only by direct observation.

At first, he felt that a single constant would take care of all automatic-ejection work. Then he realized that there would be an extra Turn in the motion sequence for semisymmetrical and nonsymmetrical parts which would not be needed for symmetrical parts which can be placed in the die in any position in which they happened to be grasped. He, therefore, worked up the two Methods Analysis Charts, Figs. 106 and 107.

It appeared at first that two formula expressions would be necessary to handle these two cases due to the extra Turn in the second sequence. In the interests of simplification, it is always desirable to have as few formulas and terms in formulas as possible; therefore the methods engineer studied his data further. At length he saw that it would be possible to add the time for Turn to the time for Positioning semi- and non-symmetrical parts in Table I, since the Turn was always to be allowed for those cases of symmetry. This meant that these two sequences could then be handled by a single formula expression as follows:

.000412 + Table I + Table II + a value for discarding bad parts

Similar reasoning was followed in developing the rest of the formula. Because the explanation of the formula derivation is contained in the formula report below, no further elaboration need be made here.

METHODS ANALYSIS CHART						
PART_____			DEPT_____		DWG_____	ITEM_____
OPERATION_____ Automatic Ejection - Symmetrical Part					DATE___	
DESCRIPTION--LEFT HAND	√ NO.	CLASS	TMU'S	DEC. HRS. +15%	√	DESCRIPTON--RIGHT HAND
Hold part		R6A	7.0		√	Reach to part in L. H.
Release part		G3	5.6		√	Grasp part from L. H.
Move to parts bin		M6C	9.7		√	Move part to die
Move to parts bin		G2	5.6		√	Regrasp part
Grasp part in bin		Table I			√	Position part in die
Hold part		R6E	8.0		√	Move hand out of way
		Table II			√	Trip press
METHODS ENGINEERING COUNCIL FORM NO. 117		TOTALS	35.9	.000412		SHEET NO. 1 OF 1 SHEETS

Fig. 106.— Methods Analysis Chart—"motion sequence—automatic ejection—symmetrical part."

The formula was derived and the report written in 1 day. Thus the entire task of developing the formula was accomplished in 2 days. If the older approach had been followed of making a time study of a variety of jobs and then trying to develop a pattern from the elemental times thus obtained, it is probable that it would have required from

DESCRIPTION--LEFT HAND	√	NO.	CLASS	TMU'S	DEC. HRS.	√	DESCRIPTON--RIGHT HAND
			R6A	7.0		√	Reach to part in L. H.
			G3	5.6		√	Grasp part from L. H.
			T180S	9.4		√	Turn part
			M6C	9.7		√	Move part to die
			G2	5.6		√	Regrasp part
			Table I			√	Position part in die
			R6E	8.0		√	Move hand out of way
			Table II			√	Trip press

METHODS ANALYSIS CHART

PART_____ DEPT._____ DWG._____ ITEM_____

OPERATION__Automatic Ejection - Semi or Non-Symmetrical Part___ DATE_____

METHODS ENGINEERING COUNCIL FORM NO. 117   TOTALS 45.3 | .00052   SHEET NO. 1 OF 1 SHEETS

FIG. 107.— Methods Analysis Chart—"motion sequence—automatic ejection—semi- or nonsymmetrical part."

3 to 4 weeks to complete the formula. The time saving that the methods-time measurement procedure makes possible in formula-derivation work is thus readily apparent.

SMALL PUNCH-PRESS FORMULA REPORT

The complete formula report for the punch-press work, which was described above, follows:

Formula MTM No. 6

PART. All small parts up to approximately 3 inches in length.

OPERATION. Form, pierce, broach, bevel, cut, flatten, size, shear, straighten, swedge, and trim.

MATERIAL. Steel, copper, brass, bronze, or aluminum.

WORK STATION. Bench presses—1½-inch stroke—Baird Machine Co. No. 1. Floor presses—1½ to 4-inch stroke—Bliss No. 18C and 19½.

ALLOWED TIME.
Each-piece Time—One Position in Die.
Automatic Ejection:
    .000412 + Table I + Table II + .000319 N

Hand Disposal:
    .000568 + Table I + Table II + Table III + .000319 N

When Two Positions in Die Are Used.
Add to Above
    .000402 + Table I + Table II + Table III
where
    N = number of times per cycle imperfect part is discarded

TABLE I.— POSITION AND RELEASE

Class of fit	Easy to handle			Difficult to handle		
	Symm.	Semi-symm.	Non-symm.	Symm.	Semi-symm.	Non-symm.
1. Loose (no pressure required)	.000081	.000093	.000137	.000121	.000175	.000205
2. Close (light pressure required)	.000203	.000189	.000269	.000232	.000310	.000330
3. Exact (heavy pressure required)	.000469	.000522	.000628	.000576	.000616	.000631

Symmetrical. Object can be positioned in an infinite number of ways about the axis that coincides with the direction of travel.

Semisymmetrical. Object can be positioned in several ways about the axis that coincides with the direction of travel.

Nonsymmetrical. Object can be positioned in only one way about the axis that coincides with the direction of travel.

TABLE II.— MACHINE TIME PER STROKE

Type of Machine	Time, Dec. Hr.
Bench press	.000288
Floor press	.000384

TABLE III.— DISENGAGE PART FROM DIE

Class of fit	Easy to handle	Difficult to handle
1. Loose (very slight effort)	.000046	.000066
2. Close (normal effort)	.000086	.000136
3. Tight (considerable effort)	.000264	.000400

APPLICATION. This formula applies to all forming, piercing, broaching, beveling, cutting, flattening, sizing, shearing, swedging, and trimming work done on bench and floor presses in Department O-3 under conditions in effect on March 29, 1946, except where tweezers or other tools are used to place part in or remove part from die.

ANALYSIS. Operators are assigned jobs by the foreman. Dies are set up by setup man so as to be ready for use when operator is ready to change jobs. If, however, it is necessary for operator to wait, waiting time is allowed.

Operator receives instructions on how to do job from setup man. Material is brought to and removed from press by a move man.

Work is inspected periodically by a roving inspector. Piece count is determined by weighing, and it is checked against register on machine.

A maintenance man is responsible for oiling and maintaining presses in proper condition. He is also responsible for proper operation of safety devices.

Allowed-time formula expressions give values that represent the time required to perform the operation with average effort and average skill. An allowance of 15 per cent has been added to all time values to cover time lost due to fatigue and personal and unavoidable delays.

To establish a time value, it is necessary to ascertain if the part is symmetrical. semisymmetrical, or nonsymmetrical, the type of press used, whether or not automatic ejection is provided, the class of fit both when positioning part to and disassembling it from die (these may not be the same), and the frequency with which defective blanks or parts are encountered. If two positions in the die are used, it is necessary to determine the class of fit for assembling in both positions. This information can best be obtained by observing briefly the operation as it is being performed in the shop.

PROCEDURE.

Automatic Ejection. Move part to die, place part in die, withdraw hand, trip press (get part from left hand while press is operating), and discard occasional bad part.

Hand Disposal. Reach to part in left hand, grasp, move part to die, place part in die, withdraw hand, trip press, reach to part in die, remove part from die, toss part aside, and discard occasional bad part.

Two-Position Die. In addition to above, after first trip press, reach to part in die, remove part from die, turn part, place in second position in die, withdraw hand, trip press.

Method and Synthesis.

Methods Analysis Chart

Part_____Dept._____Dwg._____Item_____
Operation   Automatic Ejection—Symmetrical Part   Date_____

Description— left hand	√	No.	Class	TMU	Dec. hr. +15 per cent	√	Description— right hand
			R6A	7.0		√	Move to part in left hand
			G3	5.6		√	Grasp part from left hand
			M6C	9.7		√	Move part to machine
			G2	5.6		√	Regrasp part
			Table I			√	Position part on die
			R6E	8.0		√	Move hand out of way
			Table II			√	Machine time
Total				35.9	.00041		

Methods Analysis Chart

Part_____Dept._____Dwg._____Item_____
Operation   Automatic Ejection—Semi- or Nonsymmetrical Part   Date_____

Description— left hand	√	No.	Class	TMU	Dec. hr. +15 per cent	√	Description— right hand
Hold part			R6A	7.0		√	Move to part in left hand
Release part			G3	5.6		√	Grasp part
Move to parts in bin			T180°S	9.4		√	Turn part
			M6C	9.7		√	Move part to machine
Grasp part in bin			G2	5.6		√	Regrasp part for positioning
			Table I			√	Position part
			R6E	8.0		√	Move out of way
			Table II			√	Machine time
Total				45.3	.00052		

METHODS ANALYSIS CHART

Part_____Dept._____Dwg._____Item_____
Operation   Hand Disposal—Symmetrical Part   Date_____

Description—left hand	√	No.	Class	TMU	Dec. hr. +15 per cent	√	Description—right hand
Hold part			R6A	7.0		√	Reach to part in left hand
Release part			G3	5.6		√	Grasp part from left hand
Move to parts in bin			M6C	9.7		√	Move part to die
			G2	5.6		√	Regrasp part
Grasp part			Table I			√	Position part in die
Hold part			R6E	8.0		√	Move hand out of way
			Table II			√	Trip press
			R4A	6.1		√	Reach to part in die
			G1a	1.7		√	Grasp part
			Table III			√	Disengage part from die
			M6D	5.7		√	Toss part aside
Total				49.4	.000568		

METHODS ANALYSIS CHART

Part_____Dept._____Dwg._____Item_____
Operation   Additional Work Required to Discard Imperfect Part   Date_____

Description—left hand	√	No.	Class	TMU	Dec. hr. +15 per cent	√	Description—right hand
Hold part			R6A	7.0		√	Reach to part in left hand
Release part			G3	5.6		√	Grasp part from left hand
Move to parts in bin			T180S	9.4		√	Turn part
Grasp part			M6D	5.7		√	Toss part aside
Total				27.7	.000319		

METHODS ANALYSIS CHART

Part_____Dept._____Dwg._____Item_____
Operation   Hand Disposal—Semi- or Nonsymmetrical Part   Date_____

Description— left hand	√	No.	Class	TMU	Dec. hr. +15 per cent	√	Description— right hand
Hold part			R6A	7.0		√	Reach to part in left hand
Release part			G3	5.6		√	Grasp part from left hand
Move to parts in bin			T180S	9.4		√	Turn part
			M6C	9.7		√	Move part to die
			G2	5.6		√	Regrasp part
Grasp part			Table I			√	Position part in die
Hold part			R6E	8.0		√	Move hand out of way
			Table II			√	Trip press
			R4A	6.1		√	Reach to part in die
			G1a	1.7		√	Grasp part
			Table III			√	Disengage part from die
			M6D	5.7		√	Toss part aside
Total				58.8	.000676		

METHODS ANALYSIS CHART

Part_____Dept._____Dwg._____Item_____

Operation   Additional Work Required when Two Positions in   Date_____

Die Are Used

Description— left hand	√	No.	Class	TMU	Dec. hr. +15 per cent	√	Description— right hand
			R4A	6.1		√	Reach to part in die
			G1a	1.7		√	Grasp part
			Table III			√	Disengage part from die
			T180S	9.4		√	Turn part
			G2	5.6		√	Regrasp
			M2C	4.2		√	Move part to die
			Table I			√	Position part in die
			R6E	8.0		√	Move hand out of way
			Table II			√	Trip press
Total				35.0	.000402		

INSPECTION. Parts must be placed properly in die so that the operation of the press will form, pierce, trim, etc., the piece in accordance with the requirements of the job.

PAYMENT. This formula gives the time in decimal hours which are required to perform the various punch-press operations which it covers when the operator works with average skill and effort and follows the prescribed method. It contains a 15 per cent allowance for fatigue and personal and unavoidable delays. It may be used as a basis for standards for any wage-payment plan when adjusted in accordance with the requirements of the plan.

APPROVED.

CHAPTER 28

PROBLEM SOLVING WITH METHODS-TIME MEASUREMENT—ASSEMBLY PROCEDURES

Methods engineers and the procedures they use are sometimes subjected to severe criticism when incentive earnings rise beyond reasonable expectancy. Investigation usually shows, however, that the time allowances as originally established were sound for the methods used at the time the allowances were set. Because of lack of thoroughness in operation analysis, however, the methods were easy for the operators to improve upon. The inevitable results are earnings higher than were anticipated.

The effects of out-of-line earnings are usually disturbing. Some of the more serious effects are:

1. Administration of the wage incentive plan is complicated.
2. Morale is disturbed because of inconsistencies in earnings among operators.
3. Output is restricted in an attempt to avoid the reduction of time allowances.
4. Costs are irregular.
5. Costs are unnecessarily high, resulting in greater difficulty in meeting competition.

The list of the undesirable effects of unsound allowances could be extended at length. These, however, will suffice to show the importance of correct time standards. The methods-time measurement procedure appears to be the best approach developed to date to ensure greater soundness in time allowances.

The following description of a study made on various methods of performing assembly work will serve to demonstrate the thoroughness with which methods can be investigated with the aid of the methods-time measurement procedure.

REASONS FOR STUDY

Because of the fact that various procedures are used in manufacturing for the same class of assembly work with apparent satisfaction, a factual application of methods-time data was made to develop the advantages and disadvantages of several procedures. It was hoped that on the basis of this study it would be possible to define the conditions under which various procedures should be used.

The assembly procedures chosen for study were four in number. They were as follows:

1. Pallet assembly
2. Motion-economy bin assembly
3. Batch assembly
4. Progressive assembly

Several days were spent in general observation of various setups employing these different assembly procedures. It was then decided to select a single assembly and to compare the way it would be handled under each assembly procedure. The part selected was being assembled

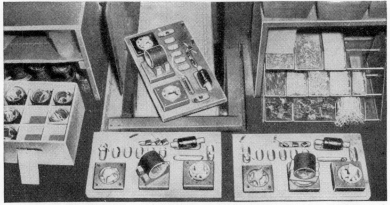

Fig. 108.— Work station in storeroom for loading pallets prior to delivering them to assemblers.

by the use of the pallet system. Because it was a fairly simple assembly, it was comparatively easy to determine by analysis and observation how the job would be done under each of the other three assembly methods.

Assembly procedures were drawn up for all four methods. The time for performing each element of each method was then determined with the aid of the methods-time data. In this way, a satisfactorily accurate comparison was obtained.

Finally, operators, supervisors, and management were questioned to determine their opinions on the relative merits of the procedures with which they were familiar. Their comments were recorded to be used in the summary of the results of the investigation.

DESCRIPTION OF METHODS INVESTIGATED

Pallet Assembly. Under the pallet assembly method, parts to be assembled are brought from the main storerooms to a matching-parts storeroom. A work station, Fig. 108, is provided at which pallets are loaded. Parts are supplied to this work station by a storekeeper. A girl then loads each pallet with all the material necessary to assemble one complete unit. Each part is placed in a definite location on the pallet. Each pallet contains one or more simple holding fixtures to facilitate assembly.

Loaded pallets are placed on a belt conveyor that conveys them to the assemblers. The assemblers remove them from the conveyor as needed. If the conveyor becomes too full, it may be stopped by the assemblers.

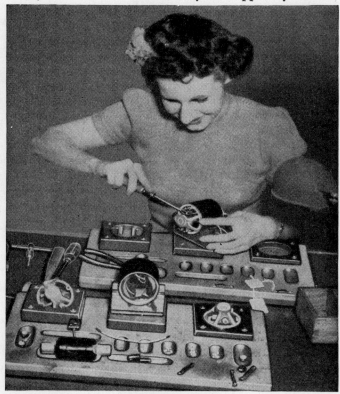

FIG. 109.— Pallet method of assembly where complete assembly operation is done on pallet.

The assembly is performed on the pallet, as shown by Fig. 109. Each operator makes a complete assembly. The final assembly is laid on the conveyor, which moves it to the inspector. If the operator spoils a part or is supplied with a defective part, the assembler calls to the pallet loader, who sends a replacement part down the conveyor. While awaiting its arrival, the assembler does other work, so that little time is lost.

Empty pallets are returned to the storeroom by a return conveyor running under the bench.

Motion-economy Bin Assembly. Under the motion-economy bin assembly method, all materials are grouped around the work station of the assembler in as great quantities as space permits. Materials are supplied direct from main storerooms by material handlers. They are stacked up around each assembler's work station. All small parts are kept in so-called "motion-economy bins." As materials are used up, they are replenished by the material handlers. Figure 110 illustrates a motion-economy bin setup.

Each operator performs the complete assembly. Completed assemblies are taken to inspection by conveyor if one is provided. Otherwise they must be carried away in boxes by material handlers.

Batch Assembly. Each operator using the batch assembly method is assigned a workbench or a large section of a workbench. Materials are supplied from the main storerooms by material handlers in large quantities. They may be placed in bins of the motion-economy type, as is shown by Fig. 111, but it is more common to leave them in their original containers.

In beginning to assemble, the operator will lay out a large number of the same kind of parts in a straight line along the bench. He will then lay a second part beside each first part. This will be repeated until all material is laid out or at least enough to perform a subassembly operation. He will then go along the line performing the same operation on each group of parts. This procedure will be repeated until all assemblies are finished. The completed assemblies will then be carried away for inspection. Because of the area occupied by this method, it is usually impractical to work seated. Hence, this must be considered as a job requiring constant standing and walking.

Progressive Assembly. Progressive work stations are set up along a bench or assembly line. The operation is begun at the first work station. The partly completed product is passed to a second work station where more work is performed. This is repeated until finally at the last work station the product emerges completely assembled.

Figure 112 shows one work station on a progressive assembly line. Material is supplied to the line from the main storerooms by material handlers. Finished assemblies are passed or taken by conveyor to an inspector stationed at the end of the line. Each operator on the line performs a portion of the assembly operation on every unit which goes down the line.

FINDINGS

It was recognized after preliminary analysis that none of the methods was going to prove superior to all the others in every respect. Therefore

Fig. 110.— Motion-economy bin setup.

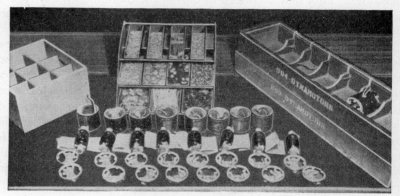

Fig. 111.— Batch assembly method.

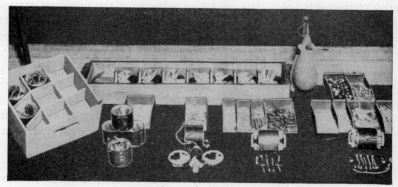

Fig. 112.—One work station on a progressive assembly line.

it was decided to compare the four methods on each of the following characteristics:

Material-handling cost
Direct labor cost
Setup cost
Quality
Degree of control of material
Operator satisfaction
Learning time
Departmental cleanliness
Control of piece count
Possibilities for special tooling
Effect of absenteeism on production
Floor space required

A description of the findings on each characteristic follows.

MATERIAL-HANDLING COST

Pallet Assembly. All materials are kept in a matching-parts storeroom located at the head of the pallet assembly line. A pallet-loading station is provided at the head end of the line. Convenient quantities of materials are arranged around the pallet-loading station. As materials are used up, the supply is replenished by a storeroom attendant from large containers of material kept in the matching-parts storeroom.

Pallets are loaded with material at the pallet-loading station. Time data showed that this required .0143 hour per pallet for the unit studied. This was the time charged to the pallet assembly method, although in most cases more time is consumed due to the fact that the storeroom operator was not required to load pallets continuously to keep up with the line. A line of six operators producing assemblies at the rate of .24 hour would require only $6 \times .0143 = .0858$ hour of pallet-loading labor. If one operator were assigned to the line, there would be idle time amounting to $.24 - .0858 = .1542$ hour per six assemblies. One operator could service two lines, but even then there would be a loss.

For purposes of comparison, only actual pallet-loading time of .0143 hour plus material-supplying time of .0013 hour, or a total of .0156 hour, was charged to the pallet method because proper layout and labor utilization would permit this figure to be approached. In all actual cases observed, however, the losses mentioned above were found to exist.

Motion-economy Bin Assembly. A matching-parts storeroom is not necessary when motion-economy bins are used. Computations were based on taking materials from regular storerooms to operators' benches. Time was allowed for distributing all materials to motion-economy bins at individual work stations and for replenishing material supplies when necessary. The time required per unit was found to be .0040 hour, about one-quarter of the time under the pallet assembly method.

Batch Assembly. It was assumed that material would be brought in quantities from the regular storerooms and distributed to the assembly benches in the original containers. This gave a material-handling time of .00225 hour, the lowest time of the four methods.

Progressive Assembly. Material-handling time for the progressive-assembly method compares favorably with the batch assembly method, but is slightly higher due to the necessity of supplying materials to containers and racks at the individual work station. Otherwise the supply procedure is the same in both cases. Material-handling time for the progressive assembly method was found to be .00256 hour per assembly.

In addition to the material handling of the materials used for assembly, the progressive assembly method requires the handling of materials from operator to operator, something not required under any other method. It was assumed that as each operator completed his work he would pass his partly completed assembly on to the next operator with a 30-inch Move. The time required for this assembly (4 Moves) was .00172 hour. Thus the total material-handling time chargeable to the progressive assembly method is .00256 + .00172, or .00428 hour per assembly.

DIRECT LABOR COST

Pallet Assembly. From the standpoint of direct assembly labor cost, the pallet assembly method is the best. All materials are furnished laid out in well-designed containers, and they may be obtained with short transport motions and simple grasps. In order to simplify direct labor-cost comparisons, only the motions that differed under the four different methods were compared. The time for performing each motion, however, was determined accurately from the methods-time data.

The pallet assembly method showed the lowest time for these motions, or .00427 hour. Because this figure by itself is meaningless, however, the labor for these motions for the pallet assembly method will be considered as zero, and the additional direct assembly labor above the pallet method will be shown for the other three methods.

Motion-economy Bin Assembly. For the motions which differed from those used for the pallet assembly method, the motion-economy bin assembly method was found to require .0035 hour more time. This was attributable largely to longer Moves and Reaches and to the presence of Search and Select when picking small parts out of motion-economy bins.

Batch Assembly. The batch assembly method requires walking up and down the line as parts are laid out on the table and afterwards. Practically every part must also be handled twice. As a result, this method requires .0075 hour more than the pallet assembly method.

Progressive Assembly. When a given assembly is worked on by several operators instead of being completed by one operator, a number of extra "pick ups" and "lay asides" are required. For this reason, the progressive assembly method requires .0043 hour more than the pallet assembly method. This assumes perfect balance among operations, which in practice is seldom obtained. A minimum loss of 5 per cent due to lack of balance can be assumed for progressive assembly setups.

SETUP COST

Pallet Assembly. The pallet assembly method requires a matching-parts storeroom at the head of the line to facilitate loading the pallets with material and a conveyor to take the loaded pallets to the operators and to return the empty pallets to the storeroom. It is also necessary to provide enough pallets so that each operator always has work ahead. These factors make the setup cost for the pallet assembly method higher than for any of the other methods. The total setup cost is as follows:

Conveyor	$321.00
Matching-parts storeroom	197.00
Pallets	78.00
Six sets, hand tools	52.50
Total	$648.50

Motion-economy Bin Assembly. If it is assumed that benches are available, all that is needed to set up for motion-economy bin assembly is one set of motion-economy bins and one set of hand tools for each operator. A conveyor may be used to take complete assemblies to the inspector. Because this requires only .0005 hour per assembly when done by a material handler, the expense of a conveyor would not be justified for the amount of activity assumed for this analysis. The cost of the motion-economy bin setup may therefore be taken to be as follows:

Six sets motion-economy bins	$120.00
Six sets hand tools	52.50
Total	$172.50

Batch Assembly. The batch assembly method requires only benches and hand tools. If it is assumed that benches are available, the total setup cost would be:

Six sets hand tools	$52.50

Progressive Assembly. Under the progressive assembly method, each operator does only a portion of the work. Therefore fewer tools are needed to turn out a given amount of work. At each work station, a few bins to hold small parts should be provided. The total cost for tools and bins is $33.80.

If a belt conveyor were provided to move work from one operator to another, a small amount of time would be saved but not enough to justify the cost of its installation.

QUALITY

No objective measurement of this factor was available during the investigation. The following conclusions, therefore, are based on analysis only.

Pallet Assembly. This method results in high quality because each operator is furnished with just the right amount of parts to make a complete assembly. There is, therefore, little likelihood of a wrong part being used or of a part being omitted. This method ranks high on the quality scale.

Motion-economy Bin Assembly. Under this method, there is a good possibility that an operator may assemble an incorrect part either because of reaching into the wrong bin or because parts have become mixed in the bins. A tendency has been observed on the part of some operators to throw defective parts that have not fitted back into the bins. Thus the same part may be handled several times. If it is eventually forced on an assembly, the resulting quality is doubtful.

There is also the possibility that parts will be omitted from the assembly. It would appear, therefore, that this method is poorest from a quality standpoint. It should be recognized, however, that this is relative quality only, for motion-economy bin assembly setups are giving satisfactory quality on a wide variety of work.

Batch Assembly. This method is likely to produce all good or all defective assemblies in a given batch. In other words, if a part is omitted at all, it will probably be omitted from every assembly in the batch. The quality produced under this method, although good, will probably not be as good as under the pallet or progressive assembly methods.

Progressive Assembly. Each operator does only a portion of the work under this method. He will, therefore, become highly proficient at doing it, with the result that high quality will be secured. The same tendency to try to use defective parts several times, which was mentioned for motion-economy bin setups, is also present at each work station on the progressive assembly line. Because each operator must keep up with the pace of the line, if one operator gets behind because of a defective part, he must increase his pace in order to catch up again. This may have an adverse effect on quality. Offsetting this is the fact that the operators who work on the parts next may detect the lowered quality and may correct the defect or may caution the offending operator. In general, it may be said that the quality obtained under the progressive assembly method is second only to that obtained under the pallet assembly method.

DEGREE OF CONTROL OF MATERIAL

Pallet Assembly. The pallet assembly undoubtedly gives the best control of materials of the four methods analyzed. All parts are kept in a controlled storeroom and are given out a set at a time. Defective parts are replaced as soon as they are found to be wrong, but a specific request must be made of the storeroom in order to obtain the needed part. Where the full utilization of material is an important factor, the pallet assembly method is the best.

Motion-economy Bin Assembly. Each operator is furnished with large quantities of material to work up into assemblies as he is able. There is very little control over material utilization. Operators can help themselves to materials from the motion-economy bins, and in all probability the parts taken will never be missed, at least until the windup of the job. For this reason this method ranks poorest from a material-control standpoint.

Batch Assembly. This method has about the same lack of material control as the motion-economy bin assembly method for the same reasons.

Progressive Assembly. Slightly better material control is provided by this method than the two preceding methods because each operator has fewer parts at his work station. The advantage, however, is relatively slight.

OPERATOR SATISFACTION

Pallet Assembly. By questioning the operators doing the assembly work, it was found that they preferred the pallet assembly method to all others. Materials come to them in the exact quantity needed, laid out in convenient fashion on the pallet. The assembly work appears to be a relatively simple, clean-cut task. The pallets themselves are rather attractive looking. It may also be true that the operators liked the method because, in the plant where this study was made, it was so new that the novelty had not altogether worn off.

Motion-economy Bin Assembly.   This method appears to be the one that is liked the least by the operators, perhaps because closer mental attention to the work is required.

Batch Assembly.   Some of the operators who had been used to using the batch assembly method stated that they could make better time using this method than any other.   This was not borne out by study and analysis, so that it may be that the operators made the common mistake of confusing effort with accomplishment.   Certainly the batch assembly method, because of the constant walking which it involves, is the most fatiguing of the four methods analyzed.

Progressive Assembly.   Because each operator performs a small part of the complete job, the tasks are relatively simple.   Many operators like the progressive assembly method for this reason.   They also tend to like the fact that they share with others the responsibility of turning out a satisfactory product.   This method ranks next to the pallet assembly method in operator satisfaction.

LEARNING TIME

Pallet Assembly.   The pallet assembly method simplifies learning time in comparison to the motion-economy bin and batch assembly methods.   Parts are laid out on the pallet in logical order.   Only enough parts to complete one assembly are provided on each pallet.   These factors simplify the job for the operator and reduce learning time.

Motion-economy Bin Assembly.   Motion-economy bins tend to arrange material in logical order.   Hence, this method is somewhat easier to learn than the batch assembly method where the operator must lay out all materials.

Batch Assembly.   This method is the most difficult to learn in that it is necessary to plan the laying out of the material for each batch assembled.

Progressive Assembly.   Because this method breaks the operation down into a series of comparatively simple tasks, learning time is reduced to a minimum.   This method is the best from the standpoint of ease of learning.

DEPARTMENTAL CLEANLINESS

Pallet Assembly.   This method is likely to result in the most satisfactory condition from a cleanliness standpoint, because materials are carefully controlled and are only issued as needed.

Motion-economy Bin Assembly.   Lack of control of material is likely to lead to the scattering of material around the area where this method is followed. At the same time, the bins do tend to keep materials arranged in orderly fashion on the top of the benches.

Batch Assembly. This method can promote a disorderly departmental appearance if the operator is not careful to keep his material lined up and his parts laid out in straight, evenly spaced lines.

Progressive Assembly. The progressive assembly area is likely to become increasingly untidy as the day progresses due to the dropping and scattering of materials about the work area. Because each operator must keep up with the line, there is less tendency to clean up the workplace from time to time than on setups where each operator can establish his own working pace.

CONTROL OF PIECE COUNT

This is a very important factor if an incentive plan is to be administered properly. Under a progressive setup an inspector is usually stationed at the end of the line. Completed parts flow down the line and the count is relatively easy to obtain. The same count applies to each operator, for each one has worked on each assembly completed.

The other three methods present greater difficulties. The count of the work produced by each operator must be obtained if it is desired to keep a record of individual performance. Thus opportunities for error and confusion exist.

POSSIBILITIES FOR SPECIAL TOOLING

Pallet Assembly. Each operator must have a complete set of tools. Each pallet must have a holding device if the assembly is to be made on the pallet. These factors limit the amount that can be expended for specialized tooling under this method.

Motion-economy Bin Assembly. Each operator must have a complete set of tools, but greater attention may be given to specialized work holders at each work station than in the case of the pallet assembly method.

Batch Assembly. Each operator must have a complete set of tools. No work holders are ordinarily used under this method. The batch assembly method offers the least opportunity for special tooling.

Progressive Assembly. This method lends itself best to special tooling. Because each operator uses only a few tools, it is economically justifiable to spend more for these tools to make them more efficient.

EFFECT OF ABSENTEEISM ON PRODUCTION

The progressive assembly method is the most adversely affected by absenteeism, because each operator must work on each assembly. If a skilled operator is absent and is replaced by an inexperienced operator, the production of the whole line will be retarded. Temporary absences from the line for personal reasons also introduce problems that are not present in the other three methods.

FLOOR SPACE REQUIRED

Pallet Assembly. The pallet-assembly method requires a matching-parts storeroom. Thus more floor space is occupied by this setup than for the motion-economy bin or progressive assembly method.

Motion-economy Bin Assembly and Progressive Assembly. These methods require approximately the same amount of floor space, which is less than that required by either of the other two methods.

Batch Assembly. Because materials are spread out in long lines prior to assembly, considerably more bench space is required for this method. It is usually the least economical method from the standpoint of space occupied.

SUMMARY OF FINDINGS

The following summary shows the ranking of each method of assembly for each of the factors analyzed. A ranking of 1 indicates the most favorable condition and a ranking of 4 the least favorable. Where two or more methods are equal the same ranking figure is shown.

Factor	Pallet assembly	Motion-economy bin assembly	Batch assembly	Progressive assembly
Material handling cost	4	2	1	3
Direct labor cost	1	2	4	3
Total material-handling and direct labor cost	4	1	3	2
Setup cost	4	3	2	1
Quality	1	4	3	2
Degree of control of material	1	3	3	2
Operator satisfaction	1	3	3	2
Learning time	2	3	4	1
Departmental cleanliness	1	2	4	3
Control of piece count	2	2	2	1
Possibilities for special tooling	3	2	4	1
Effect of absenteeism on production	1	1	1	2
Floor space required	2	1	2	1

CONCLUSION

From the summary of findings, it may be seen that no method is best in every respect. Therefore before deciding on which method to use in any situation, the factors which are the most important should be determined. Then the method that best handles these factors may be determined by referring to the table.

On an each-piece cost basis, the motion-economy bin assembly method is best. This is nearly always an important factor to consider. On the other hand, if it were necessary to set up quickly and break in new operators to turn out a job whose duration was not long, then the progressive assembly method with its low setup cost and low learning time would be indicated. If the full utilization of material due to difficulties in obtaining additional stock should be a factor of major importance, the pallet method would best meet the situation.

CHAPTER 29

PROBLEM SOLVING WITH METHODS-TIME MEASUREMENT—PERFORMANCE RATING

A search for a satisfactory method of rating the performance of the operator while time studies are being made has been under way ever since Frederick W. Taylor developed his time-study system. This phase of time study has received more attention than all the rest combined. This is as it should be, because the soundness of the time value depends on the rating.

Researches made with the aid of the methods-time measurement procedure are beginning to shed an increasing amount of light on the performance-rating problem. It is the purpose of this chapter to present and comment upon some of the most recent findings. The conclusions drawn are not presented as final, for they must be regarded as tentative only. It is hoped that they will prove stimulating to thought and will encourage others to do further research work on the performance-rating problem.

HISTORY OF THE DEVELOPMENT OF THE LEVELING PROCEDURE

In order that the recent findings on performance rating may be viewed in proper perspective, it will be desirable to review briefly the history of the development of the leveling procedure. Mathematical methods for making adjustments for differences in the performance of operators during time study were in vogue in years past, but they are now quite generally recognized as being unsatisfactory. Methods which require judgment on the part of the observer in determining the performance of the operator are better, but not all methods which introduce the element of judgment are of equal effectiveness. Recognition of this fact led to the development of the leveling principle by a group of industrial engineers. They were attempting to describe the soundest time-study procedure which could be devised, and they held frequent meetings together during which all parts of existing time-study procedures were thoroughly analyzed before being accepted.

None of the existing performance-rating methods seemed satisfactory. The mathematical methods were recognized for what they were worth.

272

The per cent selection method which was being used by their company at the time seemed better than the rest because it required an evaluation of the performance of the operator, but when it came to preparing a detailed description of the manner in which it was to be applied, it was seen that the procedure left much to be desired.

The per cent selection method is worth describing, because in effect, it is the direct ancestor of the leveling procedure. When a number of observations are made of the same element, the observed times vary from a minimum to a maximum, with a number of values in between. Under the per cent selection method, the elapsed times for each element are summarized in order of magnitude. A series of ten readings might line up as follows:

$$1—.0009$$
$$3—.0010$$
$$3—.0011$$
$$2—.0012$$
$$1—.0013$$

The engineer working up the study has to decide upon a per cent selection factor which will tell him which of these values to select. The factor chosen is supposed to be based upon his judgment of the performance of the operator, but a check of the practices of a number of experienced engineers who used this method showed that there was no uniformity of practice in arriving at the selection factor. Each man in general used low factors if a poor performance were observed and high factors if the performance was superior, but because there had been no criteria established of what constituted low or high performances or even any scale of per cent selection factors to use for various performances, there were wide variations in the results obtained by different observers.

It was obvious, therefore, that the first step which should be taken was to establish criteria of performance. The factors that determined performance were first analyzed and were tentatively set up as skill, effort, conditions, and consistency. Skill and effort were seen to have the greatest effect. The range of useful skill and effort was divided into six classes; poor, fair, average, good, excellent, and superskill, and poor, fair, average, good, excellent, and excessive effort.

In order to secure consistent results where a number of time-study men are employed, it is necessary for each man to have the same conception of each degree of skill and effort. To secure this, each degree of skill and effort was defined and then checked with a number of experienced engineers. These definitions were at length included in the book, "Time and Motion Study and Formulas for Wage Incentives," by Lowry,

Maynard, and Stegemerten. Since that time, the definitions have been revised twice to try to clear up any ambiguous points and also to express the definitions more clearly as additional information was obtained through research, analysis, and study about skill, effort, and methods.

When explaining the definitions, the average performance was considered at some length. It was decided that this should be the equivalent of the much-discussed fair day's work. It was to represent an effort level that could be easily maintained year in and year out by the physically normal operator without in any way requiring him to draw upon his reserves of energy. It was to be the effort given by the conscientious dayworker when he was working. It was to be a pace which appears somewhat slow when observed and which can be accelerated without too much difficulty under the encouragement of a wage-incentive system.

With regard to skill, the operator considered as giving an average performance was to be one qualified for the job who had been at the work long enough to do it without undue hesitation, planning, or errors. He was not expected to be noticeably good at doing the job. At the same time, he was not expected to be noticeably poor.

The conception of average performance was that it should be the performance expected from the conscientious dayworker, while working, in return for his base rate of pay if that were considered to be the going community rate for the class of work being performed. It was not related to his usual production, however, for many factors, not all controllable by him, prevent the typical dayworker from producing steadily throughout the day.

The average performance level was to represent the point of 100 per cent performance, the point at which incentive payment begins under many wage-incentive plans. It was to be a level which could be surpassed by those desiring to increase their earnings somewhat above base.

This was the conception of average performance that was originally established. It has remained the same ever since. Indeed there is no reason why having once been established, it need ever be changed. Because it is established by definition and not mathematically, it is the same on any class of work in any plant in any part of the country. It is often said that the average working pace is slower in Southern plants than in Northern plants because of temperature conditions. This may be true of the actual mathematical average, but that is no reason for changing the average performance level as established by definition. If the Southern employer wants his employees to begin earning bonuses at a lower output point than in his Northern branch, he can adjust his standards accordingly. He can add an extra percentage to the standards as determined by time study; he can make the fair performance level correspond to the point of make out; or he can accomplish the same results in a dozen different ways. The concept of the average performance level as used for performance rating should remain constant, however, if method engineers as a group are to work consistently. If all engineers have the same conception of average performance, then they will be interchangeable among departments, divisions, or plants. More important, their data, before allowances are added to take care of local conditions, will be comparable and interchangeable not only within the same company but throughout industry. The vision that Taylor had of a handbook of standard times for each element in each trade can become a reality only if a uniform concept of performance is maintained throughout industry.

With the average performance as established by definition as the reference point, it is not difficult to establish the other performance levels. The maximum level is described as "superskill" and "excessive effort." The two levels are placed between it and "average," namely, and in descending order, "excellent" and "good." The lowest level of performance to be considered as acceptable for study purposes is named "poor." The one level between it and "average" is called "fair." These levels have always seemed to be somewhat easier to define and recognize than the average level, perhaps because of the fact that they stand out more clearly because they are departures from average.

This line of reasoning led to the beginning of a new approach to the matter of performance rating. It was recognized that if an operator could be found who was working with average skill and average effort, then the time-study data secured from a study on him, averaged to eliminate minor variations, would give the time for average performance. A study of a man giving better than average performance would yield lower time values than desired, while a study of a man giving lower than the average performance would give higher time values. Consequently, adjustment would be necessary.

It seemed reasonable to suppose that numerical factors could be determined which would permit this adjustment. Good skill, for example, would raise performance a definite amount above average. A poor effort would lower it by another definite amount.

As a result, studies were made and data collected. Different operators doing the same job were studied. They were rated in accordance with the standard definitions of skill and effort, and from the data collected, the percentage of variation in performances above and below average was determined.

After months of study, the results of the project were condensed, and a set of numerical performance-rating factors was obtained. These factors were thus based upon hundreds of studies taken on a wide variety of work—since the concern in which the data were collected performed nearly every operation known to industry—by a large group of trained time-study engineers. They were established to be applied to manual operations where the factors of both skill and effort are present.

The leveling factors as established were next tested in use by the engineers of the plant. It was found that they considerably improved the consistency of time-study data. The company, therefore, decided to accept and use the leveling method.

As time went by, comments were received about the leveling method which hailed it as the greatest development since Taylor and the complete answer to the rate-setting problem—which it certainly was not—to the other extreme where those who had never had any contact with the development of the procedure reported that the leveling factors were arbitrarily pulled out of the air.

During the years which have intervened, the leveling procedure has been looked at by psychologists, physiologists, statisticians, unions, industrial engineers, and hosts of others. Some have taken exception to it. Many have used it and have found that it gives usable results if properly applied. Certainly a growing number of methods engineers have used it successfully for a number of years.

THE PITFALLS OF TERMINOLOGY

Much of the discussion of the leveling procedure has been caused by giving improper meanings to the terms used in leveling. If the terms are properly defined, many controversial points disappear.

For example, a common error is to confuse the meaning of the word "average." In leveling, it must be recognized that average skill on a given operation does not mean the average skill of all men, women, and children in the country, or the average skill of all workers in a given plant at a given moment. What is referred to is the normal skill that may be expected to be developed by a normal worker who has learned the operation and who has gained a certain amount of proficiency in doing it as a result of a period of training and practice.

The limitations of language are clearly apparent in situations of this kind. The word "average" in leveling refers to a level established by definition rather than by mathematics. In spite of the confusion which this may cause, it has seemed a better word to use from a practical standpoint than others which might be used, such as "normal" or "standard." If normal were used, for example, an unfavorable reaction might be obtained from the worker in some cases when it was explained to him that he had to give a better than normal performance to earn a bonus. One can imagine his telling his friends, "I guess you've got to be abnormal to make any money in that plant." The word "average" is much more acceptable and less likely to be misunderstood by the worker.

"Skill" is another term that can cause confusion if it is not carefully defined. A common definition is "knowledge plus ability." This is entirely too intangible for the purpose of leveling and in addition includes method in its meaning. It is impracticable to attempt to make adjustment by leveling factors for differences in time that are caused by variations in method. Therefore, "skill" must at all times be defined in its narrow sense of "proficiency at following a given method" when used in connection with leveling.

APPLICABILITY OF LEVELING FACTORS TO BASIC ELEMENTS

For many years after the development of the leveling procedure, there was an unanswered question as to whether the leveling factors that seemed to apply so well to manual operations on an over-all basis would apply equally well to the basic elements. The methods-time measurement procedure has finally supplied the answer.

It has already been reported in Chapter 3 how, even in the initial development of the data, it was found that on manual operations the leveling factors checked with remarkable closeness.

Subsequent investigations, as reported in Chapter 15, have confirmed the applicability of the leveling factors to basic elements. Thus it now seems reasonable to conclude that the leveling factors apply to the basic elements as well as to whole elements or operations. However, this conclusion is offered for manual elements only. The fact that the same leveling factors do not apply to walking has already been brought out in Chapter 12.

THE IMPORTANCE OF METHOD IN PERFORMANCE RATING

One of the points that is brought out more forcefully than ever by researches made with the methods-time data is that the determination of the proper method is of the utmost importance for the satisfactory working out of the leveling procedure. For example, during a detailed study of the effect of skill and effort on motion times, motion pictures were made of a number of operators performing the same operation. The resulting films were carefully analyzed frame by frame. It was found that not only did no two operators use exactly the same method, but that the differences were of far greater magnitude than would be suspected from mere casual observation. Not only were there differences in the easily observable externals of the job, such as the point at which the material is grasped, the manner in which it is handled, and the location of the point of disposal of the finished product, but there were other even more significant differences. Some operators were able to overlap motions so that both hands worked constantly; others tended to work first with one hand and then the other. The transport motions of some operators started from rest, accelerated, traveled, decelerated, and ended at rest. The Grasps and Releases were distinct motions requiring a measurable amount of time. Other operators blended their transport motions so that in many cases there was no deceleration and subsequent acceleration between two or even more motions. The Grasps and Releases were accomplished while the hands were in motion. No measurable time was consumed by them as they were overlapped by the transport motions.

Positioning was another important variable. It was noticeably present in the case of many operators, but others—not necessarily the most experienced—found it possible to work with such accurately controlled Moves that no Position was required.

When the output of these operators was compared, it was found that it varied greatly. The difference, however, was not attributable to skill and effort in the sense that they are used in leveling. The individual motion times when leveled with the conventional leveling factors checked accurately with the basic operation standards. The difference was caused by the fact that the poorest operator made many more motions, i.e., individual motions which require a measurable amount of time to make, than the best operator.

Even the methods used on successive cycles by the same operator varied considerably. Fumbles or false moves caused the greatest difference. Other differences were caused when the length of motion required to perform a given Reach or Move was changed by varying the motion path slightly, by overlapping Grasps and Releases on some cycles and not on others, by using different cases of Reach, Move, and Grasp from cycle to cycle, and by employing type 2 and type 3 Reaches and Moves on some cycles and not on others.

The study of the gauze-folding operation, previously described in Chapter 15, showed that the operators who were given high performance ratings tended to perform the operation more simply and with fewer basic operations than the operators with lower ratings. The following tabulation shows how the average number of basic elements employed per cycle varied with the leveling factor.

Leveling Factor	Number of Basic Elements per Cycle
123	21.8
111	26.8
111	31.7
108	31.4
106	30.3
105	29.0
105	30.8
105	28.0
105	34.7
105	33.5
105	32.0
105	41.2
102	34.7
100	36.3
100	44.2
100	39.0
100	33.5
96	45.0
95	35.3
87	44.0
86	41.7

There are several reasons why the operators giving the better performances use a simpler method. One is that many of the better operators have fewer limiting Grasps and Releases. By working quickly, they tend to perform Grasps and Releases while making a Reach or a Move. Another is that the more proficient operators simplify the operation cycle by overlapping the motions performed by the right and the left hands. A superior operator performing a limiting motion with one hand will usually perform another operation simultaneously with the other hand. An operator whose coordination is poorer will perform first one operation and then the other, thus requiring more time.

Superior operators working quickly tend to change Reaches and Moves from type 1 to type 2 or type 3 motions. They also are able to reduce positioning time. In some cases, the explanation for this in terms of methods-time data is that by aligning and orienting the part during the Move toward the destination, they are able to Position a nonsymmetrical part in the same amount of time as a semisymmetrical or a symmetrical part. At least one case has been observed where a highly skilled operator was able to eliminate a Positioning altogether. He had been doing the job for years, and he had apparently been able to learn to make his case C

Move so accurately that no subsequent Positioning was necessary for him, although four other operators who were doing the same job all required a Positioning.

Still another methods improvement introduced by superior operators results from changing the cases of a basic element. It has already been pointed out that one operator after years of practice was able to reach for an object which was not in reality in a fixed location with a case A Reach whereas several other operators employed the case B Reach, which would normally be expected. On another study, it was found that an operator picking up parts from a jumbled pile was able to grasp them with G1a Grasps. The entire cycle was less than 3 seconds, and she had been doing the job for some time. Apparently she had learned either to make a visual selection before the hand reached the pile so that she could use a G1a Grasp when she got there or had learned to grasp one part and separate it from the rest by feel without the necessity of making a visual selection.

The effect of fumbles on method is sufficiently important to justify further discussion. Most operators fumble occasionally, thus introducing unnecessary time-consuming operations. Fumbles are costly in time not only because they consume a number of frames themselves, but because they often necessitate additional basic elements to adjust the disorders caused by the fumbles. Superior operators fumble less frequently than the poorer operators. Fumbles occur most frequently in conjunction with the basic element Grasp.

The occurrence has been observed of certain inept moves which perhaps should not properly be called fumbles. An operator in attempting to grasp an object quickly may miss it altogether. It is then necessary to repeat the Grasp and at least part of the Reach.

Finally it should be pointed out that operators will sometimes introduce unnecessary, superfluous moves as a regular part of the cycle. Although the existence of unnecessary elements has often been noted by time-study men, the existence of one or two unnecessary motions is likely to go unobserved unless the observer has been trained to notice minor motions as the result of experience with the methods-time measurement procedure.

Extra motions because of fumbles, inept motions, or superfluous work are not confined to operators giving below average performances. The opportunities per cycle for fumbles are decreased in the case of the superior operators, however, because they reduce the number of basic elements employed in the various ways pointed out above.

A study made of the same operator working with different degrees of effort yielded some interesting results. The gauze-folding operator who gave the best performance was asked to slow down and give what she considered an average performance. An analysis of the motion pictures made of her showed that while performing at her best effort she had about 22 limiting basic elements per cycle, but when performing more slowly she employed 29 basic elements per cycle. Releases, which were overlapped with Moves during her best effort, were performed separately. There was less overlapping of the motions made by the right and left hands. Thus as the operator reduced her effort, she changed her method.

SOME TENTATIVE CONCLUSIONS

The findings resulting from analyses made using the methods-time data indicate the answers to many of the problems that have been causing concern among time-study men for years. Although many more investigations will have to be made before all the answers are obtained, the methods-time data approach appears to offer the key to the solution of the problems of performance rating.

In the light of the findings thus far, there are as many different methods of performing an operation as there are operators doing the job. No two operators perform in exactly the same way, for, although they may perform each major or time-study element in the same order, within each major element the basic elements will vary. These differences are often difficult to observe, but when the operations are analyzed into terms of basic elements using the methods-time measurement approach, they are found to exist.

Experience has shown that with patience it is possible to teach an operator to perform the major elements in the proper order and in what has been considered up to the present time as the proper manner. Whether or not it will be possible to teach a number of operators to perform each basic element in the same way remains to be seen. Analysis would indicate that the basic elements are performed so rapidly that the operator cannot think a sequence as fast as he can perform it. Therefore he cannot be expected to perform every basic operation exactly as a slowly thought out analysis might indicate that it should be performed. Therefore it might appear that the best that can be done is to teach the operator the general elements of the method and let him work out the basic elements he uses himself.

In the meantime, industry is faced with the task of establishing workable standards and of training operators to meet those standards. The findings of the gauze-folding study will be helpful in this connection. When the analysis work was completed, a curve was plotted of performance level vs. leveled TMU per cycle, as shown by Fig. 113. Although

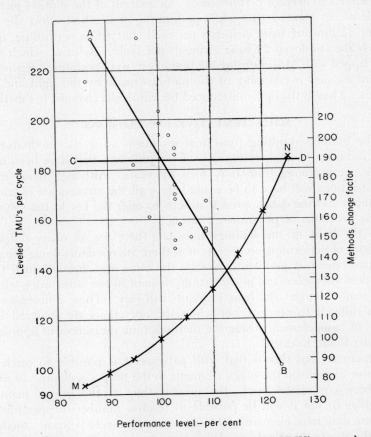

FIG. 113.— Curve of performance level against leveled TMU's per cycle— gauze-folding study.

the points were somewhat scattered due to the fact that not all operators improved their method in exactly the same way as performance increased, the points nevertheless indicated the trend, and the Curve AB was plotted. This curve shows how the leveled time per cycle decreased for the gauze-folding operation as the performance level increased, judged in terms of the leveling factors resulting from conventional skill and effort rating.

The leveling factors in all the studies made thus far have been found to give a reasonably correct gauge of speed of motions. Thus if the motions used by all operators had been the same as those used by the operators giving an average performance, the leveled TMU per cycle would have been the same for all operators and the curve of performance level vs. leveled TMU per cycle would have been the Curve *CD*. The fact that the curve plotted from the data was not *CD* but was the Curve *AB* indicates that there was another variable present. The variable, of course, was the difference in methods that was found to exist throughout. Thus although the points that determine the Curve *AB* have been adjusted for the effect of performance on speed of motions, they will also have to be adjusted for the factor of methods change if the same standard is to be established regardless of the performance studied. The Curve *MN* was therefore developed to show the methods-change factors, which would have to be applied to bring the Curve *AB* into coincidence with Curve *CD*.

Now, of course, the Curve *MN* applies only to the gauze-folding operation. On another operation, the factor of methods change might be entirely different depending upon the number of possibilities for fumbling, inept Moves, overlapping of motions, reducing the classification of Positioning, etc., which exist. Certainly in an operation involving machining time, the methods-change factor would be different for the entire cycle, and probably for the manual elements as well. Therefore the methods-change factors shown by Fig. 113 cannot be used for other operations.

The curves shown by Fig. 113 do shed some light, however, on the establishing of standards. It has been recognized that the leveling factors do not make adjustments for differences in methods, and hence time-study men endeavor to see that the proper method is in use before they begin their studies. This they can often do insofar as the general method is concerned, but up to the present time they have seldom attempted to give instructions with regard to the use of basic elements. Thus when they make their studies and apply the conventional leveling factors, they are in many cases making only part of the adjustment that should be made if the performance observed varies much above or below average. If they study a below-average performance they will arrive at a higher standard than if they study an average performance and if they study an above-average performance they will arrive at a lower standard at least on an operation like gauze folding.

This will result, of course, in inconsistent standards. Therefore until the possibility of introducing methods-change factors has been explored further, it may be advisable, where practicable, to heed the request of labor, which is so often made, and study only operators who give average or nearly average performance. Because the majority of industrial workers when time studied are found to give average or good performances, it is probable that the majority of standards established in the past are satisfactory, particularly where there has been an averaging-out process, such as occurs when a time-formula derivation is made. The few values that stand out as being inconsistent even when there has been no noticeable change in method are those where either a very poor or a very good performance was given when the time study was made. The difficulty is apparently caused by the fact that the existence of minor methods changes of the type brought out by the gauze-folding study have not heretofore been recognized rather than by any fundamental inaccuracy of the leveling method of making adjustments for variation in "speed of motions."

The minor methods changes that operators are able to introduce into a method appear to result largely from repeated performance of the same operation. Therefore, the longer a job is in operation, the greater the improvement is likely to be, particularly when the operator is working under the stimulus of a wage incentive plan and is really trying to produce. This confirms past experience which has shown that production tends to increase on a given job the longer it is in existence. Many companies have had the experience of studying and establishing standards too soon on a long-run job and later finding that earnings were much higher than was anticipated. The curves on Fig. 113 indicate this.

On the assumption that the point of average performance has been correctly chosen, the majority of operators in the gauze-folding study fell between the 100 per cent and the 111 per cent performance level. The methods-change factor in this range is 100 per cent to 125 per cent. Therefore the earnings of these operators may be expected to range from 100 to 111 per cent × 125 per cent, or 138.6 per cent, which is what they did and which is not out of line with normal incentive earnings. One operator, however, had developed herself to the point where she was able to work at a 123 per cent performance level. The methods-change factor at this point is 180 per cent. Thus her earnings possibilities on the established standard are 221 per cent. (Actually she limited her production to about 185 per cent, perhaps to avoid having the standard checked.)

A LOOK AHEAD

The solution to the problem of establishing accurate standards, therefore, appears not to lie in the devising of a new or different leveling procedure, but rather in doing a much more thorough methods job than has heretofore been done throughout industry. First of all, it will be necessary to learn through research more about methods. Then this knowledge will have to be passed on in practical form to the methods engineers of industry. It is probable that eventually it will require as much education to turn out a methods engineer as it now does to develop a mechanical or an electrical engineer.

When methods engineering itself has developed to the point where it can say with reasonable certainty not only how a given operation should be performed but also what the ultimate method should be after the job has been in existence long enough to become fully developed, then two other tasks must be faced. One is to select through proper aptitude tests—many of which are yet to be developed—operators who will be able to approach the best methods for doing the job. The other will be to use far better methods of training operators than are in general use at present, so that the learning period when productivity is low will be materially shortened.

The rewards that the successful handling of this problem offer are great. The level of productivity of individual operators will be raised without increase in effort to a point considerably beyond present levels. Production and, hence, incentive earnings among individual operators will be much more consistent, thus eliminating one major source of difficulty. Finally, by learning at last the correct time for performing all basic operations and, hence, all factory operations throughout industry, once and for all that perplexing problem of time study—What is average performance?—will be eliminated.

INDEX

287